Chasing Dreams

EDITED BY JOSH PERELMAN

Chasing Dreams

BASEBALL & BECOMING AMERICAN

CONTENTS

home

PREFACE

IVY L. BARSKY

No one has learned more about baseball during the preparations for *Chasing Dreams: Baseball and Becoming American* than I have. And I had a lot to learn. I hope that others like me who are not already "deep in the dugout" or do not have a "home field advantage" will be similarly engaged by our exhibition.

I have long been inspired by the Yiddish-language *Forverts* (*Jewish Daily Forward*) piece from 1903 in the Museum's core exhibition, where editor Abe Cahan urges his immigrant readership: if you want your children to become truly American, you must let them play baseball. Later, in 1909, the *Forverts* published a charming diagram of a baseball field with detailed descriptions (only marginally accurate) of how the game works.

I have begun to understand the magic that baseball has brought into the lives of so many. I understood, intellectually, the important role baseball has played on the leading edge of equality issues—which were being played out on the baseball field long before they became common practice or law. The authors in this volume do the work of recounting the groundbreaking, barrier-breaking progress that ensued over time in the baseball community and how that translated onto fields and in homes across the country.

The stories of *Chasing Dreams* are the stories of our Museum—stories of courage and hope, of hard work and aspiration, of leadership and service—the stories of becoming fully American.

And while many expect an exhibition and its companion volume to be focused on important proper names—and they won't be disappointed; those stories are here—the most compelling aspects of *Chasing Dreams* are the names you don't know, the fans, families, and communities who share the triumphs and disappointments, the statistics and baseball cards, the memories: Where were you on April 15, 1947, or on Yom Kippur in 1965? Or when Ken Holtzman pitched his two no-hitters, when Shawn Green hit four home runs, or when the hometown team won the World Series?

Creating an exhibition, programs, and a companion volume of this ambition and magnitude is a team sport. And we are fortunate to have had an All-Star lineup. First and foremost, now and always, is our incredibly talented and dedicated staff, led by Chief Curator and Director of Exhibtions and Collections Josh Perelman. He and Associate Curator Ivy Weingram acted as cocurators for *Chasing Dreams*, and their love for the subject matter is evident in every page of the catalogue and every inch of the exhibition. The curatorial team—Shira Goldstein, Alisa Kraut, Sasha Makuka, Claire Pingel, Ryan Bott, and Ryan Will—went above and beyond, and were joined by special designated hitter Associate Director of Development Cobi Weissbach as well as colleagues across the institution. We had a bench deep with talent, too many to name here.

Our academic advisory group for this project is composed entirely of heavy hitters. We were especially blessed to have the personal and professional leadership, knowledge, and wisdom of John Thorn, official historian of Major League Baseball, whose story is truly one of becoming American through baseball. We are grateful to the whole advisory committee: Martin Abramowitz, Rebecca T. Alpert, Adrian Burgos Jr., Jeffrey S. Gurock, Jane Leavy, Peter Levine, Daniel Okrent, William Ressler, Steven A. Riess, Allan H. "Bud" Selig, Justine Siegal, Scott Simon, and Beth S. Wenger.

Major League Baseball itself gave us invaluable support and access. We can never recognize sufficiently Commissioner Selig and John Thorn, and we really could not have realized a project of this scope and quality without Senior Vice President of Public Relations Pat Courtney. We are also grateful to David Gavant, David Kaufmann, Kim Ng, Joe Torre, and Nick Trotta.

New York Mets Chairman Fred Wilpon was an early and vocal proponent of this project. Various team owners, general managers, and administrators enthusiastically helped this project come to fruition: Ruben Amaro Jr., Philadelphia Phillies; Larry Baer, San Francisco Giants; Jon Daniels, Texas Rangers; Mark D. Lerner, Washington Nationals; Randy Levine, New York Yankees; David Montgomery, Philadelphia Phillies; Jerry Reinsdorf, Chicago White Sox; Mark Shapiro, Cleveland Indians; Matthew Silverman, Tampa Bay Rays; Janet Marie Smith, Los Angeles Dodgers; and Dr. Charles Steinberg, Boston Red Sox.

We are grateful for the exceptional help from several truly exceptional people: Della Britton Baeza, president and chief executive officer, and Rachel Robinson, Jackie Robinson Foundation; Steve Greenberg, managing director, Allen and Company; Sandy Koufax; the Honorable Ed Rendell; and longtime Museum supporter Alan Shulman.

We were able to amass an astounding group of objects, photographs, and memorabilia from our colleagues at the following institutions: African American Museum in Philadelphia; the American Jewish Historical Society; the Corey R. Shanus Collection; Daniel Harris, Ida Crown Jewish Academy; Heritage Auctions; the Jewish Historical Society of Greater Washington; Keneseth Israel Congregation; the Mercer Museum; the Museum of Jewish Heritage; the National Baseball Hall of Fame and Museum; the National Pastime Museum; the Van Pelt-Dietrich Library Center of the University of Pennsylvania.

Many thanks to the individuals who shared their enthusiasm and stellar collections: Rebecca T. Alpert; Jay and Patty Baker; Rabbi Barry and Amy Cohen Blum; George Blumenthal; Gil Bogen; Mark W. Cooper, MD, MBA; the Dreyfuss family; Barbara and Mike Epstein; Marjorie and Len Freiman; Nathan Freiman; Jonathan Fuld; Carl B. Goldberg; Al Goldis; Howard K. Goldstein, Esq.; Shawn Green; Steve Greenberg; LTC (R) Dave Grob; the Hirschfield family; Kate Harris; Jess and Naomi Hordes; Peter S. Horvitz; Ian Kinsler; Sandy Koufax; Jane Leavy; Rick Levy; Steve Mandel; Nancy Messinger; Kerry Yo Nakagawa of the Nisei Baseball Research Project; Joshua Prager; the Siegal family; Dr. Seymour Stoll; Andy Strasberg; Rabbi Michael Strassfeld; Nancy and Arn Tellem; Harvey and Ann Tettlebaum; Michael S. Wolfson; the Zeid family; and all those who posted photographs and artifacts to chasingdreamsbaseball.tumblr.com.

Worthy of special mention is Stephen Wong, a truly remarkable collector of baseball memorabilia and someone who was inspired by *Chasing Dreams* early on. He made his world-renowned collection available to the Museum and offered critical assistance to the curatorial team along the way.

We express boundless gratitude to our most generous donors. Major support for *Chasing Dreams: Baseball and Becoming American* is provided by the National Endowment for the Humanities, Major League Baseball, Judy and Fred Wilpon and the New York Mets, Annette M. and Theodore N. Lerner Family Foundation and the Washington Nationals, the Marc and Diane Spilker Foundation, Leon Wagner, Harriet and Larry Weiss, and Sam Wisnia. Additional support is provided by Oakland Athletics, John Fisher and Lew Wolff, Cozen O'Connor, Gary Goldring, Steve and Myrna Greenberg, Macy's, Michael G. Rubin, Susie and Robert Zeff, Mitchell & Ness Nostalgia Co., and other dedicated fans.

I am indebted to our board of trustees and its cochairs, Ron Rubin and Phillip Darivoff, who make this, and all that we do, possible. The success of *Chasing Dreams* and this companion volume is due to those in the box seats as well as the bleachers: curators and copywriters, funders and fans. To all those who regularly went to sleep with their transistor radios under their pillows, *Chasing Dreams* is for you.

Ivy L. Barsky
CEO and Gwen Goodman Director

INTRODUCTION

JOSH PERELMAN

I do not believe that every person, in every walk of life, can succeed in spite of any handicap. That would be perfection. But I do believe—and with every fiber in me—that what I was able to attain came to be because we put behind us (no matter how slowly) the dogmas of the past: to discover the truth of today; and perhaps find the greatness of tomorrow.

—Jackie Robinson, 1952

———

Growing up in a Conservative Jewish family in Madison, Wisconsin, I spent a good number of hours during high school participating in my synagogue's youth group. I served as religious secretary, a title that carried with it minimal distinction and few duties, a fact that perhaps says something about me and our group. Still, despite our lack of *halakhic* rigor, our chapter partook in a robust schedule of Jewish social and educational programs throughout the year, including a highly anticipated annual outing to see the Milwaukee Brewers.

Each spring, at least a baker's dozen of us would travel east on Highway 94 to claim our bleacher seats in County Stadium. We still held fast to memories of Harvey's Wallbangers and the highs of the 1982 season, and enthusiastically cheered when Robin Yount, Paul Molitor, Cecil Cooper, and Ben Oglivie took the field or Pete Vuckovich pitched. Bud Selig still controlled the Brewers, and we held him in high esteem as a Jew who had made it in a quintessentially American fashion: he owned a baseball team. To a small group of Wisconsin-bred Jewish kids, that gave solace to us. Because we viscerally felt what it meant to be a minority. We knew that we would have to explain to teachers why we would be absent from school on the High Holidays; knew that all heads would turn to us when anything related to Judaism, the Holocaust, or Israel came up in class; and knew that we lived in the only houses on our streets without Christmas lights. And we knew that part of growing up meant we would have to make choices of our own about being Jews in America.

Immersed as we were in all the issues of identity that get sorted out during teenagerhood, to be sitting with that group of Jewish kids in the bleachers, cheering the Brewers while eating snacks we had brought with us to ensure we maintained Jewish dietary laws, nothing felt more American or more Jewish. We knew about Hank, and about Sandy, and coming from liberal Madison we surely knew about Jackie. Like those seeming immortals, we knew that even as we faced the challenges of being members of an American minority group, we could also be accepted.

Chasing Dreams: Baseball and Becoming American, the title of this volume and a pioneering exhibition created by the National Museum of American Jewish History, speaks to the centrality of baseball in American culture, especially its symbolic role in the process of acculturation and integration. From the game's earliest days in the nineteenth century through today, baseball has served as a pathway for learning and understanding American values, even when the game has failed to live up to those values or as values themselves changed over time. "Baseball was a kind of secular church that reached into every class and region of the nation," wrote Philip Roth in the seminal essay that inaugurates this book. Growing up, Roth felt that baseball

Paul Molitor hits a two-run home run at Milwaukee County Stadium earning the Brewers a playoff win against the California Angels, October 8, 1982

connected him to his neighbors and his nation, bringing "millions upon millions of us together in common concerns, loyalties, rituals, enthusiasms, and antagonisms."[1]

From the major leagues to the Little Leagues, the stories that fill this volume illustrate how parents, children, and grandchildren adapted to, and sometimes challenged, what it means to be an American. As John Thorn, official historian of Major League Baseball and a contributor to this book, has eloquently written, "This great game opens up a portal to our past, both real and imagined, comforting us with intimations of immortality and primordial bliss. But it also holds up a mirror, showing us as we are."[2] Played on these shores for nearly two hundred years, baseball has been a pungent and exhilarating metaphor for America, a land of so much promise and opportunity, whose best ideals are realized through creativity and consistent, determined hard work. The game's legends and myths, heroes and flops, its struggles and its moments of triumph tell our national story. And for immigrants to this country—be they Jews, Italians, Latinos, or Japanese—baseball has long served as a pathway to learning about and understanding America.

Why have American Jews identified with, taken pride in, and felt connected to the nation's pastime? How can so few players mean so much to a small American minority community? Did baseball impact how American Jews established affinities with other racial and ethnic minorities? The authors in *Chasing Dreams* explore how values, identity, and especially race have been projected, contested, and occasionally solidified.

Many of the stories in this book illustrate how generations of Jews and other American minority groups looked to baseball as an avenue for navigating the challenges of becoming American and draw parallels to the other minority groups for whom baseball has provided an important sense of belonging and pride.

In the nineteenth and early twentieth centuries, Jewish immigrants and their families faced the challenge of making America home. Work, family life, politics, and consumer culture dominated their lives and shaped their identities. Making ends meet in difficult working conditions, combined with the emphasis Jews placed on education and social justice, shaped their attitudes toward athletics, both as recreation and as a career. Even one of the most esteemed Jewish newcomers, Rabbi Solomon Schechter, who immigrated to America to head the Jewish Theological Seminary, recognized in baseball a key to American culture, telling up-and-coming student Louis Finkelstein that "unless you can play baseball, you will never get to be a rabbi in America."[3]

Social reformers likewise supported taking up a bat and a ball, be it in city streets, vacant fields, or full-fledged ballparks, lest parents "raise [their] children to be foreigners in their own country."[4] Pursuing mainstream consumer culture served as an entryway for immigrants to feel and act American, and baseball in particular became an accessible way to identify with the dominant culture. During the era of mass migration, sports and physical fitness were considered by settlement houses, YMCAs and YM/YWHAs, to be effective methods for teaching what they considered to be appropriate American behaviors.

America's postwar economic boom led millions to relocate to suburban neighborhoods and Sun Belt cities to seek new opportunities. These moves coincided with the integration of baseball and the advent of Hank Aaron, Roberto Clemente, and Sandy Koufax, who became the new faces of baseball's ethnic diversity and idols to their communities. Hank Aaron pursued racial equality just as vigorously as he chased Babe Ruth's "unbreakable" home run record. Clemente faced racial prejudice as a dark-skinned, non-English-speaking player but overcame the barriers of prejudice to become both a baseball superstar and an icon to Spanish-speaking

Americans, both in his life and tragic death. Koufax's unparalleled athleticism (yielding millions of flashbulb memories) and celebrated decision not to pitch the first game of the 1965 World Series because it fell on Yom Kippur stand out among the proudest moments in American Jewish sports memory.

The essays in this volume provide a unique vantage on the nature of Americanization through the lens of sport and engage themes that resonate across cultures, minority populations, and American histories. They explore our collective encounter with our national pastime—with its own rites, reams of interpretations, and ever-evolving theology—and the ways in which we celebrate success and confront failure when it inevitably happens. As Marc Tracy observes in his essay, "in nearly all respects great Jewish baseball players are exactly like great non-Jewish baseball players: imperfect sometimes, but deserving of second chances when they appear open to being worthy of them." Taken together, the authors featured here attest to the elegant opening words of Ken Burns's *Baseball*, which describes a sport of "mythic contradictions." Baseball, the film's narrator explains, "reflects a host of age-old American tensions: between workers and owners, scandal and reform, the individual and the collective. It is a haunted game, where each player is measured by the ghosts of those who have gone before. *Most of all, it is about time and timelessness, speed and grace, failure and loss, imperishable hope, and coming home.*"[5]

Coming home, becoming American, can often include a warm embrace as well as facing what has been left behind. The essays in this book attest to the complexities of identity and the challenges of maintaining cultural distinctiveness in a land of uncertain and uneven opportunities. Throughout their history, American minority communities have sought freedom even as they operated with uncertainty about just how much freedom to accept. Even as they took advantage of opportunities for advancement and integration, some expressed a sense of wariness or anxiety.

Readers will find this book divided into three thematic sections, which mirror the primary themes of the Museum's exhibition—**shaping identity**, **overcoming adversity**, and **family and community**—each highlighted by an introductory essay as well as a variety of personal recollections and historical pieces that attest to baseball's

enduring impact. Many, but not all, of the authors write from the perspective of a Jewish American. In doing so, they highlight issues specific to American Jewish life, while shedding light on Jews' efforts to engage the heterogeneous communities in which they have chosen to make their homes. As a whole, *Chasing Dreams* invites readers to explore the American spirit of courage, imagination, aspiration and hard work, leadership, and service through active engagement with our national pastime.

On city streets and suburban fields, in living rooms, and from stadium bleachers, baseball has offered a symbolic metaphor for everyday life to American minority groups and their descendants. Each of the essays in **shaping identity** brings to life stories of how the game has helped immigrants seeking to understand and express their new country's ideals, culture, and behaviors at the same time that it has increasingly become a means for assimilated or geographically detached members of cultural groups to reconnect with their own cultures.

Ira Berkow, the noted sportswriter, introduces the section by highlighting how the desire to feel at home in a new and unfamiliar place is not a uniquely Jewish story, but one that is particularly resonant for Jews, who have sought ways to maintain their traditions and practices while addressing the pressures they have felt to talk, look, and act American at school, in the workplace, and on the street. Playing baseball, attending games, trading baseball cards, and following the statistics of favorite players and teams have all served as outward affirmations of the idea of America. The *Jewish Daily Forward* underscored baseball's centrality in a 1909 article, writing, "If an entire nation is crazy over something, it's not too much to ask to try and understand what it means."[6]

"What it means" is the subject Colum McCann takes on when he writes about sitting beside his son in present-day Yankee Stadium, a reminder that historic questions of immigrant adaptation are as vivid today as they were two hundred years ago. The series of essays that follow, by Beth S. Wenger, Steven A. Riess, Peter Levine, and Jeffrey S. Gurock, take a historical view of immigrant identity, exploring baseball's origins in the streets of New York City, its early Jewish stars, and the ongoing negotiation between religion and sport. Likewise, Barry M. Bloom, Steve Wulf, Curt Smith, and Eric Rolfe Greenberg testify to the role baseball played in shaping identities through business, the media, and fiction. The section also includes excerpts from two well-known works of fiction, Chaim Potok's *The Chosen* and Bernard Malamud's *The Natural*.

Aviva Kempner fondly describes the career of America's first Jewish baseball superstar, Hank Greenberg. His career began with the Detroit Tigers in the 1930s, playing for a city that was home to two of America's most prominent antisemites, Henry Ford and Father Coughlin. Coming of age during the Great Depression and witnessing the rise of the Nazis, children and grandchildren of Jewish immigrants looked to ethnic baseball players like Hank Greenberg, or Joe DiMaggio if you were Italian, whose skills on the field and conspicuous patriotism publicly attested to American minorities' commitment to their homeland.

Stephen Wong poignantly describes how a boyhood fascination with baseball grew into a lifelong passion, and even how it created opportunities at a particularly challenging moment in his life. Wong's essay describes the emotional significance of baseball memorabilia and how collecting makes possible the telling and retelling of the game's great stories.

John Thorn's introduction to **overcoming adversity** focuses on the challenges Jews, African Americans, and women have faced as they have sought integration into baseball, and America. The essays that follow point to baseball's role in addressing national struggles, including racial integration and equal rights. But they also show how urbanization, racism, class stratification, gender discrimination, and cheating have all been debated, and continue to be factors, in everyday life, and in the game. "Baseball seems to have the uncanny ability to endure through the great challenges the world brings to us," former player and widely respected author, commentator, and book contributor Doug Glanville introduces the section with an essay that picks up on one of his recent columns from *The New York Times*, in which he wrote that baseball has has figured into "not just the larger events like wars and struggles for racial equality, but internal wounds suffered by the game: from the Black Sox cheating scandal to the age of steroids."[7]

For Jews, as well as African Americans and Latinos and Dominicans and Japanese (and many others), involvement in baseball has been associated with communal efforts to overcome adversity and achieve equal rights—as players and as citizens. Jackie Robinson's debut with the Brooklyn Dodgers is no doubt the seminal event in this story and a touchstone for a number of the book's authors. Scott Simon writes poignantly that it is "tempting today, when Jackie Robinson is enshrined in halls of fame, social studies curricula, classroom calendars, songs, and statues" to diminish the struggles he endured and the threats he confronted. "But in the late 1940s," Simon reminds us, "beatings, bombings, lynchings, and shootings scarred the landscape of the United States. They could be just as public as—well, as baseball games." Similarly, Michael Berenbaum emotionally recalls Robinson's significance to him as a Brooklyn native and as a Jew: "Because Jackie was the first, he played for everyone who had been denied a chance, whose future was closed because of racism and segregation; he was the forerunner of the civil rights movement and the struggles by women and gays for equality that would follow. He would do anything to win."

The integration of baseball served as a crucial indicator of changing American values toward pluralism. As catalogue contributor Rebecca T. Alpert has written, Jackie Robinson's debut on April 15, 1947, "provided many Jewish writers and artists, rabbis and baseball fans, with a symbolic representation of their experience of assimilation into American society in the era immediately following World War II."[8] Having witnessed, from the sidelines, how easily antisemitism could turn into extermination, Jewish organizations placed themselves at the forefront of efforts to ensure civil rights and civil liberties for all American citizens. Moreover, Jews hoped that they too would benefit from the civil rights movement and through their activism prove their loyalty to American Democracy (the antithesis of Communism). In their view, a country that supported equal opportunities for African Americans would be much less likely to withhold rights from its Jewish citizens. Yet Alpert also points out that despite their good intentions, Jews often "saw the

American capacity for tolerance through their own experiences of assimilation to the white middle class," without recognizing "the enormous difference between America's brand of anti-semitism and its pervasive antiblack racism."[9]

Such complexities are present in essays by Alpert, Adrian Burgos Jr., and Shirley Povich, who show that black baseball of the 1930s involved a host of complex personal and business relationships that complicate the story of baseball's integration and transcended popular notions of the Negro League and segregation. In Philadelphia, and around the nation, Jewish entrepreneurs owned, booked, supplied, and promoted Negro League teams, forming both collaborative and competitive relationships with their African American peers. Moreover, as Burgos illustrates, just as these white businessmen profited from baseball's segregation, some, like Abe Saperstein, also scouted black talent for major league teams.

Jews too could feel the sting of prejudice, and more than a few players recall the epithets hurled at them from the stands and opposing dugouts. Michael Scott Alexander's essay returns to the infamous 1919 World Series scandal (which notably inspired the character Wolfsheim in F. Scott Fitzgerald's *The Great Gatsby*) and a time when Henry Ford used his *Dearborn Independent* as a vehicle to decry Jewish involvement in, well, almost anything, including baseball.[10] Marty Appel's very personal essay takes us to a later period, when he worked in the New York Yankees front office. He describes how he managed the complex negotiation between his Jewishness and the fact that the Yankees were once, but no longer, well known for antipathy to Jewish players and executives.

Efforts to challenge social or professional boundaries have not been limited to men. As Pamela S. Nadell and Justine Siegal illustrate, women who wanted to play baseball, own baseball teams, or open baseball-related businesses not only had to overcome prejudices of race and religion but those of gender as well. Nadell shows how women met these challenges and how baseball has expanded to recognize women as players, essential cultural consumers, and potential business partners. For example, World War II witnessed the emergence of the All-American Girls Professional Baseball League (AAGPBL) as the first professional baseball league for women. The AAGPBL provided women like Jewish All-Star outfielder Thelma "Tiby" Eisen an arena to express their patriotism in a sport usually reserved for men. Eisen nevertheless testified to the double standard women faced, stating that "They're so worried about the men...and what they do and they're fighting all the time...but if a woman does something that isn't quite right, well they're right on their backs immediately."[11] Standing on the shoulders of the AAGPBL, Justine Siegal, the first woman to pitch in major league batting practice, tells her own poignant story of breaking barriers in baseball.

Rob Ruck and Kerry Yo Nakagawa take the discussion of baseball's integration into the latter half of the twentieth century, when an influx of players of Latino heritage and from Japan continued to diversify the game. Their essays on Roberto Clemente and Ichiro Suzuki serve as critical additions to the story of baseball's role in shaping of American ethnic identities.

As our national pastime, baseball has emulated a set of values and traditions that have been transmitted across generations through **family and community** relationships. Barry Levinson, director of *The Natural* (based on the novel by Bernard Malamud), shared in an interview that, to him, family has been essential to "the introduction of the game and how it's passed on.... It's the story told seven times over, and it gets more vivid and exciting each time. That's where it all connects, from generation to generation and from father to son."[12] Levinson accurately notes the importance of intergenerational relationships to the continuity of values and traditions—in baseball, in families, and in American life—even as they have changed over time, but it's crucial to expand his observation to mothers and daughters.

Indeed, in my own family, my two daughters are my regular companions to Citizens Bank Park, home to the Philadelphia Phillies, and the hours spent there are an opportunity to be together but also to grow a love of baseball in my own family. Doug Glanville's introduction to this section of the book attests to the significance of such relationships in his own life, offering an eloquent description of how his own family and the family of baseball nourished his successes. Joshua Prager's beautiful essay describes how memories of playing catch in the backyard with his father helped him overcome a traumatic accident. And generational connections are likewise vividly illustrated in Marc Appleman's and William Choslovsky's essays.

A historical exchange between an immigrant parent and Abe Cahan, editor of the *Jewish Daily Forward*, sets the stage for essays by Doris Kearns Goodwin, Arn Tellem, Jane Leavy, and Billy Crystal. Goodwin returns to her Brooklyn childhood to describe the importance baseball played in her relationship with her father. Tellem writes about growing up outside of Philadelphia and how strong family values and an early passion for baseball set him on the path to become one of the most successful sports agents in America today. Jane Leavy, biographer of Sandy Koufax, recalls when Koufax came to her daughter's bat mitzvah as an avenue for exploring the monumental role he plays in the history of baseball, and in her own life. And Billy Crystal, an ecstatic Yankees fan, tells the story of every boy's dream come true: the opportunity to play for a day with baseball's best.

Jewish fans have made much of Jewish stars like Andy Cohen, Hank Greenberg, Sandy Koufax, and Shawn Green. Their achievements, and the groundbreaking endeavors of Jewish change makers, including journalists, owners, managers, and players, have instilled pride in Jews around the nation. Former player and now Detroit Tigers manager, Brad Ausmus, tells his story of how baseball brought him closer to his Jewishness and to leading Team Israel in the 2013 World Baseball Classic. Colin Friedman, an up-and-coming college player, relates how the support of his grandfather inspired him to become a better baseball player and a more closely identified Jew. And William Ressler draws on his extensive interviews with Jewish minor leaguers to show how the warmth of community can support young players trying to break into the big leagues. As one Jewish minor league player observed, the fans "want to have connections. They feel like we're all one and we're part of the same thing, same family, and anytime someone else succeeds…we all succeed."[13]

My connection to baseball began with the scrappy Milwaukee team Bud Selig created. He left the Brewers to become commissioner of Major League Baseball in 1998 and, as this volume is being published, enters his final year in that position. A hallmark of his tenure has been the emphasis on baseball as a "social institution," one that "must do everything it can to maintain integrity, fairness, and a level playing field."[14] But as a sport whose finest practitioners succeed barely a third of the time, baseball too has had its share of hucksters, grifters, malcontents, and charlatans. And it faces more challenges to come in resolving the legacy of the steroid era, welcoming women throughout its ranks, and openly embracing players of all sexual orientations. But one only has to look to the enduring significance of Jackie Robinson's debut, or more recently to the games that followed 9/11 or the Boston bombings, to see evidence of baseball's ability to unite the nation in bitter times. We cherish players past and present who make baseball glamorous and meaningful, and respect the minor leaguers who work tirelessly despite few rewards, and cheer the everyday heroes of who play on park fields across the United States. Whatever may come, the game will be in our souls and part of our lives as we continue to become Americans.

Notes

1   Philip Roth, "My Baseball Years," in *Reading Myself and Others* (New York: Farrar, Straus and Giroux, LLC, 1975).
2   John Thorn, "Why Baseball?" in Geoffrey C. Ward and Ken Burns, *Baseball: An Illustrated History* (New York: Knopf, 1994), 58.
3   "A Trumpet for All Israel," *Time*, 13 Oct. 1951, 54.
4   *Jewish Daily Forward*, 6 Aug. 1903.
5   Ken Burns, dir., *Baseball* (PBS, 2010). Film. Emphasis added.
6   *Jewish Daily Forward*, 27 Aug. 1909.
7   "Baseball, Faith and Doubt," *The New York Times*, 17 Aug. 2012.
8   Rebecca T. Alpert, *Out of Left Field: Jews and Black Baseball* (New York: Oxford UP, 2011), 1.
9   Alpert, *Out of Left Field*, 2.
10 "Jewish Gamblers Corrupt American Baseball," *Dearborn Independent*, 3 Sept. 1921.
11 Rebecca T. Alpert, unpublished oral history of Thelma "Tiby" Eisen, used with Alpert's permission.
12 Barry Levinson, interview by Joshua Siegel, "Reflections on *The Natural*," in *Baseball as America: Seeing Ourselves through Our National Game*, ed. John Odell (Washington, DC: The National Baseball Hall of Fame and Museum and National Geographic Society, 2002), 231.
13 Jewish Minor Leaguer "J21," interview by William H. Ressler, 5 May, 2 June, and 16 Sept. 2012.
14 "Commissioner Selig to Retire in January of 2015," Web, 26 Sept. 2013, http://mlb.mlb.com/news/article.jsp?ymd=20130926&content_id=61836386&vkey=pr_mlb&c_id=mlb.

PHILIP ROTH

My Baseball Years

IN ONE of his essays George Orwell writes that though he was not very good at the game, he had a long hopeless love affair with cricket until he was sixteen. My relations with baseball were similar. Between the ages of nine and thirteen, I must have put in a forty-hour week during the snowless months over at the neighborhood playfield—softball, hardball, and stickball pick-up games—while simultaneously holding down a full-time job as a pupil at the local grammar school. As I remember it, news of two of the most cataclysmic public events of my childhood—the death of President Roosevelt and the bombing of Hiroshima—reached me while I was out "playing ball." My performance was uniformly erratic; generally okay for those easygoing pick-up games, but invariably lacking the calm and the expertise that the naturals displayed in stiff competition. My taste, and my talent, such as it was, was for the flashy, whiz-bang catch rather than the towering fly; running and leaping I loved, all the do-or-die stuff—somehow I lost confidence waiting and waiting for the ball lofted right at me to descend. I could never make the high-school team, yet I remember that, in one of the two years I vainly (in both senses of the word) tried out, I did a good enough imitation of a baseball player's *style* to be able to fool (or amuse) the coach right down to the day he cut the last of the dreamers from the squad and gave out the uniforms.

Though my disappointment was keen, my misfortune did not necessitate a change in plans for the future. Playing baseball was not what the Jewish boys of our lower-middle-class neighborhood were expected to do in later life for a living. Had I been cut from the high school itself, *then* there would have been hell to pay in my house, and much confusion and shame in me. As it was, my family took my chagrin in stride and lost no more faith in me than I actually did in myself. They probably would have been shocked if I had made the team.

Maybe I would have been too. Surely it would have put me on a somewhat different footing with this game that I loved with all my heart, not simply for the fun of playing it (fun was secondary, really), but for the mythic and aesthetic

Roy Perry, *Camp Moodna, "Who's Up First?"* gelatin silver print, Mountainville, New York, ca. 1940

dimension that it gave to an American boy's life—particularly to one whose grandparents could hardly speak English. For someone whose roots in America were strong but only inches deep, and who had no experience, such as a Catholic child might, of an awesome hierarchy that was real and felt, baseball was a kind of secular church that reached into every class and region of the nation and bound millions upon millions of us together in common concerns, loyalties, rituals, enthusiasms, and antagonisms. Baseball made me understand what patriotism was about, at its best.

Not that Hitler, the Bataan Death March, the battle for the Solomons, and the Normandy invasion didn't make of me and my contemporaries what may well have been the most patriotic generation of schoolchildren in American history (and the most willingly and successfully propagandized). But the war we entered when I was eight had thrust the country into what seemed to a child—and not only to a child—a struggle to the death between Good and Evil. Fraught with perilous, unthinkable possibilities, it inevitably nourished a patriotism grounded in moral virtue and bloody-minded hate, the patriotism that fixes a bayonet to a Bible. It seems to me that through baseball I was put in touch with a more humane and tender brand of patriotism, lyrical rather than martial or righteous in spirit, and without the reek of saintly zeal, a patriotism that could not so easily be sloganized, or contained in a high-sounding formula to which you had to pledge something vague but all-encompassing called your "allegiance."

To sing the National Anthem in the school auditorium every week, even during the worst of the war years, generally left me cold. The enthusiastic lady teacher waved her arms in the air and we obliged with the words: "See! Light! Proof! Night! There!" But nothing stirred within, strident as we might be—in the end, just another school exercise. It was different, however, on Sundays out at Ruppert Stadium, a green wedge of pasture miraculously walled in among the factories, warehouses, and truck depots of industrial Newark. It would, in fact, have seemed to me an emotional thrill forsaken if, before the Newark Bears took on the hated enemy from across the marshes, the Jersey City Giants, we hadn't first to rise to our feet (my father, my brother, and I—along with our inimical countrymen, the city's Germans, Italians, Irish, Poles, and, out in the Africa of the bleachers, Newark's Negroes) to celebrate the America that had given to this unharmonious mob a game so grand and beautiful.

Just as I first learned the names of the great institutions of higher learning by trafficking in football pools for a neighborhood bookmaker rather than from our high school's college adviser, so my feel for the American landscape came less from what I learned in the classroom about Lewis and Clark than from following the major-league clubs on their road trips and reading about the minor leagues in the back pages of *The Sporting News*. The size of the continent got through to you finally when you had to stay up to 10:30 P.M. in New Jersey to hear via radio "ticker-tape" Cardinal pitcher Mort Cooper throw the first strike of the night to Brooklyn shortstop Pee Wee Reese out in "steamy" Sportsman's Park in St. Louis, Missouri. And however much we might be told by teacher about the stockyards and the Haymarket riot, Chicago only began to exist for me as a real place, and to matter in American history, when I became fearful (as a Dodger fan) of the bat of Phil Cavarretta, first baseman for the Chicago Cubs.

Baseball, as played in the big leagues, was something completely outside my own life that could nonetheless move me to ecstasy and to tears.

Not until I got to college and was introduced to literature did I find anything with a comparable emotional atmosphere and aesthetic appeal. I don't mean to suggest that it was a simple exchange, one passion for another. Between first discovering the Newark Bears and the Brooklyn Dodgers at seven or eight and first looking into Conrad's *Lord Jim* at age eighteen, I had done some growing up. I am only saying that my discovery of literature, and fiction particularly, and the "love affair"—to some degree hopeless, but still earnest—that has ensued, derives in part from this childhood infatuation with Baseball. Or, more accurately perhaps, baseball—with its lore and legends, its cultural power, its seasonal associations, its native authenticity, its simple rules and transparent strategies, its longueurs and thrills, its spaciousness, its suspensefulness, its heroics, its nuances, its lingo, its "characters," its peculiarly hypnotic tedium, its mythic transformation of the immediate—was the literature of my boyhood.

Baseball, as played in the big leagues, was something completely outside my own life that could nonetheless move me to ecstasy and to tears; like fiction it could excite the imagination and hold the attention as much with minutiae as with high drama. Mel Ott's cocked leg striding into the ball, Jackie Robinson's pigeon-toed shuffle as he moved out to second base, each was to be as deeply affecting over the years as that night—"inconceivable," "inscrutable," as any night Conrad's Marlow might struggle to comprehend—the night that Dodger wild man, Rex Barney (who never lived up to "our" expectations, who should have been "our" Koufax), not only went the distance without walking in half a dozen runs, but, of all things, threw a no-hitter. A thrilling mystery, marvelously enriched by the fact that a light rain had fallen during the early evening, and Barney, figuring the game was going to be postponed, had eaten a hot dog just before being told to take the mound.

This detail was passed on to us by Red Barber, the Dodger radio sportscaster of the forties, a respectful, mild Southerner with a subtle rural tanginess to his vocabulary and a soft country-parson tone to his voice. For the adventures of "dem bums" of Brooklyn—a region then the very symbol of urban wackiness and tumult—to be narrated from Red Barber's highly alien but loving perspective constituted a genuine triumph of what my English professors would later teach me to call "point of view." James himself might have admired the implicit cultural ironies and the splendid possibilities for oblique moral and social commentary. And as for the detail about Rex Barney eating his hot dog, it was irresistible, joining as it did the spectacular to the mundane, and furnishing an adolescent boy with a glimpse of an unexpectedly ordinary, even humdrum, side to male heroism.

Of course, in time, neither the flavor and suggestiveness of Red Barber's narration nor "epiphanies" as resonant with meaning as Rex Barney's pregame hot dog could continue to satisfy a developing literary appetite; nonetheless, it was just this that helped to sustain me until I was ready to begin to respond to the great inventors of narrative detail and masters of narrative voice and perspective like James, Conrad, Dostoevsky, and Bellow.

WHY BASEBALL BEGINS
IN THE SPRING

MARC
TRACY

In December 1999, during one of the two or three deadest months of the year for baseball, *Sports Illustrated*—having put the more seasonally appropriate Dan Marino on its cover—deemed a baseball player with only two full seasons to his credit worthy of a feature-length profile. Partly it was that outfielder Shawn Green, having been traded from the Toronto Blue Jays to the Los Angeles Dodgers, was poised to take his place in the heart of a lineup also stacked with the likes of Gary Sheffield, Eric Karros, and Adrian Beltre. Partly it was that Green had signed one of the biggest contracts in baseball history.

But mainly, just judging by what the article itself focused on, the justification for so many print inches was that Green seemed set to become the most notable—and notably—Jewish ballplayer since his fellow Dodger Sandy Koufax retired in 1966. (Incidentally, the article repeatedly misidentifies Rod Carew—who married a Jewish woman but never converted—as a "member of the tribe.") "If Green had a dollar for every bar mitzvah he was invited to over his first five years in the big leagues," author Michael Bamberger noted, "he'd be rich." Bamberger quoted Green's mother in the hometown paper, the *Orange County Register*, saying: "If Shawn doesn't make the majors, he'll just become a doctor." Accompanying the article was a photograph of Green at Canter's, the legendary deli in Los Angeles's Fairfax neighborhood, flanked by three *bubbes* and his table stacked with pastrami, matzah ball soup, pickles, rye bread, and Dr. Brown's Cream Soda. You get the picture, *nu*?

But after the neo-Borscht Belt routine was complete, Bamberger closed on a profound, important, and original thought. Not only did Shawn Green have "all the stuff to become a hero to his people," the author concluded, "He has all the stuff to become a hero, period."

On that final note—the close so abrupt it literally had to be spelled out—Bamberger revealed the central tension of what it means to be a Jew in baseball today, and what it means for Jewish fans to root for a Jew in baseball. On the one hand, a Jewish major leaguer carries an element of *dayenu* to him. He has a uniform? It is enough. On the other hand, if baseball, America's pastime and all that, is ripe space for assimilation and acceptance, then the last thing Jewish ballplayers should do is

On the one hand, a Jewish major leaguer carries an element of *dayenu* to him. He has a uniform? It is enough.

Shawn Green and *bubbes* pose for a *Sports Illustrated* profile, December 13, 1999

stand out for being Jewish, particularly if it's because they lack any other good reason to stand out. Jewish ballplayers are great for giving little Jewish boys and girls something to aspire to, and that is true even if their aspiration is not to play for the Dodgers. But nobody aspires to hit .219—or to do the equivalent of .219—in music, business, or (yes) medicine.

Green—a lifetime .283 hitter who slugged a formidable 328 home runs—became a hero, period, as well as to his people. But the tension can cut in the other direction as well. Never has this been so laceratingly brought home to Jewish fans than in the case of Ryan Braun.

The Milwaukee Brewers' Braun was—is, perhaps—unequivocally a superstar. He was a slugger on a competitive team. He won the Most Valuable Player Award. He signed a long-term contract to play for his small-market franchise through his prime years rather than hold out for a juicy deal from one of the megaspenders on the coasts. Is he handsome? Not that it should matter (unless it should), but yes.

And then, over the course of eighteen months, much of it came apart. Braun's name cropped up in connection with a shady Miami-area clinic that was connected to banned substances. A mishandled test prolonged the retrospectively inevitable: Braun was suspended for sixty-five games without pay for violating the leagues' substance policies; his 2013 season ended in July. Braun's name is now uttered in the same breath as Alex Rodriguez's, and it seems destined to be for years.

And what was really bad—both generally and For The Jews—was that also, without any solid grounding in evidence, Braun accused the man

Even baseball fans, the most sentimental group of people this side of people who cry at operas, have learned to reaccept players tainted by illicit performance-enhancing drugs.

Ryan Braun of the Milwaukee
Brewers, April 27, 2012

responsible for collecting his urine of antisemitism. It was the grotesque mirror image of a perfect ethnic moment. It was as if Jewish fans' sense of dissatisfaction, disappointment, and betrayal simply could not be *permitted* to go unarticulated. Braun—whose mother is not Jewish, who did not have a bar mitzvah, who had seemed at best reluctant to be embraced by the Jewish community (no deli spread for him)—had his most prominently Jewish moment only when it seemed to be maximally convenient for him. Really, it is difficult to conceive of a way the whole thing could have gone down worse.

Braun will be back. He will probably remain good, even great. (He says, credibly, that he took the banned substance in order to recover more rapidly from an injury—which is no legal defense, but does constitute a substantial distinction from the sluggers of the 1990s who loaded up on steroids in order to slam inhuman quantities of home runs.) But can he be a hero again—to his people, and to the world?

Actually, the latter question is easily answered: Yes. Even baseball fans, the most sentimental group of people this side of people who cry at operas, have learned to reaccept players tainted by illicit performance-enhancing drugs. Mark McGwire, of all people, has quietly rejoined the ranks of the tolerated as a hitting coach for the St. Louis Cardinals. You can be sure Braun will be tested again, and you can be nearly as sure he will pass. He will continue to be a good team player (how good the team will be is a different story) and a good citizen of Milwaukee. A few weeks after his suspension came down, he admitted guilt; gave a comprehensive accounting of what he did; and apologized to his teammates, his fans, and the urine collector. I suspect this will be enough for many. It should be enough for everyone.

But will it be enough for most Jews? It is harder to say. If Braun does as he pledged to do in his apology—stay on the straight and narrow: "be part of the solution"—then Jews ought to forgive him. In fact, Jews who hold back their forgiveness would be failing as Jewish baseball fans, who should make peace with the fact that in nearly all respects great Jewish baseball players are exactly like great non-Jewish baseball players: imperfect sometimes, but deserving of second chances when they appear open to being worthy of them.

Actually, Jews who refuse Braun their compassion might not be upholding their obligations as Jews, either. When, in August 2013, Braun apologized and then reached out to his teammates and fans, going so far as to call some Brewers season ticket holders, a rabbi friend of mine keenly espied the timing of it all and noted that Braun was simply getting a few weeks' head start on the annual Yom Kippur ritual of *teshuvah*—the repentance, the atonement, the asking for mercy. Maimonides taught that if the victim of the sin is stubborn enough to resist repeated entreaties for forgiveness, the victim himself becomes sinful. Which is another way of saying that there is a reason baseball begins in the spring.

Sandy Koufax pitching in Dodger Stadium, July 20, 1965

IRA BERKOW

WHAT WOULD

Koufax

HAVE SAID?

A View of How Baseball
Played a Role in Shaping Jewish
Identity in America

AT AGE 73, Sandy Koufax, hair more salt than pepper, looked fit enough to hurl a few shutout innings in a tight ballgame. Nattily dressed in a navy blazer, white button-down shirt, and wine-red tie, his understated but warmly appealing manner immediately recognizable to his millions of fans, he sat for a 2009 film interview for the documentary *Jews and Baseball: An American Love Story*, for which I was the scriptwriter. The interview was conducted by the film's director, Peter Miller, in his apartment on the west side of Manhattan. Miller and Koufax were seated facing each other, a video camera above Miller's shoulder focusing on Koufax. The conversation turned to Koufax's striking out fifteen New York Yankees for the Los Angeles Dodgers in the first game of the 1963 World Series, a World Series record.

That sunny October afternoon Yankee Stadium looked immense to Koufax. "You're playing the Yankees in Yankee Stadium, which is an amazing feeling," he recalled. "The stadium is so tall and then so close to the field, as opposed to other ballparks, it almost feels like you're at the bottom of the Grand Canyon." Whitey Ford, the Yankees' starting pitcher, "came out and struck out the side in the first inning," continued Koufax. "So I came out and struck out the side. It kind of made it feel like, OK, the game is on...."

And so it was. Koufax began to dominate. Yogi Berra, who was coaching at first base for the Yankees, remembered feeling "lonely there." "No one was coming to see me," he recalled, because most of the Yankee batters were returning to the dugout, their bats useless against Koufax's sizzling fastball and tumbling-off-a-table curveball. To say nothing of his knee-buckling changeup as well as control that would make a pub dart-thrower envious.

I was sitting on a couch nearby, a few feet from Koufax and next to his wife, Jane. During a break in filming, I took the opportunity to speak with Koufax.

"Sandy," I said, "are you aware of James Thurber's line that the majority of American males go to bed at night dreaming of striking out the Yankee batting order?"

"No," he said. "I hadn't heard that."

"But you did it."

He shrugged, as if to say, "That's nice."

"Did you ever dream of doing anything like that?" I continued.

"No, I never have."

That response hung in the air for a moment.

"Well, Sandy," I said, "what *do* you dream about?" A throw-away line, to be sure.

He smiled. "Her," he said, pointing to Jane.

Everyone in the room laughed. Jane beamed. Koufax, not known for his prowess at the plate, had hit this one out of the park.

I tell this story because it is so revealing of Koufax as well as of the Jewish condition and tradition in America.

Here was a "clutch moment" of sorts—Koufax was certainly used to dealing with crises, with games on the line—and perhaps this was also a moment of indecision, and the Jewish baseball icon chose the right thing to say. He came at it from an unusual, unexpected angle, underscored with a, well, Yiddish sense of humor, as he deflected the question away from himself. Similarly, over the last six thousand years Jews have sought to overcome, resolve, or sidestep situations by brains, by

---

Mark Twain had a similar take when, in 1890, he commented that baseball had become "the very symbol, the outward and visible expression of the drive and push and rush and struggle of the raging, tearing, booming nineteenth century."

Sandy Koufax

of the world of baseball. The "national pastime" would take a passionate hold among newly arrived Jewish citizens and their offspring, a hold that continues to the present day. As the esteemed scholar and author Jacques Barzun, French-born but an Americanized citizen, wrote in 1954, "Whoever wants to know the heart and mind of America had better learn baseball."

Mark Twain had a similar take when, in 1890, he commented that baseball had become "the very symbol, the outward and visible expression of the drive and push and rush and struggle of the raging, tearing, booming nineteenth century." Bart Giamatti, the late commissioner of baseball, echoed both earlier writers in 1998, when he wrote in *A Great and Glorious Game*, "[In the early part of the twentieth century,] baseball became business as Business and wealth and population boomed across the country, as millions of immigrants poured in, as the tempo of life quickened and the country flexed its muscles. Baseball, increasingly played with increased skill, caught the mood of America and rode it…. [F]or the immigrant, the game was a club to belong to, another fraternal organization, a common language in a strange land. For so much of expanding and expansive America, the game was a free institution with something for everyone."

Jews, as well as other European immigrants, blacks, Hispanics, and Asians found significant truth in the idea that baseball opens the doors to feeling American. For example, in the 1920s Jews flocked to the Polo Grounds to see the rookie second baseman Andy Cohen play for the New York Giants while Italians cheered Yankee second baseman Tony Lazzeri, one of the first Italian star major leaguers, calling from the stands, "Poosh 'em up, Tony" in the hope that their Italian hero would advance the runners whenever he came to bat. Growing up in Chicago, I remember going to Wrigley Field with my father in 1948 to see the Cubs play the Brooklyn Dodgers. I remember the great block of Negroes (as blacks were generally referred to in those days) all sitting together in the

innovation, by wit, by self-possession, even by, yes, muscle, and sometimes with their lives hanging in the balance—which, to say the least, wasn't quite the case with Koufax's response to my question.

At one end of the spectrum, it was nothing more than a cute, though surely sagacious, response. On the other, it might well be fodder for, as is almost everything else, a Talmudic discussion. At this point I will leave it to Hebraic scholars to continue the discourse if, in fact, one is to be had.

From their earliest moments in America, Jews faced a preponderance of obstacles amid strivings, from their first attempt to settle on these shores in the seventeenth century (initially barred from entry by Peter Stuyvesant, the antisemitic governor of New Amsterdam, later called New York, who referred to Jews as "a repugnant race") to their various travails in "Columbus's Land" (as immigrants were wont to refer to America) to their entrance into, and discovery, as it were,

right-field grandstands (and nowhere else in the stadium), attired in their Sunday-best suits and dresses and hats, and heartily, if politely, cheering for Jackie Robinson.

The prejudice and ignorance that Robinson had to confront when he broke the seventy-year-long color barrier in the major leagues has been well documented. Some fifteen years after Robinson had established himself as one of baseball's greatest players, I interviewed Dixie Walker, then spring training batting coach for the Dodgers. Walker, a Southerner from Alabama, had been a teammate of Robinson and outspoken in the beginning about his aversion to playing with a black man. "Not only did some of us feel that a Negro was inferior to a white, but we thought they couldn't take the pressure, that they didn't have ice water in their veins," said Walker. "It didn't take long for Jackie, and a lot of the others—Mays, Aaron, Newcombe—to prove us totally wrong."

As a sportswriter, I remember the intense interest and pride that Latinos took in the success, for example, of the future Hall of Fame Pittsburgh Pirate outfielder Roberto Clemente, who became one of Puerto Rico's most revered native citizens. Cubans have exulted in fellow countrymen who succeeded in the major leagues, like Tony Oliva, Minnie Miñoso, and Aroldis Chapman. And Dominicans have had hundreds of players to cheer for, among them Juan Marichal and the brothers Jesus, Matty, and Moises Alou. Venezuelans look to White Sox shortstops Chico Carrasquel and Hall of Famer Luis Aparicio, Mexicans to Fernando Valenzuela and Sergio Romo, and Panamanians to Rod Carew and Mariano Rivera.

I remember the remarkable flock of Japanese reporters crowding into the press box to send back transmissions to fans in Japan hungry for information about their countrymen who had joined the major leagues, from pitcher Hideo Nomo to catcher Kenji Johjima to infielder Kazuo Matsui to outfielders Hideki Matsui and Ichiro Suzuki. Pretty much the same held for the South Korean major leaguers, like outfielder Shin-Soo Choo and pitcher Chan Ho Park, and the Taiwanese, including pitcher Chien-Ming Wang and infielder Chin-Lung Hu.

On opening day 2013, 241 players, or 28.2 percent of those on major league rosters, were born outside of the fifty states in the United States, representing fifteen countries or territories, including two from the most distant country, Australia, Oakland Athletics pitchers Grant Balfour and Travis Blackley. Although rugby and cricket are the major sports in Australia, both Balfour and Blackley discovered baseball as young boys and took to its "complexity," as Balfour described it. Baseball has been in Australia since 1850, when American gold miners first brought the game over, but it never gained truly widespread popularity. But some two dozen Aussies have indeed found their way to the big leagues, including Sydney-born Trent Oetjien, former Los Angeles Dodgers outfielder. He said that growing up he was intrigued by the "faster pace of baseball." "Cricket's a little slow, and it can take a couple of days to complete a match," he said. "I wasn't too into that." (The great Irish playwright George Bernard Shaw, taking note of the two sports, saw it somewhat similarly, if drolly: "Baseball has the great advantage over cricket in being sooner ended.")

Baseball's origins, to be sure, stretch back farther than the game played by those American miners in Australia. Fact is, no one knows exactly when or where baseball began—most likely in the eighteenth century with a version called one o' cat or rounders, though it would hardly be recognized in American ballparks today. But by the middle of the nineteenth century, baseball was emerging as the most popular sport in America, played in sandlots in the country and empty lots in the city. America was made up of people from every other place on earth, and as each new group arrived, they too found baseball.

At the end of the Civil War, the Jewish population in America was a quarter million, one-half of one percent of the nation. One of the first players to receive money for playing baseball—twenty dollars from the Philadelphia Athletics in 1866—was a Jew of Dutch origin, the outfielder Lipman Emanuel Pike. When the first professional baseball league, the National Association of Professional Baseball Players, was organized in 1871, Lipman Pike was its star. He led the league in home runs the first three years of its existence, hitting as many as six home runs in a season.

When Barry Bonds became the all-time leader in career home runs in 2007, I was charmed to come across a timetable of big-league career home-run leaders. Bonds broke Henry Aaron's record of 755, Aaron broke Babe Ruth's record of 714, and so

St. Louis Brown Stockings, 1876. Lipman Pike, one of America's first baseball stars, is seated at center, holding a bat

on to the first career home-run leader, Lipman Emanuel Pike, known as "Iron Batter" for his stunning ability at the plate. Pike hit a total of twenty home runs in his sixteen-year career, a seemingly low number, but baseball was different in those days: the ball softer, the outfield stands more distant, pitchers using the spitball (disallowed today), yet he still sent more baseballs soaring over the fences than any of his contemporaries.

It has not been recorded, to my knowledge, whether Pike endured any antisemitic treatment. He was respected enough to be named a player-manager for the Troy (New York) Haymakers, the first Jew to become a professional baseball manager. Still, it is instructive to know that Jewish big-league players in the early part of the twentieth century (some with very short careers and only a handful of games, and others who played for a number of years)—such as the five-foot-four, 145-pound St. Louis Cardinals shortstop Reuben Ewing (born in Odessa, Ukraine), Philadelphia Phillies pitcher Harry ("Klondike") Kane, Chicago

White Sox pitcher Ed Corey, Cincinnati Reds star infielder Sam Bohne, and Yankees third baseman Phil Cooney—all decided to change their names when they entered professional baseball. Each one of them, as it happens, was born Cohen or Cohn. At the time that Harry Kane made his debut in the major leagues, on August 8, 1902, a story in *The Sporting News* noted, "His name is Cohen and he assumed that of Kane, when he became a semi-professional, because he fancied that there was a popular and professional prejudice against Hebrews as ball players."

One who did not change his name was second baseman Andy Cohen, who came up to the New York Giants in 1926. He once told me about a minor league game in which he was being harassed by a fan who loudly called him "Christ killer." Finally, Cohen had had enough. He went to the edge of the stands and, bat in hand, shouted, "Come down here and I'll kill you, too!"

Another time, after Cohen made a very good catch in the field, a fan in the stands shouted, "Just

Hank Greenberg with his award for Most Valuable Player, Briggs Stadium, 1936

He once told me, "it was still hard enough trying to hit a major league fastball without thinking that the Jewish community was looking over my shoulder."

like all you Jews—you'll take anything you can get your hands on." Cohen felt differently this time. "I didn't mind that so much," he said. "It was actually a backhanded compliment."

Despite the increased assimilation of Jews in America, primarily after World War II—when glass ceilings were removed in corporations, quotas permitting only a certain number of Jews in colleges, including several in the Ivy League, exposed and eliminated; housing and country club restrictions eased somewhat—some Jew-baiting and discrimination in and around baseball still existed.

A young Navy ensign, fresh from battle in the South Pacific, returned stateside after the war and embarked on a baseball career, and two years later, in 1947, at age twenty-three, made it to the major leagues as a third baseman with the Cleveland Indians (though he did not stick with the big club until two years later, eventually becoming a four-time American League All-Star, unanimously elected Most Valuable Player of his league in 1953, and one of the best sluggers in baseball during his ten seasons). This was Albert (Al) Leonard Rosen, who grew up in Miami but in a racially and ethnically mixed area, and from the time he was a small boy felt, or was made to feel, intensely about his Jewishness, so much so that he said, "There were times I considered changing my name to sound even more Jewish—a name maybe like Rosenthal or Rosenstein."

"Being a Jew in the limelight is a heavy burden," Rosen said. "To be someone that your community, your friends, your associates look up to unwaveringly. When I was a baseball player, I always felt like I wanted to be the Jew that all other Jews could be proud of. I knew the newspapers wrote about what I did and didn't do not only on the field, but off the field as well. And I just felt that it was very important to the Jews that were following my career—even the Jews who didn't know anything about baseball but were proud of their heritage—to have someone they could be proud of."

Hank Greenberg, who would become the first Jewish baseball superstar, came up to the major leagues nearly two decades before Rosen, with the Detroit Tigers. It was 1930; the nation was in the throes of the Great Depression; and antisemitism, which was rife in America, would, with the rise of Adolf Hitler, grow to unimaginably tragic proportions in Europe.

Greenberg, named the American League's Most Valuable Player in 1935, was continually sought after by the Detroit Jewish community for appearances, dinners, and other events. The child of Orthodox parents, he had grown up in the Bronx and wanted to be "a good baseball player, not a good Jewish baseball player." He tried to shrug off that burden—an added burden, as he saw and felt it. "While I was very aware not to do anything that would embarrass the Jewish people," he once told me, "it was still hard enough trying to hit a major league fastball without thinking that the Jewish community was looking over my shoulder."

That changed by 1938, when Greenberg pursued Babe Ruth's hallowed record of sixty home runs in a single season. As he was belting home fifty-two, fifty-three, fifty-four, fifty-five, he said he was acutely aware of the plight of Jews in Europe. "As time went by, I came to feel that if I, as a Jew, hit a home run, I was hitting one against Hitler," he said. With five games to go in the season, Greenberg had fifty-eight home runs. He did not hit another, though he got several hits and some long outs and foul balls. He was walked a handful of times, but no more than any other slugger of his caliber. It is widely thought by conspiracy theorists that the opposing pitchers did not want a Jew to break Babe Ruth's record, so they pitched around him.

Greenberg, who died in 1986 at age seventy-five, disputed that supposition. "I had enough chances," he said. "I just didn't do it." The facts, as I understand them, bear that out. One example Greenberg liked to raise was his fifty-seventh home run, against the St. Louis Browns. He had hit a ball over the center fielder's head, and it bounced against the wall and rolled back toward the infield. Greenberg, not a speedy runner, thought he could get an inside-the-park home run. The third-base coach tried to hold him up, but Greenberg ignored him, thinking he could beat the relay. The throw came in to the catcher and, recalled Greenberg, "I was out by a mile." However, the home-plate umpire, an Irishman named Bill McGowan ("my good friend," said Greenberg), called him safe. The Browns' catcher leaped up and protested, but to no avail. Home run number fifty-seven was entered into the record book.

"Hank Greenberg was the perfect standard-bearer for Jews," Shirley Povich, a Jew and the great sports columnist for the *Washington Post*, said. "He was smart, he was proud—and he was *big*."

Yet both Greenberg and Rosen battled antisemitism in their time—even engaging in fistfights with other players over insulting remarks (Rosen, in fact, was quite handy with his fists, having been a Golden Gloves middleweight champion while still in high school). On the other hand, Koufax, who came along several years after Greenberg and overlapped with Rosen only briefly, said he experienced none that he was aware of.

However, Ike Davis, the New York Mets' first baseman, had a stunning though different awakening into his Jewish identity. Putting together a family tree while in high school in Scottsdale, Arizona, Davis discovered that many of the relatives on his mother's side had perished in the Holocaust (his mother—the former Millie Gollinger—is Jewish while his father, Ron, a former major league pitcher, is Baptist). Davis consulted his great aunt, who survived the Holocaust, and she told him of the horrors members of his family had endured during Hitler's regime. "That's when I realized how brutal it was and how many people were killed," Davis said. His grandfather on his father's side landed in France on D-day in 1944 and later helped liberate one of the concentration camps. Davis said that his grandfather's experience in Europe made it easier for him to accept the Jewish girl his son brought home, who would become his wife and eventually Ike's mother.

Although Davis has not asked to be a representative for Jewish causes, he understands that, particularly among New York City's expansive Jewish population, he is held up as a contemporary standard-bearer of Jewish baseball heritage.

"But I'm not trying to be a role model for any religious reasons," he told Dave Waldstein of *The New York Times*. "I'm trying to be a role model, period, for everyone, by just being a good person, a responsible person who leads the best life he can. That's for everyone, I think."

Rarely has a Jewish baseball player been involved in a controversy that puts him in a negative light, but that happened during the 2013 season: Ryan Braun, the star outfielder for the Milwaukee Brewers, admitted to having taken performance-enhancing drugs during the 2011 season, when he was named the National League's Most Valuable Player.

"I was shocked and deeply disappointed by those revelations," said the eighty-nine-year-old Al Rosen by telephone from his home in Rancho Mirage, California. "Ryan Braun was this clean-cut, impressive young man, and had a reputation comparable to, say, Derek Jeter. Braun is a special kind of athlete, and if you're a Jew in that category, you have two kinds of people following you—those who admire you and want you to succeed, and those who want you to fall on your face because of who you are. As a Jew, I especially follow the progress of Jewish ball players. And I revel in their success, as I reveled in Ryan Braun's. He's a tremendous player, but he broke the rules of the game. Being a Jewish athlete is a kind of calling. Imagine, you've reached a level that only a very few reach, and so many wish they could. So I think you have an added responsibility."

Jews take satisfaction not only in the legitimate achievements of Jewish baseball players on the field, but also, in certain cases, their erudition. These are, after all, the "People of the Book." Perhaps the most learned of the twenty-first-century Jewish major leaguers is Craig Breslow, a Yale graduate with a bachelor's degree in molecular biophysics and biochemistry. Breslow, a left-handed pitcher for the Boston Red Sox, had been admitted to the New York University School of Medicine several years ago, but deferred acceptance because of his "love of the game." In 2010 *The Sporting News* named Breslow the "smartest athlete in sports," topping a list of twenty. From Trumbull, Connecticut, he was brought up with a sense of Jewishness by his parents, Abe and Anne Breslow, both teachers. "Being Jewish is more difficult in baseball...but I try to do what I can in terms of paying attention to holidays," he said. While pitching on Yom Kippur, for example, Breslow noted that he "was also fasting." Breslow has traveled extensively in the big leagues since his 2005 debut—San Diego, 2005; Red Sox, 2006; Cleveland Indians, 2008; Minnesota Twins, 2008–9; Oakland Athletics, 2009–11; Arizona Diamondbacks, 2012; and back to Boston. Breslow's journeys illustrate that

Al Rosen awaits a pitch during spring training in Tucson, Arizona, photograph by Hy Peskin for *Sports Illustrated,* April 18, 1955

APRIL 18, 1955
25 CENTS

Sandy Koufax celebrates pitching a perfect game, September 9, 1965

regardless of impressive brain matter and a ninety-two-mile-an-hour fastball, making it in the major leagues is still a tough go.

Among Jews of great wisdom in baseball, there have been none like the inscrutable Morris (Moe) Berg: spy, scholar, catcher.

In the baseball press boxes at Shea Stadium and Yankee Stadium in the late 1960s and early 1970s, Berg sat in a black suit, black tie, black shoes—the ensemble never varied; his black hair with a touch of gray at the temples, black eyebrows rather closely knit, warm smile, elegant demeanor, and high intelligence created an air of mystery that he often fostered. I would often sit with him and listen to both his insights on the goings-on on the ball field before us and his stories of long ago.

Berg's seventeen years in the major leagues with the Dodgers, Indians, Senators, White Sox, and Red Sox produced a lifetime batting average of .243 with eleven stolen bases and six home runs. He was, wrote Terry Hauser in a letter to me, "unmatched for marginality."

Berg, who died at age seventy in 1972, had extended his big-league playing career because managers liked having him around for his wisdom. He knew the pitchers and could help the hitters. On occasion he could knock a pitch off the left-field wall. Berg, the son of Ukrainian Jewish immigrants, graduated from Princeton University, where he had been a star shortstop and graduated magna cum laude with a major in languages. He was also a graduate of the Sorbonne, and then studied law at Columbia University and passed the bar while a starting catcher for the White Sox in 1929. Two anecdotes about Berg have met the test of time: "Moe could speak twelve languages but couldn't hit in any of them" and, kidded by other players, including Hank Greenberg, "Moe, you have seven college degrees but you always call the wrong pitch."

Moe told me of the time he returned to Princeton and requested to meet with Albert Einstein, then an esteemed faculty member of the Institute for Advanced Study. They met at Einstein's residence on campus, drinking tea from glasses, and the professor played the violin for Berg. At one point, Einstein said to his guest, "You teach me baseball, and I'll teach you the theory of relativity." But Einstein then added, "We'd better forget it. You will learn mathematics faster than I would learn baseball."

Berg was not only a wise baseball player, but he was also a spy. In 1934, while on tour as a player with an All-Star team in Japan (Moe was brought along with Babe Ruth and others, but as an interpreter), he disguised himself in a kimono (black, of course) and from rooftops snapped photos of industrial plants in Tokyo that were supposedly helpful to American bombing missions during World War II. It was also said that Berg, working with the Office of Strategic Services, a precursor to the Central Intelligence Agency, was sent to a conference in Zurich in December 1944 where Germany's leading scientist, Werner Heisenberg, might indicate that the Nazis had a devastating weapon, perhaps the atomic bomb. If so, Berg, who was fluent in German, had instructions to assassinate Heisenberg on the spot. The scientist revealed no such new weapon, and Berg, as the story goes, spared his life.

"Moe," I asked him, "is the story true?" In his customary fashion, he put his finger to his lips, and said, "Shh," even some twenty-five years after the alleged fact.

I once asked Moe if he had ever written for publication. "Only once," he said. "A treatise on Sanskrit."

Not true. One day shortly after our conversation, I was browsing in a secondhand bookstore and ran across an old collection of *Atlantic Monthly* articles; one, written in 1940, was titled "Pitchers and Catchers." The author was Moe Berg.

The piece was all Moe: smart, insightful, and fun. Such as: "At first, the superspeed of Grove obviated the necessity of pitching brains. But, when his speed began to fade, Lefty turned to his head. With almost perfect control and the addition of his fork ball, Lefty fools the hitter with his cunning. With Montaigne, we conceive of Socrates in place of Alexander, of brain for brawn, wit for whip...."

When I next saw Berg at the ballpark, I said, somewhat perplexed, "Moe, you told me you never wrote for publication." And I produced the book.

He looked at it, looked at me, and smiled.

"You caught me," he said.

The complexities of identity, of what we hide and what we show, and the complications of fitting in have been as much a part of our national pastime as they have been for all American minorities. This piece began with an anecdote about Sandy Koufax, and it seems fitting to conclude with one that may

Moe Berg

say something about how being Jewish shaped his understated, but very real, identity. The fact that Koufax did not pitch on Yom Kippur, which happened to fall on the first day of the 1965 World Series, was a matter of pride for Jews across the country. "I had always taken Yom Kippur off, and felt I should do the same, even if it was the World Series," Koufax said. Koufax pitched Game 2 against the Minnesota Twins, lost, then won Game 5, returning with just two days rest to pitch a three-hit shutout, 2–0, to give the Dodgers the World Series victory.

I had heard an anecdote about that Series and wondered about its veracity. Don Drysdale, the other ace on the Dodgers pitching staff along with Koufax, started Game 1 and was removed by manager Walt Alston in the second inning in the midst of a six-run scoring outburst by the Twins. One day in the 1980s, when Drysdale was a broadcaster, I ran into him and asked if the story was true. "Yes," he said. "When Alston came to the mound to take me out of the game, I handed him the ball and said, 'I know what you're thinking, Skip. You're wishing I was a Jew.'"

This is not the only example, to be sure, of how Jews have often succeeded in America and in the national pastime, but few, from where I sit, are funnier.

At one point, Einstein said to his guest, "You teach me baseball, and I'll teach you the theory of relativity." But Einstein then added, "We'd better forget it. You will learn mathematics faster than I would learn baseball."

C O L U M   M c C A N N

WHAT BASEBALL DOES TO THE SOUL

It was long before baseball ever enchanted me, and long before I ever knew anything of the Yankees, and long before I learned that a pitch could swerve, yet it came back to me, years later, sitting in the bleachers at Yankee Stadium, a curveball from the past.

It was 1975. I was 10 years old. I stood onboard a ferry in Dun Laoghaire, Ireland. I was traveling with my father to England for the weekend. We crossed the Irish Sea, the night blanket-black above us. On deck, men in flat caps worked hard at their coughs.

In Liverpool, dawn rose in increments of gray. We boarded a train for London. I had to hush. We were Irish after all. There were bombs going off in Britain in those days. The train swerved through a landscape that seemed exotic and familiar by turns. London, then, was a confusion of red post boxes, terraced houses and chimneystacks.

We made our way out to Highbury, where my favorite team, Stoke City, was playing against Arsenal. Portions of the game still decorate my memory with splinters of despair and joy—my team drew, 1–1—but it is not the game that later made sense to me.

On the way out of Highbury, my father and I bought a bottle of Powers whiskey. He seldom drank, my father, and the purchase surprised me. We stopped, then, to buy a carton of cigarettes and I knew that the world was shifting somehow: my father never smoked.

"How'd you like to see your grandfather?" he asked.

I had never met my grandfather Jack McCann. He was, I knew, a character—a man given to the Irish trinity of drink and song and exile.

We took a bus to Pimlico Road, tramped up the wide staircase of a decrepit nursing home. My father handed me the bottle of whiskey. "Go on in and give that to your grandda," he said.

A shadow in the bed. He glanced up and said, "Ah, another bleedin' McCann." But he perked up when he saw the bottle, reached out and tousled my hair.

He was a fabulous ruin, my grandfather. I sat on the bed beside him and—suddenly glamorous with whiskey—he told his stories. The greyhounds. The horses. The days with Big Jack Doyle. I sat in my red and white Stoke City shirt, stunned that this was a history that could belong to me.

What I recall is my father lifting me onto his shoulders, late that night, into a foreign city, toward the railway station, and home. A number of stray soccer fans were still singing under the station's eaves.

Down, 3–1. Bottom of the ninth. One on. Nobody out. The Yankees against the Minnesota Twins. Game 2 of the American League Division Series, October 2009. A-Rod is at the plate. The air has that chewy sense of hope. There is always call for a miracle.

"It's gonna happen, Dad."

This is what baseball can do to the soul: it has the ability to make you believe in spite of all other available evidence. My son, John Michael, is 10 years old. We are in the bleachers. He leans in to me and says that the pitch is going to come in high and fat. It's still a new language to me. The pitch is thrown, and indeed it does—it comes in high and fat, and 94 miles per hour. A-Rod leans into it like he's about to fell a tree and smacks the ball and it soars, that little sphere of cowhide rising up over the Bronx, and it is a moment unlike any other, when you sit with your son in the ballpark, and the ball is high in the air, you feel yourself aware of everything, the night, the neon, the very American-ness of the moment.

And then it strikes you that the ball has an endless quality of fatherhood to it.

We all know these moments. They don't come along very often, but when they do they open up your lungs to the bursting point. It's not simply me sitting with my son in the Bronx, but it's my father sitting with me in London, too, and maybe him with his own father in Dublin, and it all comes back to me, the pure and reckless joy of the past, Arsenal, Stoke City, the dark corners of a nursing home, the slippery deck of a ferry boat and how every moment is carried into other moments.

I stood in the bleachers as A-Rod rounded the bases with that slightly nonchalant grin: a Dominican kid born in Washington Heights had just brought me home.

Baseball is often talked about as the American game, but there is something wildly immigrant about it too. No other game can so solidly confirm the fact that you are in the United States, yet bring you home to your original country at the same time.

If soccer is the world's game, then baseball belongs to those who have left their worlds behind. This is not so much nostalgia as it a sense of *saudade*—a longing for something that is absent.

I have been in New York for 18 years. Every time I have gone to Yankee Stadium with my two sons and my daughter, I am somehow brought back to my boyhood. Perhaps it is because baseball is so very different from anything I grew up with.

The subway journey out. The hustlers, the bustlers, the bored cops. The jostle at the turnstiles. Up the ramps. Through the shadows. The huge swell of diamond green. The crackle. The billboards. The slight air of the unreal. The guilt when standing for another nation's national anthem. The hot dogs. The bad beer. The catcalls. Siddown. Shaddup. Fuhgeddaboudit.

Learning baseball is learning to love what is left behind also. The world drifts away for a few hours. We can rediscover what it means to be lost. The world is full, once again, of surprise. We go back to who we were.

I slipped into America via baseball. The language intrigued me. The squeeze plays, the fungoes, the bean balls, the curveballs, the steals. The showboating. The pageantry. The lyrical cursing that unfolded across the bleachers.

As the years went on, baseball surrounded me more and more. My son began listening to the radio late at night, under the covers. There was something gloriously tribal about the

> # No other game can so solidly confirm the fact that you are in the United States, yet bring you home to your original country at the same time.

PREVIOUS

Chien-Ming Wang pitches at Yankee
Stadium, April 18, 2009

ABOVE

Fans arriving at the Yankee Stadium
subway station at 161 Street for a
"Subway Series" between the New
York Yankees and the New York Mets,
June 8, 2012

Yankees for him. He learned to imitate John Sterling, the radio announcer. *It is high, it is far, it is gone. An A-bomb from A-Rod.* He began playing the game too, and so I would walk to Central Park with him. How far was my own father on the street behind me, juggling a soccer ball at his feet? How far was my dead grandfather?

We become the children of our children, the sons of our sons. We watch our kids as if watching ourselves. We take on the burden of their victories and defeats. It is our privilege, our curse too. We get older and younger at the same time.

I never meant to fall in love with baseball, but I did. I learned to realize that it does what all good sports should do: it creates the possibility of joy.

Sometimes, when walking home from the subway, after being at Yankee Stadium, I have the feeling that a whole country has been knocked around inside me. I am Irish, but I am also American. I am both father and son.

I cherish these moments. It confirms that life is not static. There is so much more left to be lived. There are times that my own boys are so tired that I have to put them on my shoulder and carry them. They are brought forward by the past.

I still recall the night of the A.L.D.S. game against Minnesota. A-Rod tied it up in the ninth. Teixeira closed out the game in the 11th. My son beamed, ear to ear. I think the stars over the Bronx shook that night. The potholes on 161st Street applauded. The 4 train ran on Champagne.

And me, well, I took a little journey a long way home.

THE *FORVERTS* EXPLAINS BASEBALL TO JEWISH IMMIGRANTS

BETH S. WENGER

In late August, at the height of the baseball season in 1909, the *Forverts*—the *Jewish Daily Forward*—printed an article, complete with a diagram of a baseball diamond, designed to teach Jewish immigrants about the American game of baseball.[1] Edited by the well-known socialist and author Abraham Cahan, the Yiddish newspaper reached approximately two hundred thousand readers, most of them immigrant Jews. The *Forverts* advanced socialist politics, kept readers informed of national and international issues, and was a backbone of the Jewish labor movement. But its pages also carried lighter fare, including a popular advice column known as the Bintel Brief, as well as copious advertisements for American consumer goods. Cahan fervently believed that immigrants could (and should) learn about American customs and habits, and he determined to accomplish that task through the medium of Yiddish and in the pages of his newspaper. American sports, so much a part of the national cultural fabric, thus found their way into many columns and editorials in the *Forverts*.

Just six years before the *Forverts* printed its 1909 explanatory column about the game of baseball, the anxieties of immigrant Jews about their children's desire to play the national pastime had already emerged in the newspaper's Bintel Brief advice column. Whether the letter printed in the paper was truly submitted by a concerned immigrant Jewish father or whether it was the creation of an editorial staff eager to address Jewish participation in American sports remains an open question. Whatever the authorship of the letter, it clearly testifies to immigrant Jews' uneasiness with American sports. The father inveighs to the editor with serious concerns about the "foolish and wild game" that his son plays with such passion. The father remains incredulous that in such a sophisticated country even adults play this nonsensical game. "They run after a piece of suede and fight with each other like small boys." The wildness that the father perceived in the game of baseball was not the vision that he had fashioned for his son in America. While the editor sympathized with the father's feelings and noted that many immigrant parents shared similar sentiments, he advised Jewish immigrants to "let the boys play baseball and become excellent at the game. Why not? It should not interfere with

The Polo Grounds grandstand, October 8, 1908

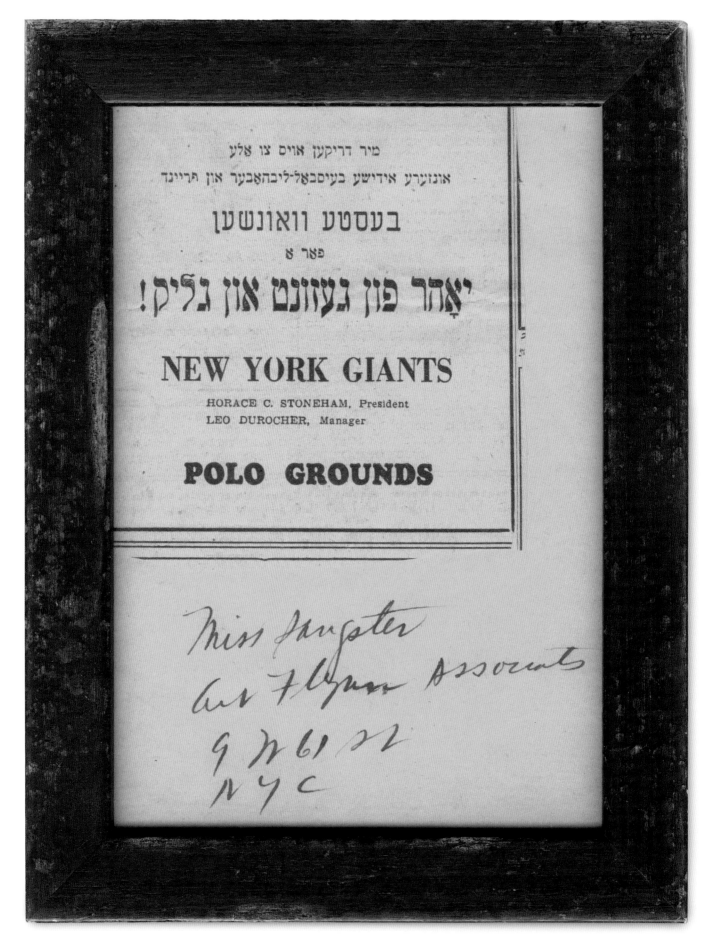

their studies and they should not become dragged down to bad company. In a healthy body lives a healthy mind." The editor underscored that Jewish children ought not be made to feel inferior by their lack of physical prowess, and in his primary message to all immigrant parents, he exhorted them, "[Let] us not raise the children to grow up foreigners in their own birthplace."[2]

Both amateur and professional sports may have appeared to immigrant Jews as dangerous or uncultured or merely a waste of time, but their children almost unanimously and wholeheartedly embraced America's games. Indeed, Abraham Cahan's Bintel Brief correctly predicted that participation in sports would help the children of immigrants fit in to their new homeland and identify as Americans.

> **Both amateur and professional sports may have appeared to immigrant Jews as dangerous or uncultured or merely a waste of time, but their children almost unanimously and wholeheartedly embraced America's games.**

By all accounts, young Jewish boys in particular were enamored with the American game of baseball. They attended games as fans and faithfully followed the outcomes. They played stickball in the streets and also honed their skills in the open spaces of city parks. The children of immigrants would not have needed the primer offered by the *Forverts* in 1909. They understood the nuances and rhythms of American baseball and came to know the game by playing it, by reading about it (increasingly in English-language newspapers rather than in the Yiddish press), and later by listening to it on the radio.

In hindsight, what is most striking about the *Forverts*'s 1909 column about baseball is how utterly foreign the game appears to the writers. To them, America's pastime remains exotic, and they admit their own inability to grasp it fully. They offer a wholly convoluted explanation of the game that would make little sense to any novice attempting to learn the fundamentals of baseball. So, the question remains, why do we find a column like this in America's most widely circulated Yiddish newspaper at the turn of the century? The columnist explains it simply enough: "If an entire nation is crazy over something, it's not too much to ask to try and understand what it means."[3] In other words, the editors of the *Forverts* may have possessed only the most rudimentary knowledge about America's game of baseball, but they recognized its cultural import and its impact for future generation of American Jews.

Ad taken out in the *Jewish Daily Forward* by the New York Giants "extend[s] to all our Yiddisha baseball lovers and friends best wishes for a year of health and joy," signed by manager Leo Durocher and owner Horace Stoneham, ca. 1940s/1950s

Notes

1   "The Fundamentals of the Base-Ball 'Game' Described for Non-Sports Fans," *Jewish Daily Forward,* Aug. 1909.
2   *Jewish Daily Forward,* 6 Aug. 1903.
3   "The Fundamentals of the Base-Ball 'Game.'"

"THE FUNDAMENTALS OF THE BASE-BALL 'GAME' DESCRIBED FOR NON-SPORTS FANS"

Uptown, on 9th Avenue and 155th Street is the famous field known as the "Polo Grounds." Every afternoon, 20 to 35 thousand people get together there. Entrance costs from 50 cents to a dollar and a half. Thousands of poor boys and older people go without some of their usual needs in order to pay for tickets. Professional teams play baseball there and the tens of thousands of fans who sit in row after row of seats all around the stadium, go nuts with enthusiasm. They jump, they scream, they simply go wild when one of "their" players does well, or, they are pained or upset when they don't succeed.

A similar scene takes place every day in another place—in the Washington Heights. And the exact same thing goes on in Brooklyn, in Philadelphia, in Pittsburgh, in Boston, in Baltimore, in St. Louis, in Chicago—in every city in the United States. And the news-papers print the results of these games and describe what happened and tens of millions of people run to read it with gusto. They talk about it and they debate the issues.

> To us immigrants, this all seems crazy, however, it's worthwhile to understand what kind of craziness it is.

And here we're only talking about the "professional games": practically every boy, nearly every youth, and not a few middle-aged men play baseball themselves, belong to baseball clubs, and are huge fans. Every college, every school, every town, nearly every "society," and every factory has its own baseball "team."

Millions are made from the professional games. In connection to this, there is a special kind of "political" battle between different cities. A good professional player gets eight to ten thousand dollars for one season. Some of them are educated, college-educated people.

To us immigrants, this all seems crazy, however, it's worthwhile to understand what kind of craziness it is. If an entire nation is crazy over something, it's not too much to ask to try and understand what it means.

We will therefore explain here what baseball is. But, we won't do it using the professional terminology used by American newspapers to talk about the sport; we must apologize, because we're not even able to use this kind of language. We will explain it in plain, "unprofessional" and "unscientific" Yiddish.

So what are the fundamentals of the game?

Two parties participate in the game. Each party is comprised of nine people (such a party is called a "team"). One party takes the field, and the other plays the role of an enemy; the enemy tries to block the first one and the first one tries to defend itself against them; from now on we will call them, "the defense party" and the "enemy party."

The "defense party" also takes the field and plays. Two of the team players play constantly while the other seven stand on guard at seven different spots. What this guarding entails will be described later. Let us first consider the two active players.

One of them throws the ball to the other, who has to grab it. The first one is called the "pitcher" (thrower) and the second is called the "catcher" (grabber).

Each time, the "catcher" throws the ball back to the "pitcher." The reader may therefore ask, if so, doesn't it happen backwards each time—the catcher becomes a pitcher and the pitcher becomes a catcher? Why should each one be called with a specific name—one pitcher and one catcher?

We will soon see that the way in which the catcher throws the ball back is of no import. The main thing during a game is how the pitcher tries to throw the ball to the catcher.

The enemy party, however, seeks to thwart the pitcher.

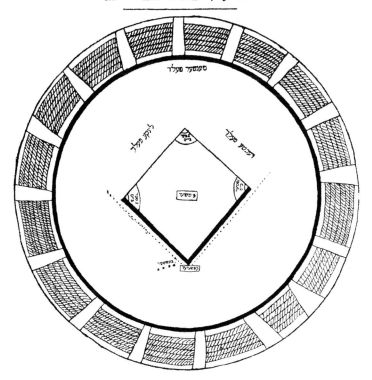

TOP

Jewish Daily Forward masthead

ABOVE

This Yiddish baseball diagram, detailing the player positions on a baseball field, was published alongside the article, "The Fundamentals of the Base-Ball 'Game' Described for Non-Sports Fans," in the *Jewish Daily Forward*, 1909

This occurs in the following way:

One of the team's nine members stands between the pitcher and the catcher (quite close to the catcher) with a thick stick ("bat") and, as the ball flies from the pitcher's hand, tries to hit it back with the stick before the catcher catches it.

This enemy player is called "batter." The place where he stands is designated by a number of little stars (****).

(The other eight players on the enemy team, in the meantime, do not participate. They each wait to be "next.") Imagine now, that the "batter," meaning the enemy player, finds the thrown ball with his stick and sends it flying. If certain rules, which we will discuss later, aren't broken, this is what can happen with the ball: if one of the "guards" catches the hit ball while it is still in the air, then the opposition of the "batter" is completely destroyed and the batter must leave his place; he is eliminated (he is "out"). He puts down the "bat" and another member of his party takes his place.

The roles of the seven guards of the defense party are also specific: they must try and catch the hit ball in order to destroy the enemy's attempt to hinder them and to get rid of the player doing the obstructing. They stand at various positions because one can never know in which direction the ball will fly. They watch the different trajectories in which the ball might fly, so a guard can be there ready to catch it.

The readers can see the way the seven guards are distributed in our picture.

The official field on which the game is played is a four-sided, four-cornered one. This is in the center of our picture. (The two round lines which go around it represent the tens of thousands of seats for the audience. That is how it usually is for the big professional games. It actually looks like a giant circus with a roof only for the audience. The field, with all the players, is under the open sky.)

THE STREET GAME

BASEBALL AS RECREATION

STEVEN A. RIESS

Ever since baseball was first spoken of as the national pastime in 1856, watching and playing the game has been an enormously popular leisure activity. Baseball started out as a recreational sport and initially had several variations.[1] Baseball historian John Thorn has suggested that a game like baseball may date back as far as the mid-1730s, although the first record he uncovered of a game called "baseball" dates back to 1791, when it was banned in Pittsfield, Massachusetts. Even then, the game had recognized rules and conventions, although flexible depending on the physical space available, it did not yet feature record keeping, statistics, or a formal structure. It simply provided enjoyment for its participants and was played for fun and sociability.[2]

The first bat-and-ball games came from England and included cricket, one o' cat, and rounders. In the United States three ball games emerged that used four bases: townball; the Massachusetts game; and the New York game, or baseball, which eventually became the most popular.[3] The first baseball clubs dated to the late 1830s, and their players drew up the first set of official rules in 1845. People enjoyed the excitement and camaraderie of the game, which did not need a perfect playing field, was easier to play than cricket, and featured frequent changes from offense to defense. It emerged at a time when the main sports were horse racing, boxing, and cockfighting, all decried by the middle class because of their violence, gambling, and perceived lack of greater social purpose. Social and moral reformers at the time advocated for the creation of new amusements, like team ball sports, that were "re-creational," promoting "uplifting" behavior and values.[4] They considered baseball a great alternative to other amusements because it seemed to promote morality, character, public health, and teamwork. With the formation of the first amateur league in 1858, baseball began to evolve into an important commercialized and professionalized spectator sport.[5]

Informal recreational baseball was the training ground for kids to learn to catch, throw, and hit a baseball. Youthful ballplayers learned a great deal from their unstructured baseball experiences, forming their own teams at the playing field and adjusting the rules if there were not enough players or the space was inadequate. Baseball historian Harold

Stickball Team, 1935

The Second Great Match Game for the Championship, 1867. The Athletic Base Ball Club of Philadelphia and the Atlantics of Brooklyn vie for the championship, October 22, 1866. Lipman Pike is seated to the lower right

Seymour argued that boys playing ball "formed the foundation of the entire structure of baseball."[6]

The exclusively male baseball fraternity of the late nineteenth century included native-born whites and blacks, as well as second-generation Germans and Irish. The latter, who wanted to become Americanized, often got started on ethnic teams in their own neighborhoods and played among themselves and against rival ethnic clubs.[7]

Immigrants from Eastern and Central Europe who arrived during the era of mass migration brought with them little familiarity with organized team sports. They encouraged their sons to get jobs and discouraged breaking with their traditional culture. Jewish immigrants particularly condemned ball playing as a threatening American distraction that took time away from work and study, and worried that it could be physically dangerous. They considered baseball a foolish activity played by men in short pants trying to hit a ball with a stick and running around in circles. Entertainer Eddie Cantor recalled that his grandmother's worst curse was "you baseball player, you." In 1903, an immigrant father wrote to the Yiddish *Forward* about his opposition: "It makes sense to teach a child to play dominoes or chess. However, what is the point of a crazy game like baseball?... Here in educated America adults play baseball. They run after a leather ball like children. I want my boy to grow up to be a *mensch*, not a wild American runner...." Editor Abraham Cahan responded, writing, "Let your boys play baseball and play it well, as long as it does not interfere with their education or get them into bad company.... Chess is good, but the body needs to develop also.... Baseball develops the arms, legs, and eyesight. It is played in the fresh air. The wild game is football.... [B]aseball is not dangerous."[8]

Jewish, Italian, and Polish boys wanted to play baseball because it was fun, was a popular topic for conversation, marked them as real Americans, and was supported by public school teachers and settlement-house workers, who considered the game "one of the best means of teaching our boys American ideas and ideals."[9] Baseball, however, did not readily fit into their crowded neighborhoods, and the cost of equipment made it difficult for immigrants and their children to afford the sport. In 1897, Sears, Roebuck charged forty cents for mitts, ten cents for a bat, and five cents for a ball. City boys often fared better in basketball, boxing, and track—urban sports with few costs for practice or participation.[10]

Many children living in cities were first exposed to baseball by playing punchball, stoopball, or stickball (with a rubber ball) in crowded alleys, on streets, or in school yards, making up their own ground rules. Comedian George Burns remembered playing in the early 1900s in New York's Lower East Side: "Our playground was the middle of Rivington Street. We only played games that needed very little equipment.... When we played baseball, we used a broom handle and a rubber ball. A manhole cover was home plate, a fire hydrant was first base, second base was a lamp post, and Mr. Gitletz, who used to bring a kitchen chair down to sit and watch us play, was third base. One time I slid into Mr. Gitletz; he caught the ball and tagged me out."[11]

Stickball became especially popular once larger schoolyards were constructed, such as in the Bronx during the 1920s, and also in suburbs after World War II, wherever there was a large paved area. Teams needed only a couple of players. The batter would be stationed by a wall where a strike zone was painted. Tom Williams, who played the game in the 1950s at P.S. 52, recalled: "[G]rounders that got through were singles; pop flies that did not get caught were singles. Anything hitting below the second floor windows on the apartment across the street were singles. Second floor to bottom of fourth floor windows was a double. Fourth floor to the top of the fifth floor was a triple, and on or over the roof a home run."[12]

A better option was softball, invented in 1887 by Chicagoan George Hancock for indoor play. An outdoor version emerged eight year later. Chicago became a center of the outdoor game, known since 1907 as "playground ball," with thirty-five-foot baselines and twelve- or fourteen-inch balls. Today Chicago is the center of gloveless sixteen-inch softball. Slow-pitch softball was played in the early 1900s at settlement houses, public parks, and summer camps. Fast-pitch softball became popular in the 1920s among men and women, especially in industrial sports programs. In the 1930s, it was the second most popular women's sport, after bowling.[13]

Youth baseball became more accessible in the 1920s, by which time 460 municipalities had built over 2,500 public fields. During the Depression, New Deal programs constructed 360 baseball and 8,800 softball fields. Boys played on teams sponsored by settlement houses and ethnic organizations like the Young Men's Hebrew Association as well as on teams they made up themselves. Jewish youth in major cities mainly

Entertainer Eddie Cantor recalled that his grandmother's worst curse was "you baseball player, you."

played other Jewish teams, but those in smaller cities often competed against gentile squads. Considerable support for teenage baseball came from the American Legion, which used the sport to promote patriotism and Americanization. It had five hundred thousand players by 1935.[14]

In 1939 Carl Stotz organized Little League to provide young boys with an organized, adult-supervised baseball experience. It became most successful in suburban, middle-class neighborhoods, where there was space to play and considerable parental support. There are now about one hundred eighty thousand teams for boys and girls around the world. Was this a good trade-off for the initiative and creativity kids developed in their own informal play?[15]

Baseball remained the national pastime until the 1970s, when it was supplanted by professional football, mainly because of television coverage. Baseball is still played by more people than any other team sport (twenty-six million compared to twenty-three million for soccer), and is second overall only to bowling (forty-six million), and probably no activity bonds children to their parents as much as playing "catch." Furthermore, despite the cost of an average ticket ($27.73), seventy-four million people attended Major League Baseball games in 2013, triple the attendance of any professional league in the world.[16]

napa tanned glove leather, felt lined and padded, leather bound, buttoned wrist, and heel pad. Shipping weight, 14 ounces.

No. 6H6961 To fit left hand. Price....40c

No. 6H6961R To fit right hand; for left handed players. Price....41c

Infielder Glove, to fit left hand, made of finest colored sheepskin, palm is felt lined and padded, well stitched seams, button wrist. Price.............16c

No. 6H6966R To fit right hand; for left handed players. Price....17c
Shipping weight, 3 ounces.

. C. Higgins League Ball.

anteed for 12 Innings.

6883 The J. C. Higgins League universally used that it requires Introduction. It is the only league anteed for twelve innings against earing or losing its shape. Best r center, finest wool yarn ever put all, specially tanned selected horse- ng, sewed with thread 25 per cent an used in any other ball. It is standard of material that makes Higgins ball superior to all others. the J. C. Higgins trade mark as e guarantee. Each ball wrapped paper and tinfoil, and packed in sealed boxes. Sold only by us. weight, 8 ounces.
r dozen, $9.50; each........85c

No. 6H6884 The Reach Official American League Ball. Officially adopted by the American League and officially recognized by the National League. Sold everywhere for $1.25. Shipping weight, 8 ounces. Price..........$1.17

6885 The ague Ball. many inter- es; conforms ecifications of al League pping weight. Regular price. 95c

6886 Spalding League Balls for wish them. Shipping weight, 8 rice..........$1.15

6888 Professional League Ball. ater, wool yarn wrapped, good over, regulation size and weight. eparate box. Guaranteed for nine ipping weight, 8 ounces. 60c

6889 Boys' League Ball. Rub- yarn wrapped, horsehide cover. A grade ball, 8½ inches in circum- ght, 4½ ounces. Shipping weight. Price..........44c

890 Pitchers' Pride Ball. A horsehide cover; well made; each ate box, sealed. A fine ball for ping weight, 8 ounces. 22c

892 Boy Scout Baseball, leather the best ever offered for the ping weight, 7 ounces. 9c

C. Higgins Indoor League Ball.

No. 6H6894 The J. C. Higgins Indoor Ball. Best horsehide cover, best curled hair, made in exact accordance with ial the regulations of the ague National Association of Indoor Ball Leagues.

The J. C. Higgins Line of Baseball Bats.

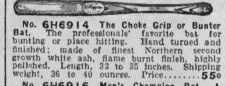

No. 6H6912 J. C. Higgins Professional League Bats. Made from selected second growth white ash and have just the right taper from end to end, giving them proper swing and balance. This bat is hand made and finely finished, showing the clear, straight grain of the wood. No better bat on the market. Length, 32 to 36 inches. Shipping weight, 36 to 42 ounces. Price..........60c

No. 6H6913 Same as above, with tape wound handle. Price..........62c

No. 6H6914 The Choke Grip or Bunter Bat. The professionals' favorite bat for bunting or place hitting. Hand turned and finished; made of finest Northern second growth white ash, flame burnt finish, highly polished. Length, 32 to 35 inches. Shipping weight, 36 to 40 ounces. Price..........55c

No. 6H6916 Men's Champion Bat. A good, durable, well balanced ash bat. Length, 32 to 36 inches. Shipping weight, 35 to 40 ounces. Regularly sells for 50 cents. Price..........35c

No. 6H6917 Amateur Youths' Bat. Made of white ash, flame burnt finish, well shaped, balanced and highly polished. Length, 32 and 33 inches. Shipping weight, 33 to 36 ounces. Price..........20c

No. 6H6919 Boys' Choice Bat. Made of selected hardwood, green finished, with red band and black stripes in middle of bat. Length, 30 inches. Shipping weight, 24 oz. Price..........9c

No. 6H6910 Regulation Indoor Bat. Made of second growth white ash, flame burnt finish, highly polished. Shipping weight, 22 ounces. Price..........32c

Neck Protecting Mask, $2.10.

Men's League Mask with neck protector, electric welded steel wire frame, much stronger, lighter and smoother in finish than the old style construction. Every wire is welded to the one which it crosses, making a solid joint. The neck piece is very strongly braced. All nicely finished in dull black enamel, fitted with full length leather side pads well stuffed and laced to the frame so strongly that they cannot be torn off. Leather adjustable forehead strap, molded chin rest and elastic head strap. Shipping weight, 44 ounces.
No. 6H6970 Price..........$2.10

Professional League Mask, $1.85.

Men's Professional League Mask, electric welded steel wire frame. All joints in the frame are electric welded, making solid joints and the frame much more rigid than in the old style mask. This mask is full size, dull black enamel finish and fitted with full length leather pads, also forehead pad at the top of the frame instead of head straps. Pads laced to frame, molded leather chin rest, elastic head band making this mask more comfortable and better finished than any other. Shipping weight, 38 ounces.
No. 6H6971 Price..........$1.85

Men's Professional League Mask. Electric welded frame. Black enameled, which prevents the reflection of the light; temple and cheek pads, with head strap and chin rest; an A1 quality mask; 10½ inches long, 7½ inches wide. A strong mask. Shipping weight, 35 ounces.
No. 6H6977 Price..........$1.25

No. 6H6978 Men's

Notes

1 Michael Chubb and Holly R. Chubb, *One Third of Our Time? An Introduction to Recreation Behavior and Resources* (New York: Wiley, 1981), 4–7, Web, http://www.humankinetics.com/excerpts/excerpts/definitions-of-leisure-play-and-recreation

2 John Thorn, *Baseball in the Garden of Eden: The Secret History of the Early Game* (New York: Simon & Schuster, 2011), xii, 23, 55–59.

3 On early ball games in the United States, see David Block, *Baseball before We Knew It* (Lincoln: U of Nebraska P, 2005).

4 On the rise of a positive sports ideology, see John R. Betts, "Mind and Body in Early American Thought," *Journal of American History* 54 (March 1968): 787–805.

5 Thorn, *Baseball in the Garden of Eden*, 1–104; Melvin L. Adelman, *A Sporting Time: New York City and the Rise of Modern Athletics, 1820–70* (Urbana: U of Illinois P, 1986), 91–142; George B. Kirsch, *Baseball and Cricket: The Creation of American Team Sports, 1838–72* (Urbana: U of Illinois P, 1989); Warren Goldstein, *Playing for Keeps: A History of Early Baseball* (Ithaca: Cornell UP, 1989); Ronald Story, "The Country of the Young: The Meaning of Baseball in Early American Culture," in *Baseball History from Outside the Lines: A Reader*, ed. John E. Dreifort (Lincoln: U of Nebraska P, 2001), 19–33.

6 Harold Seymour and Dorothy Seymour, *The People's Game* (New York: Oxford UP, 1990), 3, vol. 3 of *Baseball*.

7 Steven A. Riess, *Touching Base: Professional Baseball and American Culture in the Progressive Era*, 2nd ed. (Urbana: U of Illinois P, 1999), 46–47, 159, 184–86. See also Larry R. Gerlach, "German Americans in Major League Baseball: Sport and Acculturation," in *The American Game: Baseball and Ethnicity*, ed. Lawrence Baldassaro and Lawrence Johnson (Carbondale: Southern Illinois UP, 2002), 27–54; and Richard F. Peterson, "'Slide, Kelly, Slide': The Irish in American Baseball," in Baldassaro and Johnson, *The American Game*, 55–67.

8 Steven A. Riess, *City Games: The Evolution of American Urban Society and the Rise of Sports* (Urbana: UP of Illinois, 1989), 93–117; quotes are from Irving L. Howe, *World of our Our Fathers* (New York : Harcourt Brace Jovanovich, 1976), 182, 259. Howe cited the story of one Jewish boy who wanted to play: "I couldn't tell my father I played ball, so my mother would sneak out my baseball gear and put it in the candy store downstairs." See Irving L. Howe and Kenneth Libo, *How We Lived, 1880–1930* (New York: R. Marek, 1979), 51–52.

9 Riess, *Touching Base*, 29–30, 187–92; Riess, *City Games*, 100–113. Quote is from a Chicago settlement house worker, quoted by columnist Huge Fullerton, in *Atlanta Constitution*, July 1909. On the Jewish experience in baseball, see Peter Levine, *Ellis Island to Ebbets Field: Sport and the American Jewish Experience* (New York: Oxford UP, 1992), 87–143, 235–47; Steven A. Riess, "From Pike to Green with Greenberg In Between: Jewish Americans and the National Pastime," in Baldassaro and Johnson, *The American Game*, 116–41; Burton A. Boxerman and Benita W. Boxerman, *Jews and Baseball*, 2 vols. (Jefferson: McFarland, 2007–2010); Peter Miller, dir. and prod., *Jews and Baseball: An American Love Story* (New York: Docudrama Films, 2011). On Italians, see Lawrence Baldassaro, *Beyond DiMaggio: Italian Americans in Baseball* (Lincoln: U of Nebraska P, 2011). On the Polish experience, see Neal Pease, "Diamonds out of the Coal Mines: Slavic Americans in Baseball," in Baldassaro and Johnson, *The American Game*, 242–61.

10 On the price of sporting goods, see, e.g., 1897 *Sears, Roebuck & Co. Catalogue*, rpt. (New York: Skyhorse, 2007), 595.

11 Riess, *City Games*, 48; George Burns, *The Third Time Around* (New York: Putnam, 1980), 9–10. Al Schacht, a New York boy who played in the majors from 1919 to 1921, though best known as the "Clown Prince of Baseball," provides a lot of information about his early baseball experiences from the sandlots through high school in *My Own Particular Screwball: An Informal Autobiography* (Garden City: Doubleday, 1955), 17–74. On punchball, see Jeffrey S. Gurock, *Jews in Gotham: New York Jews in a Changing City, 1920–2010* (New York: New York UP, 2012), 41–42.

12 Tom Williams, "Stickball," *For Displaced, Misplaced, and Nostalgic Ex-Bronxites*, Web, 27 Sept. 2013, http://bronxboard.com/diary/diary.php?f=Stickball; "Stickball: A Crash Course for the Essential Urban Game," Web, 27 Sept. 2013, http://www.streetplay.com/rulesheets/pdf/stickballsheet.pdf.

13 Amateur Softball Association of America, Web, 21 Sept. 2013 http://www.asasoftball.com/about/; Levine, *Ellis Island to Ebbets Field*, 97. See also Chaim Potok, *The Chosen* (New York: Simon & Schuster, 1967), whose narrative is significantly based on the softball games of Orthodox New York teenagers in the late 1940s; and Jeffrey S. Gurock's reminiscences of Sunday morning softball in the Catskills in the late 1960s, in Larry Ruttman, *American Jews & America's Game: Voices of a Growing Legacy in Baseball* (Lincoln: U of Nebraska P, 2013), 431.

14 Levine, *Ellis Island*, 68–70, 96; Seymour and Seymour, *The People's Game*, 85–90; The American Legion, "History of American Legion Baseball," Web, 5 Oct. 2013, http://www.legion.org/baseball/history.

15 Lance Van Auken and Robin Van Auken, *Play Ball!: The Story of Little League Baseball* (University Park: Pennsylvania State UP, 2001); "Little League World Series: Little League World Series History," Web, http://espn.go.com/sports/llws13/story/_/id/9550886/little-league-world-series-history.

16 "MLB Average Ticket Price & Fan Cost Index for All 30 Baseball Teams," Web, 3 Oct. 2013, http://www.kshb.com/dpp/sports/baseball/mlb-average-ticket-price--fan-cost-index-for-all-30-baseball-teams. See also Web, 3 Oct. 2013, http://www.kshb.com/dpp/sports/baseball/mlb-average-ticket-price--fan-cost-index-for-all-30-baseball-teams#ixzz2garRLg3a.

Page from the 1912 Sears, Roebuck, and Co. catalogue advertising baseball equipment

"HERO OF THE DAY"

THE SHORT CAREER OF ANDY COHEN

PETER LEVINE

For Jewish immigrants and their children who were eager to become American, following and playing baseball provided an easy opportunity to do so. As Abraham Cahan, the editor of the *Jewish Daily Forward*, wrote in 1903, "let your boys play baseball and play it well.... Let us not so raise our children that they should grow up foreigners in their own birthplace."

Cahan's encouragement came at a time when professional baseball magnates eagerly sought ethnic talent in hopes of attracting new immigrants to their ballparks. Nowhere did these two impulses of recruiting new talent and new fans coincide more forcefully than in 1920s New York, the home of a vast Jewish immigrant population and the stomping grounds of the greatest baseball player and team of the day—Babe Ruth and the New York Yankees.

Determined to compete with the Yankees both on the field and at the box office, John McGraw, the manager of the New York Giants, went on the hunt for good Jewish ballplayers. Enter Andy Cohen.

Andy first arrived in New York for a brief stint, midway through the 1926 season. After thirty-two games, McGraw shipped him off to the

ABOVE

Polo Grounds, New York, 1913

OPPOSITE

"Andy Cohen Drinks Toddy!"
June 14, 1928, *Morgen Zhurnal*
(Jewish Morning Journal)

Buffalo Bisons in the International League, where he remained through the 1927 season. Cohen had a spectacular year, hitting .355, and he was named shortstop to the league's All-Star team. But it was not until he took over second base for the Giants in 1928 that he became baseball's first Jewish star.

On opening day 1928, a chilly, gray April afternoon, Andy led the Giants to a 5–2 victory over the Boston Braves before thirty thousand fans at the Polo Grounds. Starting at second base—a position recently vacated by the legendary Rogers Hornsby, who had been traded by the Giants to the Braves during the offseason—Andy scored twice, knocked in two runs, and put out Hornsby on grounders to second twice.

Immigrant Jewish fans who flocked to the ballpark that day celebrated the moment. As Andy remembered it, at the end of the game thousands of Jewish fans rushed onto the field, lifted him on their shoulders as if he were a Jewish bridegroom, and literally carried him around the Polo Grounds until he was rescued by teammates who escorted him up the clubhouse steps in center field.

The *American Hebrew* extolled Andy as the "hero of the day" and marked him as destined to become "the greatest Jew in organized baseball." Westbrook Pegler, writing in the *Chicago Tribune*, noted that if Cohen succeeded at second base, "the Giant firm could do business in the Jewish trade alone."

Although hardly free of ethnic slurs, an anonymous parody of "Casey at the Bat" captured the excitement of the day and explicitly made clear the connections between Cohen and his Jewish constituency.

Cohen at the Bat

The outlook wasn't cheerful for the Giants yesterday
They were trailing by a run with but four innings left to play.
When Lindstrom flied to Richbourg and Terry weakly popped,
It looked as though those Bostons had the game as good as copped.
But Jackson smacked a single over Eddie Farrell's pate
And from the stands and bleachers the cry of "Oy, Oy" rose,
For up came Andy Cohen half a foot behind his nose.
There was ease in Bob Smith's manner and a smile on Hornsby's face,
For they figured they had Andy in the tightest sort of place.
It was make or break for Andy, while the fans cried "Oy, Oy, Oy,"
And it wasn't any soft spot for a little Jewish boy.
And now the pitcher has the ball and now he lets it go.
And now the air is shattered by the force of Casey's blow.
Well nothing like that happened, but what do you suppose?
Why little Andy Cohen socked the ball upon the nose.
Then from the stands and bleachers the fans in triumph roared.
And Andy raced to second and the other runner scored.
Soon they took him home in triumph amidst the blare of auto honks.
There may be no joy in Mudville, but there's plenty in the Bronx.

Even with its obvious antisemitic flavor, reflective of the real discrimination and prejudice Jews faced in the United States, the poem's

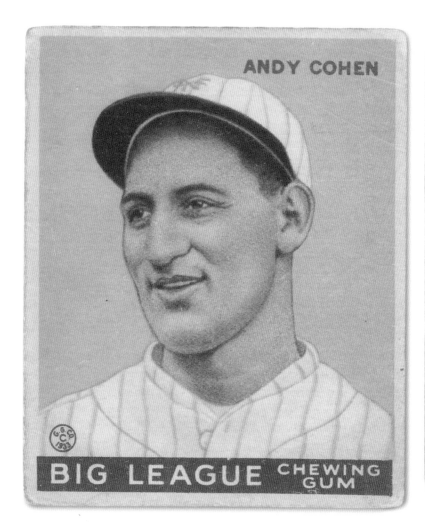

cloaking of Andy with the mantle of Casey, that immortal American icon, cast him as an American hero capable of appealing to Jew and gentile alike.

Andy lasted only two seasons in New York, playing a respectable second base and batting over .270, before embarking on a thirty-year career as player and coach in the minor leagues. He ended his baseball life by helping to found and coach men's baseball at the University of Texas at El Paso along with his younger brother, Syd, who also pitched briefly in the majors for the Washington Senators. An unlikely location for two Jewish ballplayers, but the brothers were so revered that the El Paso baseball venue, Cohen Stadium, was named in their honor.

Like his brother, Syd also began his career in the minor leagues, including a stint with the Mexican-based Nogales Internationals in 1931 in the Arizona-Texas League. Fluent in Spanish and dark in complexion, Syd played as Pablo Garcia in an attempt to placate local Mexican fans who thought there were too many American ballplayers on the roster.

Syd's claim to fame was that he pitched the last strikeout to Babe Ruth *and* served him his last home run before leaving the Yankees to finish his career with the Boston Braves. By the time Syd came along, however, another Jewish ballplayer, Hank Greenberg, had caught the attention of Jewish fans. But Andy had set the table for Hank. Wherever Andy played, Jewish fans rushed to the ballpark to cheer him. Although he did not

ABOVE LEFT

Andy Cohen, New York Giants, 1933

ABOVE RIGHT

Syd Cohen, San Francisco Seals, 1928

escape antisemitic remarks from opponents, or newspaper cartoons that highlighted his "hook nose" and "thick eyebrows," Andy relished his time as a Jewish American baseball hero. Fondly, he remembered how loyal Jewish fans asked to sit right on second base so that they could be near their hero. And how the Yiddish *Jewish Daily Forward* carried Giants box scores and news of his latest exploits on its front page, even publishing the following notice on a day the Giants were not scheduled to play: "No game today, Andy must be sick."

Andy Cohen's brief stay in the big leagues encouraged Jews who dreamed of participating fully in American life that such futures were possible—in or out of baseball. Some of those who covered Cohen's moment in the sun even implied that his presence might serve as a middle ground between Jews and gentiles, lessening fears that an alien immigrant population could not be absorbed into the American mainstream. A *New York Evening World* article about Cohen, titled "Still His Name and Nose Have Made Things Hard," noted that he had overcome these obstacles and established himself as a proper American ballplayer "with exactly the correct mixture of modesty and self assurance...with nothing crawling about his nature." The fact that he grew up in Texas and attended the University of Alabama only enhanced his credibility as a model of assimilation who managed to make his mark in the great American game of baseball. Gentiles fearful that Eastern European Jewish immigrants might overrun the country could only hope that other Jews might follow his example.

> Andy Cohen's brief stay in the big leagues encouraged Jews who dreamed of participating fully in American life that such futures were possible – in or out of baseball.

Certainly, many Jewish immigrants chose to stay cloaked in traditional culture and religion, shunning any interest in things American—including baseball; however, many more eagerly sought to embrace American ways and American possibility, even as they did not deny their cultural identities as Jews. Especially for these people, and most emphatically for their children, Andy Cohen's accomplishments served as a passport for learning more about American culture and values. In a very public and visible way, his brief triumph in the quintessential American sport helped diminish stereotypes about Jewish weakness. It also encouraged Jews to feel more comfortable, both as Americans and as Jews, in a world about to enter a time of increasing antisemitism at home and the Nazi menace abroad. As the poem said, no mean feat for "a little Jewish boy."

For fuller treatment of Andy and Syd Cohen's story and for full citations of all material quoted here, see Peter Levine, *Ellis Island to Ebbets Field: Sport and the American Jewish Experience* (New York: Oxford UP, 1992), 100–116, and Tilden Edelstein, "Cohen at the Bat," *Commentary* (Nov. 1983): 53–56.

BASEBALL AND JUDAISM

FRIENDS AND FOES

JEFFREY
S.
GUROCK

It was a Sabbath of celebration in October 2005 as Congregation Brith Sholom–Beth Israel commemorated 150 years of service to the Orthodox community of Charleston, South Carolina. Rabbi Ari Sytner ascended the pulpit to express his community's thanks to the Almighty for his goodness in "keeping them alive and sustaining them" to reach this milestone occasion. But they were taken aback, and then laughed appreciatively, when Rabbi Sytner concluded his *b'racha* with the words "to see the Red Sox defeat the New York Yankees." Some days earlier, Boston had overcome, in almost miraculous fashion, a 3–0 deficit to win the American League playoffs and moved on to the World Series. The clever rabbi had grabbed his audience's attention with a sports metaphor, and now they were "on deck" to listen attentively to his religious and historical messages. He had also demonstrated his skill as a "switch-hitter," evidencing his comfort with popular secular culture and Judaism's sacred traditions. Somewhere Solomon Schechter was smiling!

"Remember this, unless you can play baseball, you will never get to be a rabbi in America."

More than eighty years earlier, the founder of twentieth-century Conservative Judaism in America had promoted the strategy of using baseball to elevate a rabbi's stature in the eyes of Americanized congregants and, through the national pastime, gain entrée into the hearts, minds, and souls of the men and women in his pews. As the story goes, sometime in the early 1910s, Schechter was walking down the street with his favored rabbinical student, Louis Finkelstein, and stopped at a news kiosk "to check out the latest World Series scores." Recognizing how important the sport was to American Jews, Schechter asked his disciple: "Can you play baseball?" When the callow young scholar replied, "No," Schechter chided him: "Remember this, unless you can play baseball, you will never get to be a rabbi in America." (Finkelstein family lore has it that Schechter actually asked him whether he "knew" about the national pastime. Apparently the young rabbinic scholar, who was no athlete, had heard of New York Giants star Mel Ott even if he called him Mel "Odd.") Whatever version of Schechter's admonition is correct, the importance of his charge remains the same and has endured as a talking point for generations.[1]

Myriad other rabbis have noted the Fall Classic in their High Holiday sermons in an attempt to achieve the remarkable feat of turning a cultural foe into a religious friend of Judaism. Baseball is one of this country's most potent phenomena that has for generations taken Jewish youngsters and their parents, men and women, away from synagogue life. During the period of mass Jewish immigration to America around the turn of the twentieth century, it was a rite of passage for kids to slip away from their parents, who wanted them to be in *shul*, to meet up with their pals for games of stickball. One early Jewish social worker, who worked among these street kids at the time Schechter and Finkelstein went for their iconic stroll, wrote critically about a "half-baked second generation" of "cocksure and smart guys" who knew "batting averages to a 'T'" but were "indifferent to, if not ashamed of Jewish life."[2]

The absence of the sports minded from the sanctuary has been most apparent during the Jewish prime-time Rosh Hashanah–Yom Kippur season. Many a season-ticket-holding synagogue member has chosen to sit in the stands rather than stand at the altar. One rabbi, who in 1968 served a suburban St. Louis congregation when Cardinals ace Bob Gibson dominated on the mound, recalled that after he denied semiserious requests that the holiest day in the Jewish calendar be postponed one day so as not to interfere with worshippers' desire to see their hero pitch, these devoted ball fans did their spiritual leader one better. They showed up in *shul* with transistor radios in their pockets and hooked themselves into the broadcast with tiny earphones. Momentarily, the nonplussed rabbi thought that he was ministering to a mass of audio-challenged synagogue goers. Certainly, they were hard of hearing of the ground rules of Jewish law.[3]

Prayer minyan at a Miami Marlins baseball game, September 17, 2011

Very recently, at least in New York, the power of Jewish communal pressure combined with the fact that many of the game's substantial patrons care about major Jewish holidays has sensitized the Lords of Baseball to Judaism's clock and calendar when scheduling important games. The latest triumph for those concerned with Jewish religious practice took place in 2009, when a classic matchup between the Red Sox and Yankees that had been slated for a one o'clock first pitch on the afternoon before Yom Kippur was moved to eight o'clock that evening to garner a larger national audience for ESPN; communal protest resulted in the return of the game to its original starting time. Rabbi Sytner and millions of other Jews were thus able to eat their prefast meal while taking in the ballgame, with time to spare before Kol Nidre services. The Jewish community had come a long way from the time in 1934

Many a season-ticketholding synagogue member has chosen to sit in the stands rather than stand at the altar.

when Hank Greenberg was pressured to play on Rosh Hashanah and Yom Kippur.[4]

But even if the High Holiday dilemma can be solved on an ongoing basis, both in Gotham and ultimately elsewhere, for fans and players, there is the enduring weekly problem of Sabbath prayer versus Little League play. Rabbis of all movements have noted that, years ago, kids broke from their elders on holy days to participate in their informal street games. Today's Jewish parents often carpool their children to various sporting activities and make up large parts of the cheering section. Perhaps the best bet for rabbis today, argued one clerical colleague recently, was to "show up in the afternoon of some of their [Saturday] games" and with a nonjudgmental demeanor show the players and their parents that "he was not just interested in them when they were in synagogue (same with their parents) but in them in general."[5]

In communities with a critical mass of Jews who want to play within the lines of the faith's ground rules, "kosher" Little Leagues have been established as workable solutions. In these Sunday leagues, youngsters are not challenged to choose between religious commitments and team allegiance. Perhaps "A League of Our Own," an all-girls softball association in Riverdale, New York, is the most imaginative of such creations. For the past twenty years (1994–2014), this "never on Saturday" loop has allowed religious Jewish athletes who are female the chance to enjoy the game on a level playing field with fidelity to their tradition. As important, in opening up the lineup to all girls, including less observant Jews and non-Jews, they have brought kids of all creeds into friendly, spirited competition and friendships outside the lines.[6]

On balance, however, none of these leagues has ever come close to capturing the allegiance of the majority of any community's baseball-enthused Jewish youths. And while, when their teams are run well, they possess many of the accoutrements of the regular groups—like uniforms, trained coaches, and officials—they ultimately do not speak to the Jewish child and parent who harbor dreams of making it to the Big Show. As in so many encounters between Judaism and secular culture, for those who wish to be fully integrated into worlds beyond their faith difficult choices remain and will endure.

Notes

1. "A Trumpet for All Israel," *Time*, 13 Oct. 1951: 54.
2. Isaac Berkson, *Theories of Americanization: A Critical Study with Special Reference to the Jewish Group* (New York: Columbia U Teachers Coll., 1920), 185–86.
3. Jeffrey S. Gurock, "Baseball, the High Holidays and American Jewish Status and Survival," in *What Is Jewish about America's "Favorite Pastime"; Essays and Sermons on Jews, Judaism and Baseball*, ed. Marc Lee Raphael and Judith Z. Abrams (Williamsburg: Coll. of William and Mary, 2006), 28.
4. "Game Moved Back to 1 P.M." *ESPN.com*, 1 Sept 2009.
5. Jeffrey S. Gurock, *Judaism's Encounter with American Sports* (Bloomington: Indiana UP, 2005), 172.
6. Gurock, *Judaism's Encounter*, 173.

THE Chosen

A NOVEL BY Chaim Potok

Original cover for Chaim Potok's
The Chosen, 1967

CHAIM POTOK

The Chosen

DAVEY Cantor, one of the boys who acted as a replacement if a first-stringer had to leave the game, was standing near the wire screen behind home plate. He was a short boy, with a round face, dark hair, owlish glasses, and a very Semitic nose. He watched me fix my glasses.

"You're looking good out there, Reuven," he told me.

"Thanks," I said.

"Everyone is looking real good."

"It'll be a good game."

He stared at me through his glasses. "You think so?" he asked.

"Sure, why not?"

"You ever see them play, Reuven?"

"No."

"They're murderers."

"Sure," I said.

"No, really. They're wild."

"You saw them play?"

"Twice. They're murderers."

"Everyone plays to win, Davey."

"They don't only play to win. They play like it's the first of the Ten Commandments."

I laughed. "That yeshiva?" I said. "Oh, come on, Davey."

"It's the truth."

"Sure," I said.

"Reb Saunders ordered them never to lose because it would shame their yeshiva or something. I don't know. You'll see."

"Hey, Malter!" Mr. Galanter shouted. "What are you doing, sitting this one out?"

"You'll see," Davey Cantor said.

"Sure." I grinned at him. "A holy war."

He looked at me.

"Are you playing?" I asked him.

"Mr. Galanter said I might take second base if you have to pitch."

"Well, good luck."

"Hey, Malter!" Mr. Galanter shouted. "There's a war on, remember?"

"Yes, sir!" I said, and ran back out to my position at second base.

We threw the ball around a few more minutes, and then I went up to home plate for some batting practice. I hit a long one out to left field, and then a fast one to the shortstop, who fielded it neatly and whipped it to first. I had the bat ready for another swing when someone said, "Here they are," and I rested the bat on my shoulder and saw the team we were going to play turn up our block and come into the yard. I saw Davey Cantor kick nervously at the wire screen behind home plate, then put his hands into the pockets of his dungarees. His eyes were wide and gloomy behind his owlish glasses.

I watched them come into the yard.

There were fifteen of them, and they were dressed alike in white shirts, dark pants, white sweaters, and small black skullcaps. In the fashion of the very Orthodox, their hair was closely cropped, except for the area near their ears from which mushroomed the untouched hair that tumbled down into the long side curls. Some of them had the beginnings of beards, straggly tufts of hair that stood in isolated clumps on their chins, jawbones, and upper lips. They all wore the traditional undergarment beneath their shirts, and the tzitzit, the long fringes appended to the four corners of the garment, came out above their belts and swung against their pants as they walked. These were the very Orthodox, and they obeyed literally the Biblical commandment *And ye shall look upon it*, which pertains to the fringes.

In contrast, our team had no particular uniform, and each of us wore whatever he wished: dungarees, shorts, pants, polo shirts, sweat shirts, even undershirts. Some of us wore the garment, others did not. None of us wore the fringes outside his trousers. The only element of uniform that we had in common was the small, black skullcap which we, too, wore.

They came up to the first-base side of the wire screen behind home plate and stood there in a silent black-and-white mass, holding bats and balls and gloves in their hands. I looked at them. They did not seem to me to present any picture of ferocity. I saw Davey Cantor kick again at the wire screen, then walk away from them to the third-base line, his hands moving nervously against his dungarees.

Mr. Galanter smiled and started toward them, moving quickly on the balls of his feet, his skullcap perched precariously on the top of his balding head.

A man disentangled himself from the black-and-white mass of players and took a step forward. He looked to be in his late twenties and wore a black suit, black shoes, and a black hat. He had a black beard, and he carried a book under one arm. He was obviously a rabbi, and I marveled that the yeshiva had placed a rabbi instead of an athletic coach over its team.

Mr. Galanter came up to him and offered his hand.

"We are ready to play," the rabbi said in Yiddish, shaking Mr. Galanter's hand with obvious uninterest.

"Fine," Mr. Galanter said in English, smiling.

The rabbi looked out at the field. "You played already?" he asked.

"How's that?" Mr. Galanter said.

"You had practice?"

"Well, sure—"

"We want to practice."

"How's that?" Mr. Galanter said again, looking surprised.

"You practiced, now we practice."

"You didn't practice in your own yard?"

"We practiced."

"Well, then—"

"But we have never played in your yard before. We want a few minutes."

"Well, now," Mr. Galanter said, "there isn't much time. The rules are each team practices in its own yard."

"We want five minutes," the rabbi insisted.

"Well—" Mr. Galanter said. He was no longer smiling. He always liked to go right into a game when we played in our own yard. It kept us from cooling off, he said.

"Five minutes," the rabbi said. "Tell your people to leave the field."

"How's that?" Mr. Galanter said.

"We cannot practice with your people on the field. Tell them to leave the field."

"Well, now," Mr. Galanter said, then stopped. He thought for a long moment. The black-and-white mass of players behind the rabbi stood very still, waiting. I saw Davey Cantor kick at the asphalt floor of the yard. "Well, all right. Five minutes. Just five minutes, now."

"Tell your people to leave the field," the rabbi said.

Mr. Galanter stared gloomily out at the field, looking a little deflated. "Everybody off!" he shouted, not very loudly. "They want a five-minute warm-up. Hustle, hustle. Keep those arms going. Keep it hot. Toss some balls around behind home. Let's go!"

The players scrambled off the field.

The black-and-white mass near the wire screen remained intact. The young rabbi turned and faced his team.

He talked in Yiddish. "We have the field for five minutes," he said. "Remember why and for whom we play."

Then he stepped aside, and the black-and-white mass dissolved into fifteen individual players who came quickly onto the field. One of them, a tall boy with sand-colored hair and long arms and legs that seemed all bones and angles, stood at home plate and commenced hitting balls out to the players. He hit a few easy grounders and pop-ups, and the fielders shouted encouragement to one another in Yiddish. They handled themselves awkwardly, dropping easy grounders, throwing wild, fumbling fly balls. I looked over at the young rabbi. He had sat down on the bench near the wire

> He talked in Yiddish. "We have the field for five minutes," he said. "Remember why and for whom we play."

screen and was reading his book.

Behind the wire screen was a wide area, and Mr. Galanter kept us busy there throwing balls around.

"Keep those balls going!" he fist-thumped at us. "No one sits out this fire fight! Never underestimate the enemy!"

But there was a broad smile on his face. Now that he was actually seeing the other team, he seemed not at all concerned about the outcome of the game. In the interim between throwing a ball and having it thrown back to me, I told myself that I liked Mr. Galanter, and I wondered about his constant use of war expressions and why he wasn't in the army.

Davey Cantor came past me, chasing a ball that had gone between his legs.

"Some murderers," I grinned at him.

"You'll see," he said as he bent to retrieve the ball.

"Sure," I said.

"Especially the one batting. You'll see."

The ball was coming back to me, and I caught it neatly and flipped it back.

"Who's the one batting?" I asked.

"Danny Saunders."

"Pardon my ignorance, but who is Danny Saunders?"

"Reb Saunders' son," Davey Cantor said, blinking his eyes.

"I'm impressed."

"You'll see," Davey Cantor said, and ran off with his ball.

My father, who had no love at all for Hasidic communities and their rabbinic overlords, had told me about Rabbi Isaac Saunders and the zealousness with which he ruled his people and settled questions of Jewish law.

I saw Mr. Galanter look at his wristwatch, then stare out at the team on the field. The five minutes were apparently over, but the players were making no move to abandon the field. Danny Saunders was now at first base, and I noticed that his long arms and legs were being used to good advantage, for by stretching and jumping he was able to catch most of the wild throws that came his way.

Mr. Galanter went over to the young rabbi who was still sitting on the bench and reading.

"It's five minutes," he said.

The rabbi looked up from his book. "Ah?" he said.

"The five minutes are up," Mr. Galanter said.

The rabbi stared out at the field. "Enough!" he shouted in Yiddish. "It's time to play!" Then he looked down at the book and resumed his reading.

The players threw the ball around for another minute or two, and then slowly came off the field. Danny Saunders walked past me, still wearing his first baseman's glove. He was a good deal taller than I, and in contrast to my somewhat ordinary but decently proportioned features and dark hair, his face seemed to have been cut from stone. His chin, jaw and cheekbones were made up of jutting hard lines, his nose was straight and pointed, his lips full, rising to

"Some murderers," I grinned at him. "You'll see," he said as he bent to retrieve the ball. "Sure," I said. "Especially the one batting. You'll see." The ball was coming back to me, and I caught it neatly and flipped it back.

a steep angle from the center point beneath his nose and then slanting off to form a too-wide mouth. His eyes were deep blue, and the sparse tufts of hair on his chin, jawbones, and upper lip, the close-cropped hair on his head, and the flow of side curls along his ears were the color of sand. He moved in a loose-jointed, disheveled sort of way, all arms and legs, talking in Yiddish to one of his teammates and ignoring me completely as he passed by. I told myself that I did not like his Hasidic-bred sense of superiority and that it would be a great pleasure to defeat him and his team in this afternoon's game.

The umpire, a gym instructor from a parochial school two blocks away, called the teams together to determine who would bat first. I saw him throw a bat into the air. It was caught and almost dropped by a member of the other team.

During the brief hand-over-hand choosing, Davey Cantor came over and stood next to me.

"What do you think?" he asked.

"They're a snooty bunch," I told him.

"What do you think about their playing?"

"They're lousy."

"They're murderers."

"Oh, come on, Davey."

"You'll see," Davey Cantor said, looking at me gloomily.

"I just did see."

"You didn't see anything."

"Sure," I said. "Elijah the prophet comes in to pitch for them in tight spots."

"I'm not being funny," he said, looking hurt.

"Some murderers," I told him, and laughed.

The teams began to disperse. We had lost the choosing, and they had decided to bat first. We scampered onto the field. I took up my position at second base. I saw the young rabbi sitting on the bench near the wire fence and reading. We threw a ball around for a minute. Mr. Galanter stood alongside third base, shouting his words of encouragement at us. It was warm, and I was sweating a little and feeling very good. Then the umpire, who had taken up his position behind the pitcher, called for the ball and someone tossed it to him.

He handed it to the pitcher and shouted, "Here we go! Play ball!"

We settled into our positions.

Mr. Galanter shouted, "Goldberg, move in!" and Sidney Goldberg, our shortstop, took two steps forward and moved a little closer to third base. "Okay, fine," Mr. Galanter said. "Keep that infield solid!"

A short, thin boy came up to the plate and stood there with his feet together, holding the bat awkwardly over his head. He wore steel-rimmed glasses that gave his face a pinched, old man's look. He swung wildly at the first pitch, and the force of the swing spun him completely around. His earlocks lifted off the sides of his head and followed him around in an almost horizontal circle. Then he steadied himself and resumed his position near the plate, short, thin, his feet together, holding his bat over his head in an awkward grip.

The umpire called the strike in a loud, clear voice, and I saw Sidney Goldberg look over at me and grin broadly.

"If he studies Talmud like that, he's dead," Sidney Goldberg said.

Still from the 1982 film adaptation of
The Chosen showing Danny Saunders
(Robby Benson) and Reuven Malter
(Barry Miller)

I grinned back at him.

"Keep that infield solid!" Mr. Galanter shouted from third base. "Malter, a little to your left! Good!"

The next pitch was too high, and the boy chopped at it, lost his bat and fell forward on his hands. Sidney Goldberg and I looked at each other again. Sidney was in my class. We were similar in build, thin and lithe, with somewhat spindly arms and legs. He was not a very good student, but he was an excellent shortstop. We lived on the same block and were good but not close friends. He was dressed in an undershirt and dungarees and was not wearing the four-cornered garment. I had on a light-blue shirt and dark-blue work pants, and I wore the four-cornered garment under the shirt.

The short, thin boy was back at the plate, standing with his feet together and holding the bat in his awkward grip. He let the next pitch go by, and the umpire called it a strike. I saw the young rabbi look up a moment from his book, then resume reading.

"Two more just like that!" I shouted encouragingly to the pitcher. "Two more, Schwartzie!" And I thought to myself, Some murderers.

I saw Danny Saunders go over to the boy who had just struck out and talk to him. The boy looked down and seemed to shrivel with hurt. He hung his head and walked away behind the wire screen. Another short, thin boy took his place at the plate. I looked around for Davey Cantor but could not see him.

The boy at bat swung wildly at the first two pitches and missed them both. He swung again at the third pitch, and I heard the loud *thwack* of the bat as it connected with the ball, and saw the ball move in a swift, straight line toward Sidney Goldberg, who caught it, bobbled it for a moment, and finally got it into his glove. He tossed the ball to me, and we threw it around. I saw him take off his glove and shake his left hand.

"That hurt," he said, grinning at me.

"Good catch," I told him.

"That hurt like hell," he said, and put his glove back on his hand.

The batter who stood now at the plate was broad-shouldered and built like a bear. He swung at the first pitch, missed, then swung again at the second pitch and sent the ball in a straight line over the head of the third baseman into left field. I scrambled to second, stood on the base and shouted for the ball. I saw the left fielder pick it up on the second bounce and relay it to me. It was coming in a little high, and I had my glove raised for it. I felt more than saw the batter charging toward second, and as I was getting my glove on the ball he smashed into me like a truck. The ball went over my head, and I fell forward heavily onto the asphalt floor of the yard, and he passed me, going toward third, his fringes flying out behind him, holding his skullcap to his head with his right hand so it would not fall off. Abe Goodstein, our first baseman, retrieved the ball and whipped it home, and the batter stood at third, a wide grin on his face.

The yeshiva team exploded into wild cheers and shouted loud words of congratulations in Yiddish to the batter.

Sidney Goldberg helped me get to my feet.

"That *momzer*!" he said. "You weren't in his way!"

"Wow!" I said, taking a few deep breaths. I had scraped the palm of my right hand.

"What a *momzer!*" Sidney Goldberg said.

I saw Mr. Galanter come storming onto the field to talk to the umpire. "What kind of play was that?" he asked heatedly. "How are you going to rule that?"

"Safe at third," the umpire said. "Your boy was in the way."

Mr. Galanter's mouth fell open. "How's that again?"

"Safe at third," the umpire repeated.

Mr. Galanter looked ready to argue, thought better of it, then stared over at me. "Are you all right, Malter?"

"I'm okay," I said, taking another deep breath.

Mr. Galanter walked angrily off the field.

"Play ball!" the umpire shouted.

The yeshiva team quieted down. I saw that the young rabbi was now looking up from his book and smiling faintly.

A tall, thin player came up to the plate, set his feet in correct position, swung his bat a few times, then crouched into a waiting stance. I saw it was Danny Saunders. I opened and closed my right hand, which was still sore from the fall.

"Move back! Move back!" Mr. Galanter was shouting from alongside third base, and I took two steps back.

I crouched, waiting.

The first pitch was wild, and the yeshiva team burst into loud laughter. The young rabbi was sitting on the bench, watching Danny Saunders intently.

"Take it easy, Schwartzie!" I shouted encouragingly to the pitcher. "There's only one more to go!"

The next pitch was about a foot over Danny Saunders' head, and the yeshiva team howled with laughter. Sidney Goldberg and I looked at each other. I saw Mr. Galanter standing very still alongside third, staring at the pitcher. The rabbi was still watching Danny Saunders.

The next pitch left Schwartzie's hand in a long, slow line, and before it was halfway to the plate I knew Danny Saunders would try for it. I knew it from the way his left foot came forward and the bat snapped back and his long, thin body began its swift pivot. I tensed, waiting for the sound of the bat against the ball, and when it came it sounded like a gunshot. For a wild fraction of a second I lost sight of the ball. Then I saw Schwartzie dive to the ground, and there was the ball coming through the air where his head had been, and I tried for it but it was moving too fast, and I barely had my glove raised before it was in center field. It was caught on a bounce and thrown to Sidney

The next pitch left Schwartzie's hand in a long, slow line, and before it was halfway to the plate I knew Danny Saunders would try for it. I knew it from the way his left foot came forward and the bat snapped back and his long, thin body began its swift pivot.

Goldberg, but by that time Danny Saunders was standing solidly on my base and the yeshiva team was screaming with joy.

Mr. Galanter called for time and walked over to talk to Schwartzie. Sidney Goldberg nodded to me, and the two of us went over to them.

"That ball could've killed me!" Schwartzie was saying. He was of medium size, with a long face and a bad case of acne. He wiped sweat from his face. "My God, did you see that ball?"

"I saw it," Mr. Galanter said grimly.

"That was too fast to stop, Mr. Galanter," I said in Schwartzie's defense.

"I heard about that Danny Saunders," Sidney Goldberg said. "He always hits to the pitcher."

"You could've told me," Schwartzie lamented. "I could've been ready."

"I only *heard* about it," Sidney Goldberg said. "You always believe everything you hear?"

"God, that ball could've killed me!" Schwartzie said again.

"You want to go on pitching?" Mr. Galanter said. A thin sheen of sweat covered his forehead, and he looked very grim.

"Sure, Mr. Galanter," Schwartzie said. "I'm okay."

"You're sure?"

"Sure I'm sure."

"No heroes in this war, now," Mr. Galanter said. "I want live soldiers, not dead heroes."

"I'm no hero," Schwartzie muttered lamely. "I can still get it over, Mr. Galanter. God, it's only the first inning."

"Okay, soldier," Mr. Galanter said, not very enthusiastically. "Just keep our side of this war fighting."

"I'm trying my best, Mr. Galanter," Schwartzie said.

Mr. Galanter nodded, still looking grim, and started off the field. I saw him take a handkerchief out of his pocket and wipe his forehead.

"Jesus Christ!" Schwartzie said, now that Mr. Galanter was gone. "That bastard aimed right for my head!"

"Oh, come on, Schwartzie," I said. "What is he, Babe Ruth?"

"You heard what Sidney said."

"Stop giving it to them on a silver platter and they won't hit it like that."

"Who's giving it to them on a silver platter?" Schwartzie lamented. "That was a great pitch."

"Sure," I said.

The umpire came over to us. "You boys planning to chat here all afternoon?" he asked. He was a squat man in his late forties, and he looked impatient.

"No, sir," I said very politely, and Sidney and I ran back to our places.

Danny Saunders was standing on my base. His white shirt was pasted to his arms and back with sweat.

"That was a nice shot," I offered.

He looked at me curiously and said nothing.

"You always hit it like that to the pitcher?" I asked.

He smiled faintly. "You're Reuven Malter," he said in perfect English.

He had a low, nasal voice.

"That's right," I said, wondering where he had heard my name.

"Your father is David Malter, the one who writes articles on the Talmud?"

"Yes."

"I told my team we're going to kill you *apikorsim* this afternoon." He said it flatly, without a trace of expression in his voice.

I stared at him and hoped the sudden tight coldness I felt wasn't showing on my face. "Sure," I said. "Rub your tzitzit for good luck."

I walked away from him and took up my position near the base. I looked toward the wire screen and saw Davey Cantor standing there, staring out at the field, his hands in his pockets. I crouched down quickly, because Schwartzie was going into his pitch.

It was hot, and I was sweating beneath my clothes. I felt the earpieces of my glasses cutting into the skin over my ears, and I took the glasses off for a moment and ran a finger over the pinched ridges of skin, then put them back on quickly because Schwartzie was going into a windup. I crouched down, waiting, remembering Danny Saunders' promise to his team that they would kill us *apikorsim*. The word had meant, originally, a Jew educated in Judaism who denied basic tenets of his faith, like the existence of God, the revelation, the resurrection of the dead. To people like Reb Saunders, it also meant any educated Jew who might be reading, say, Darwin, and who was not wearing side curls and fringes outside his trousers. I was an *apikoros* to Danny Saunders, despite my belief in God and Torah, because I did not have side curls and was attending a parochial school where too many English subjects were offered and where Jewish subjects were taught in Hebrew instead of Yiddish, both unheard-of sins, the former because it took time away from the study of Torah, the latter because Hebrew was the Holy Tongue and to use it in ordinary classroom discourse was a desecration of God's Name. I had never really had any personal contact with this kind of Jew before. My father had told me he didn't mind their beliefs. What annoyed him was their fanatic sense of righteousness, their absolute certainty that they and they alone had God's ear, and every other Jew was wrong, totally wrong, a sinner, a hypocrite, an *apikoros*, and doomed, therefore, to bum in hell. I found myself wondering again how they had learned to hit a ball like that if time for the study of Torah was so precious to them and why they had sent a rabbi along to waste his time sitting on a bench during a ball game.

Standing on the field and watching the boy at the plate swing at a high ball and miss, I felt myself suddenly very angry, and it was at that point that for me the game stopped being merely a game and became a war. The fun and excitement was out of it now. Somehow the yeshiva team had translated this afternoon's baseball game into a conflict

> ## "I told my team we're going to kill you apikorsim this afternoon." He said it flatly, without a trace of expression in his voice.

between what they regarded as their righteousness and our sinfulness. I found myself growing more and more angry, and I felt the anger begin to focus itself upon Danny Saunders, and suddenly it was not at all difficult for me to hate him.

Schwartzie let five of their men come up to the plate that half inning and let one of those five score. Sometime during that half inning, one of the members of the yeshiva team had shouted at us in Yiddish, "Burn in hell, you *apikorsim!*" and by the time that half inning was over and we were standing around Mr. Galanter near the wire screen, all of us knew that this was not just another ball game.

Mr. Galanter was sweating heavily, and his face was grim. All he said was, "We fight it careful from now on. No more mistakes." He said it very quietly, and we were all quiet, too, as the batter stepped up to the plate.

We proceeded to play a slow, careful game, bunting whenever we had to, sacrificing to move runners forward, obeying Mr. Galanter's instructions. I noticed that no matter where the runners were on the bases, the yeshiva team always threw to Danny Saunders, and I realized that they did this because he was the only infielder who could be relied upon to stop their wild throws. Sometime during the inning, I walked over behind the rabbi and looked over his shoulder at the book he was reading. I saw the words were Yiddish. I walked back to the wire screen. Davey Cantor came over and stood next to me, but he remained silent.

We scored only one run that inning, and we walked onto the field for the first half of the third inning with a sense of doom.

Dov Shlomowitz came up to the plate. He stood there like a bear, the bat looking like a matchstick in his beefy hands. Schwartzie pitched, and he sliced one neatly over the head of the third baseman for a single. The yeshiva team howled, and again one of them called out to us in Yiddish, "Burn, you *apikorsim!*" and Sidney Goldberg and I looked at each other without saying a word.

Mr. Galanter was standing alongside third base, wiping his forehead. The rabbi was sitting quietly, reading his book.

I took off my glasses and rubbed the tops of my ears. I felt a sudden momentary sense of unreality, as if the play yard, with its black asphalt floor and its white base lines, were my entire world now, as if all the previous years of my life had led me somehow to this one ball game, and all the future years of my life would depend upon its outcome. I stood there for a moment, holding the glasses in my hand and feeling frightened. Then I took a deep breath, and the feeling passed. It's only a ball game, I told myself. What's a ball game?

Reprinted by permission of Mrs. Adena Potok.

STEPHEN WONG

THE HEART AND SOUL OF BASEBALL

One Sunday afternoon in the autumn of 1982, during my sophomore year at the Lawrenceville School in New Jersey, I wandered into the basement of the school library to find some books for a history paper. Walking through one of the aisles, I noticed that several of the bookshelves were stacked with volumes of the school yearbook, which was (and still is) called Olla Podrida. I was staring at an archival collection of almost every yearbook since the 1885 inaugural issue, and I was fascinated. I began flipping through a number of them, starting with the 1967 edition, because I wanted to see what pop star Huey Lewis (Lawrenceville class of '67) looked like as a senior in high school. Gradually, I made my way back to the books from the early part of the twentieth century. In one of the yearbooks, stuck between two pages, I came across a brittle newspaper containing the following poem:

> These are the saddest of possible words:
> "Tinker to Evers to Chance."
> Trio of Bear Cubs and
> Fleeter than birds,
> "Tinker to Evers to Chance."
> Ruthlessly pricking our gonfalon bubble,
> Making a Giant hit into a double,
> Words that are weighty with nothing but trouble:
> "Tinker to Evers to Chance."

I had no idea who Tinker, Evers, and Chance were, nor did I understand what "gonfalon bubble" meant. But being a former Little Leaguer, a San Francisco Giants fan, and an avid buyer of contemporary baseball cards, I knew the poem had to do with baseball; and the names of the three players, along with the lilting rhythm of the poem, greatly appealed to me.

This poem piqued my curiosity. Who were these three players, and why were they important enough to be the subjects of a poem? What was the "gonfalon bubble"? To find out, I went to a bookstore in nearby Princeton and bought a copy of Lawrence Ritter's *Glory of Their Times*, which I had heard was a wonderful book based on interviews with ballplayers who played in the early twentieth century. From reading

"Curiosity is, in great and generous minds, the first passion and the last."
Samuel Johnson

Joe Schwartz, *Stickball Game,*
ca. 1930s

an interview with Fred Snodgrass, who played with the New York Giants between 1908 and
1915, I learned that Tinker, Evers, and Chance were the shortstop, second baseman, and first
baseman, respectively, for the Chicago Cubs during that era. They were celebrated, across
the baseball world as well as in the poem, for their uncanny ability to turn double play after
double play. In his interview, Snodgrass recalled, among other memorable plays, Evers's role in
the famous "Merkle's Boner" play, in which the Giants baserunner Fred Merkle forgot to touch
second base, a gaffe that ultimately cost the Giants the pennant in 1908. Not only did Evers,
notice that Merkle failed to touch second, he also made sure the umpire was aware of it.

Although it should not have been such a surprise to me that there was more to baseball
and baseball players than meets the eye on television broadcasts, somehow this "behind-the-
scenes" perspective was a revelation. Rather than satisfying my curiosity about Tinker, Evers
and Chance, Ritter's book left me wanting to know more. I wanted to learn not only about the
1908 Chicago Cubs, but also about players and teams that I already knew were legendary,
such as Shoeless Joe Jackson and the 1919 Chicago "Black Sox," Christy Mathewson and
the early twentieth-century New York Giants, and Jackie Robinson and the 1950s Brooklyn
Dodgers. So I began to read other classics, including W.P. Kinsella's *Shoeless Joe,* Eric Rolfe
Greenberg's *The Celebrant,* and Roger Kahn's *The Boys of Summer.* During college and law
school, I spent weekend afternoons curled up with A. Bartlett Giamatti (*The Green Fields
of the Mind*), Gay Talese (*The Silent Season of a Hero*), and John Updike (*Hub Fans Bid Kid
Adieu*), as well as what W.P. Kinsella calls the "sun-drenched baseball prose" of Roger Angell,
which appeared in the *New Yorker* from time to time.

For many baseball fans, watching all of their teams' games is all it takes for them to "live
and breathe" baseball. For others, the passion grows into a desire to collect the physical

objects involved in the game, as well as the objects made to commemorate baseball and its players. I know; this happened to me. In the decade after I found the "Tinker to Evers to Chance" poem and read Ritter's book, I read every baseball book I could get my hands on, and started to purchase old baseball cards so I could see images of the players I had been reading about. I also started to buy old scorecards at baseball memorabilia conventions because I loved the nostalgic advertisements they featured.

For the past thirty years building a collection of historically significant baseball artifacts has been at the center of my life. There has been an overwhelming sense of joy in this endeavor, but it's hard to pinpoint why I have been so passionate and committed to it. Poet Marianne Moore seemed to offer some guidance in the first stanza of her 1961 poem, "Baseball and Writing," that would ultimately lead me to find the answer:

> "Fanaticism? No. Writing is exciting
> and baseball is like writing.
> You can never tell with either
> how it will go
> or what you will do."

Stephen Wong before a Little League game, Los Altos Hills, California, 1975

―――――――――――――

Not long after Ty Cobb died in 1961, Lawrence Ritter, an economist at New York University, began a journey that would last five years and take him more than seventy-five thousand miles across the United States and Canada. He was looking for old-time baseball players who could tell him about their lives in the big leagues in the 1890s and the early years of the twentieth century. According to Ritter, "It seemed to me then that someone should do something, and do it quickly, to record for the future the remembrances of a sport that has played such a significant role in American life." Ritter recorded conversations with twenty-two ballplayers, including Rube Marquard, "Wahoo Sam" Crawford, Fred Snodgrass, Smokey Joe Wood, Babe Herman, Paul Waner, and Lefty O'Doul. Each of them, in talking to Ritter, vividly re-created what it was like to play in the majors during the era of Cobb, Honus Wagner, Tris Speaker, and Christy Mathewson, as well as later legends such as Babe Ruth, Lou Gehrig, and Jimmie Foxx. Ritter compiled his interviews in *Glory of Their Times: The Story of the Early Days of Baseball Told by the Men Who Played It* (1966), one of baseball's landmark literary masterpieces and the same book I purchased in Princeton during high school.

In February 2003, with war looming in Iraq and Severe Acute Respiratory Syndrome (SARS) on the rise in Hong Kong where my family has lived since the 1980s, my personal world was in crisis as well. Burnt out after six and a half years in finance, I had left my job and was at loose ends about my future. One evening during this time, I decided to cheer myself up (once again) with baseball and Duke Ellington. I pulled out *The Glory of Their Times* from the bookshelf and sat down with a glass of wine and Duke's "Creole Rhapsody" purring softly in the background. While reading the book's original preface, I kept thinking how rewarding those five years on the road must have been for Ritter, and how exciting it must have been to travel all those miles in pursuit of a dream.

Slowly it dawned on me that I might consider a baseball journey of my own. The timing seemed ideal. Only seven months earlier, baseball and America had lost one of their beloved icons, Ted Williams, and 2003 was the year in which baseball would celebrate the hundredth anniversary of the World Series, the seventieth anniversary of the All-Star Game, and the eightieth anniversary of the opening of Yankee Stadium. I thought how wonderful it would be, as a passionate collector of baseball memorabilia, to visit, professionally photograph, and write about some of the world's finest private collections of rare and important artifacts from baseball's rich history. What a delight it would be to meet with people who, like me, have dedicated a significant part of their lives to collecting and preserving some of the game's most precious relics; to learn more about, and share in, their joy and fascination with the objects in their collections; to listen to their stories about how they got started in collecting and why they chose particular themes or types of artifacts in which to specialize; to reminisce with them about special moments in baseball history, both on and off the field.

That evening's epiphany led me to research, write, and publish *Smithsonian Baseball: Inside the World's Finest Private Collections* (2005). I wanted to shine a spotlight on some of the finest and most comprehensive private collections in each major segment of baseball memorabilia. My primary focus was on the period starting before the Civil War and ending in the 1960s. For the most part, artifacts from this period are significantly scarcer and more valuable than those from later eras.

For many baseball fans, watching all of their teams' games is all it takes for them to "live and breathe" baseball.

By July 2003, when Smithsonian Books expressed interest in publishing *Smithsonian Baseball*, my photographer and I were on our way to the first photo shoot in Los Angeles. During the next six months, we traveled to nineteen other cities and towns throughout the country. Drives from Haddonfield, New Jersey, to Pittsburgh; Cincinnati to St. Louis via Louisville; and Memphis to Clarksdale, Mississippi, were long but always rewarding.

In January 2004, I flew back to Hong Kong to finish the research and writing. The passenger sitting next to me on the plane, a man who looked to be in his mid-forties, introduced himself and we started chatting. When he asked what I did for a living, I told him that I had been writing a book on private collections of historical baseball artifacts. He asked me what kind of objects would be featured. When I told him a few of the highlights, his eyes widened in disbelief. Across the aisle, I noticed an elderly gentleman wearing a Boston Red Sox cap so weathered it looked as though its prime coincided with Carl Yastrzemski's. Seated next to him was a young boy, probably his grandson, also wearing a Red Sox cap. The boy kept tugging at the man's sleeves to show him his baseball cards. I turned back to my window and thought about all the miles I had traveled during the past six months, and about why I had taken such a chunk out of my life (more than two and half years) to complete the book. I reminisced about finding the "Tinkers to Evers to Chance" poem in the basement of my high school library, reading *The Glory of Their Times* for the very first time, and how I had spent a lifetime collecting baseball memorabilia. I realized then that my journey was not only about commemorating these astounding collections. It was about being part of the heart and soul of baseball. As author Tom Stanton wrote in *The Road to Cooperstown*: "Baseball's appeal isn't complicated or confusing. It's about the beauty of a game; it's about heroes and family and friends; it's about being part of something larger than yourself, about belonging; it's about tradition—receiving it and passing it; and it's about holding on to a bit of your childhood."

That is how I feel. The collection is my way of expressing it.

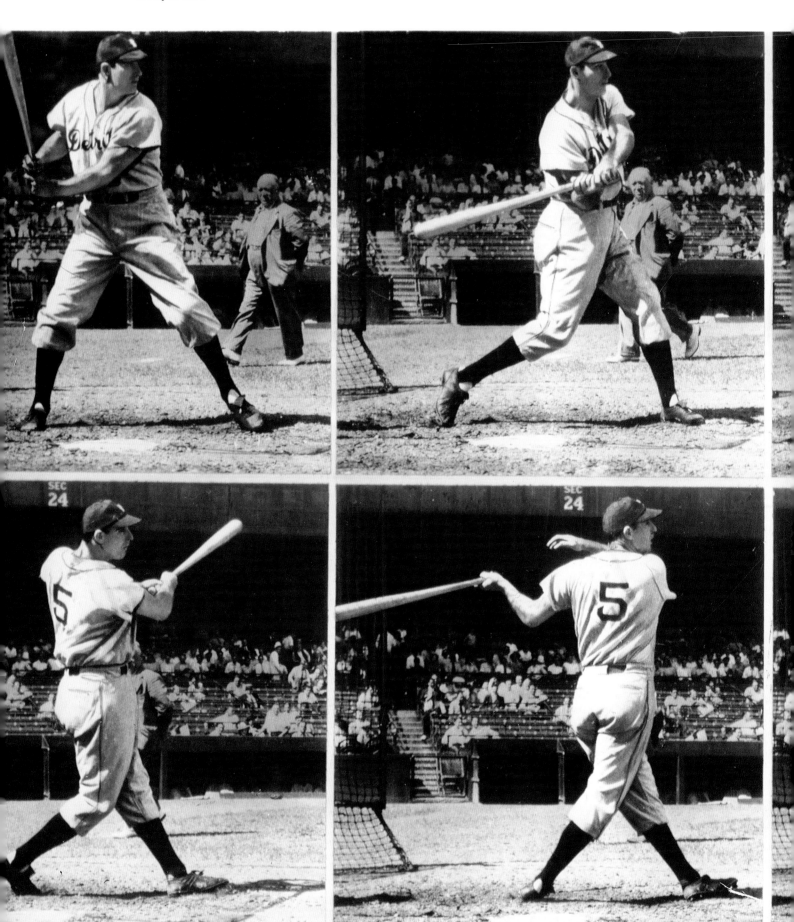

HAMMERIN' HANK GREENBERG

CALL HIM THE HERO OF HEROES

AVIVA KEMPNER

Hall of Famer Hank Greenberg is famous for challenging Babe Ruth's 1938 record of sixty home runs by hitting fifty-eight out of the park. Paradoxically, Hammerin' Hank is most revered in Jewish homes for actually not showing up to play a game, and instead attending services on Yom Kippur in 1934.

Greenberg was born Hyman in New York City on January 1, 1911; his mother, Sarah, used to tease him that the New Year's celebrations were for his birthday. Greenberg's father, David, who owned a cloth-shrinking plant, moved the family from Greenwich Village to a home across from Crotona Park in the Bronx when Hank was six years old. This fateful move provided the budding athlete with a conveniently located baseball field. Greenberg became so devoted to the game he would be chewed out for being late to evening meals, except on Friday nights, when he made sure to be on time for Shabbat dinner.

Scouted for his power at the plate while still in high school, Greenberg passed on the chance of being a Yankee after seeing power hitter Lou Gehrig covering first base, and he figured it would be years before he ever played. The nearby New York Giants mistakenly never called him for a tryout. The good-looking, six-foot-four rookie was drawn instead to a Detroit stadium favorable to home-run hitters and signed with the Tigers in 1929. His parents wanted him to attend college, but the dream of playing professional baseball trumped an advanced degree. So, against his father's wishes, Greenberg dropped out after his first year at New York University.

Leaving the Big Apple for the first time, Greenberg headed to the minor leagues. Playing mostly with Southern natives, the New Yorker encountered players who had never met a Jew before. One player naively asked him, "Where are your horns?" The ignorance of and prejudice toward Jews intensified once Greenberg reached Detroit in 1933. Detroit was home to the car inventor and manufacturer Henry Ford, notorious for distributing antisemitic literature at his dealerships. The Motor City also saw the rise of Father Charles Coughlin, who preached virulent hatred against Jews and African Americans on the radio to millions of followers. In other cities as well Greenberg's appearances gave rise to antisemitic taunting.

Just imagine going to work every day and hearing slurs yelled at you. That is exactly the hostile atmosphere Greenberg played in during the Golden Age of Baseball. Fellow player Birdie Tebbetts said, "Hank was abused more than anyone except Jackie Robinson." There was always some "leather lung...yelling at me," Greenberg recalled in an interview. But the proud Jewish player used those catcalls as "a spur to make me do better."

The existence of such tremendous domestic antisemitism makes Greenberg's decision on how to cope with the convergence of the High Holy Days and the conclusion of the competitive 1934 baseball season especially admirable. The Tigers were in a hot pennant race, and coming in first had eluded them since 1909. The team could not afford to lose their top home-run and RBI producer, even for a day.

First he had to decide what to do about Rosh Hashanah. The local papers were full of stories debating whether the power hitter would play on the Jewish New Year. Rabbis were asked for their advice for the slugger. One Orthodox rabbi claimed it was acceptable for Greenberg to play if no money was exchanged for ticket purchases and kosher food was served.

The *Detroit News* consulted a local Reform rabbi on Greenberg's behalf, who cited references in the Talmud that allowed for playing on a holiday in the street. So Greenberg decided to split the day. He went first to Rosh Hashanah services and then showed up at the stadium to play. Detroit's starting pitcher, Elden Auker, was surprised to see him arriving in a suit after davening at *shul*. Greenberg's prayers were rightly answered. He hit two solo home runs to help the Tigers beat the Red Sox 2–1. Never mind that, according to sportscaster Dick Schaap, "the rabbi knew that the Talmud really said that it was the Roman children who played on Rosh Hashanah, but didn't tell Hank that part of it."

The following day, the *Detroit Free Press* carried a headline addressed to "Mr. Greenberg" and read "Leshono tovo tikosayvu," or "Happy New Year" in Hebrew letters. (Who knows how they ever secured the metal type for this ancient language?)

When Yom Kippur arrived, Greenberg faced a real dilemma unlike that of any other baseball player before or after. Sure, fellow Jewish Hall of Famer Sandy Koufax chose not to pitch on Yom Kippur during the 1965 World Series, but pitchers always rotate what games they play; however, a team needs to have its ace hitter playing every day. Plus, Greenberg was playing at the time of the greatest domestic antisemitism, making his decision more challenging and more courageous.

The Jewish first baseman chose to honor his Romanian-born parents by trekking to synagogue instead of suiting up, even though the Tigers were in a raging pennant race. When he arrived at Detroit's Shaarey Zedek synagogue, he was applauded, and young boys chased after him as he walked down the steps. Not surprisingly, the Tigers lost.

Using his faith instead of his strong arms, the newly found hero of the Jewish community taught America about a minority religious practice that was unknown to most. Greenberg gained the respect of the entire community, as reflected in the last lines of the ode by Edgar Guest published in the October 4 *Detroit Free Press*:

Using his faith instead of his strong arms, the newly found hero of the Jewish community taught America about a minority religious practice that was unknown to most.

PREVIOUS

Hank Greenberg's mighty swing, Yankee Stadium, August 30, 1938

ABOVE

Hank Greenberg with his mother, Sarah Greenberg, at breakfast, Bronx, New York, 1936

Hank Greenberg's war department identification card, issued after his voluntary reenlistment following the bombing of Pearl Harbor, 1944

"We shall miss him on the infield and shall miss him at the bat /
    But he's true to his religion—and I honor him for that!'"

The Tigers went on to win the pennant in 1934, 1935, 1940, and 1945. The team captured World Series titles in 1935 and 1945. Except in 1935, when he broke his wrist, Greenberg's hitting contributed greatly to the Tigers' winning performances.

In 1938, Greenberg almost surpassed Babe Ruth's record sixty home runs. Even though many Jewish fans believe Greenberg was pitched bad balls because he was Jewish, the two-time Most Valuable Player (MVP) denied such a bias. Greenberg, who revered Ruth, later claimed, "What a thrill just to even get a shot at it."

Back in the Bronx, those mothers who had claimed for years that Greenberg was a "bum" for playing baseball now acted with total respect toward his mother; Mrs. Greenberg was now treated as "Queen of the Bronx." Greenberg was idolized for being big and strong, belying the "nebbish" stereotype. The kvelling for Greenberg knew no bounds. Young Jewish women, wanting to marry him, stalked him where he played and offered him marriage proposals. One fan even concocted a plan to ask the naïve Greenberg to help her do her math homework.

As his career progressed, Greenberg went on to rack up great stats. He hit a .313 lifetime average, won the MVP title in 1935 and 1940 at two different positions, and had the third most RBIs in a single season, with 183 in 1937. He also slugged 331 home runs and played both first base and the outfield.

When the Nazis rose to power in Europe in the late 1930s, the symbol of a powerful Jewish hitter rose in significance. Greenberg's son Stephen said his father felt that "every time he would hit a home run, he would feel doubly proud because he felt like he was hitting a home run against Hitler." No wonder Greenberg became a beacon of hope to American Jewry.

Hankus Pankus, as he was known, became the first major league player drafted by the military in May 1941. Once in the army, Greenberg did not play for four and a half years. To the joy of those in the stadium

Joe DiMaggio and Hank Greenberg in Yankee Stadium, September 3, 1939

awaiting his return in 1945, the out-of-shape slugger pounded a home run in his first game back in July. One Jewish fan celebrated by dancing precariously around the roof of a protruding press box.

In the last game of the 1945 season, Greenberg pounded a grand slam in the ninth inning and the Tigers won 6-3 against the St. Louis Browns. That game clinched the pennant; and Hank's performance, after not playing for so many years, was one of the greatest comebacks in sports history.

Senator Carl Levin recalls how as a boy he read the next day's exuberant newspaper coverage that started off: "Call him the hero of heroes, call him the champion of champions, call him the hero of Bengal-town." Decades later an elderly female fan approached Greenberg at a lunch and declared, "I want you to know you did more for the Jewish people than anyone else during World War II. You were a symbol of our strength."

After the 1946 season, Tigers owner Walter Briggs traded Greenberg to the Pittsburgh Pirates. Of this controversial 1947 trade, one Jewish fan, Don

Shapiro, lamented, "It was like your *bubbe* moved to Mississippi." But the trade also made Hank the first player to earn $100,000.

As fate would have it, 1947 was the last year of the Jewish player's career and the first year for the great African American player, Dodgers first baseman Jackie Robinson. The rookie was facing far greater prejudice than even Greenberg had ever encountered from his fellow and opposing players and from the stands. Greenberg, unlike most opposing players, welcomed Robinson. During one game, they collided at first base and thousands of fans gasped. Greenberg held out a hand and treated Robinson with empathy and respect. Afterwards, Robinson told newspaper reporters, "Mr. Greenberg is class, it stands out all over him." Greenberg retired in 1947, and was elected to the Hall of Fame in 1956.

Upon his retirement, Greenberg went to work with the colorful Bill Veeck, who owned the Cleveland Indians, eventually becoming the team's general manager. They signed Larry Doby, the first African American player in the American League, and during Greenberg's tenure the team featured several black ballplayers, including the great Satchel Paige. Greenberg was instrumental in bringing success to the Indians, who won the pennant in 1954.

Veeck and Greenberg became close friends, and their partnership continued. Greenberg was appointed vice president of the Chicago White Sox, and in 1959 became part owner, along with Veeck. The '59 White Sox won the American League pennant with a very diverse roster.

During one game, they collided at first base and thousands of fans gasped. Greenberg held out a hand and treated Robinson with empathy and respect.

Fans also closely followed the great baseball player's personal life. Greenberg created headlines when he eloped with Caral Gimbel, heiress to the department store family, in 1945. They had three children and later divorced, in 1959. Their son, Stephen, played in the minor leagues and became deputy commissioner of Major League Baseball from 1990 until 1993. He now advises new baseball ownerships. Their second son, Glenn, heads an investment firm, and daughter Alva is an art dealer.

Greenberg married actress Mary Jo Tarola in 1966 and moved with her to Los Angeles. Always competitive, he played the stock market and tennis, and Jewish fans still sought him out. Actor Walter Matthau plotted to have lunches often at the Beverly Hills Tennis Club just so he could schmooze with his childhood hero. Greenberg died on September 4, 1986, from cancer.

Eighty years after the Hebrew Hammer's widely applauded decision to sit out a game, his bravery still evokes prideful discussions in Jewish homes. Influenced by Greenberg's precedent, Judge Ruth Bader Ginsburg claims the Supreme Court does not hear cases on Yom Kippur.

Growing up, my brother Jonathan and I would hear our father recite the story of Hank Greenberg's 1934 Yom Kippur observance on our way to synagogue. No wonder I thought Greenberg was an integral part of Kol Nidre services—his historic observance proves how much baseball is a religion in America.

DIVERSITY IN
THE OWNER'S BOX

───

BARRY
M.
BLOOM

When the Braves left Milwaukee for Atlanta after the 1965 season, a young University of Wisconsin history major vowed that Major League Baseball (MLB) would certainly return. That man, Allan "Bud" Selig, whose family was well known in the abandoned city for its ownership of several thriving automobile dealerships, set about the process of wooing baseball back to Milwaukee. Barely five years later, his perseverance paid off. The expansion Seattle Pilots—a franchise that had been scorned in its first year, losing ninety-eight games and drawing a scant 677,944 at the decrepit Sick's Stadium—had declared bankruptcy.

Selig and a group of partners agreed to purchase the team, but there was still a question of whether it had to remain in Seattle. During the spring of 1970, as the Pilots trained in Arizona, a bankruptcy judge was asked to determine the financial standing of the one-year-old ball club. On the eve of the season opener, the truck loaded with all the Pilots' baseball equipment was routed to Las Vegas, where the driver was told to await a verdict. If the judge ruled in favor of Seattle, the truck would head to the Pacific Northwest, while an adverse ruling for that city would send the equipment and players hurtling toward the Northeast. The judge ruled that the franchise was indeed bankrupt and ordered it sold to Selig. And that's the way MLB's ninth commissioner wound up ascending from a minority owner of the Braves to having principal ownership of the team that from then on would be known as the Brewers.

Selig, with his European Jewish background, joined a group of baseball owners as diverse as the sport that had evolved around them. From Effa Manley, who owned the Newark Eagles in the Negro Leagues, to Arte Moreno, the current owner of the Los Angeles Angels, and Magic Johnson, the Hall of Fame basketball player who is now a partner in the Los Angeles Dodgers, baseball owners have a rich ethnic background and have worked mightily for the privilege of owning a team.

All the above were firsts. Selig was the first Jewish baseball commissioner. Manley was the first woman elected to the National Baseball Hall of Fame. Moreno was the first Mexican American to wholly own a major league team. And Johnson, a star member of the "Showtime" Lakers of the 1980s, was the first African American to have an out-front ownership position with a major league team.

Johnson was certainly aware of the significance of his purchasing an ownership stake in the Dodgers. He did so after the team was transferred to a new ownership group, on May 1, 2012, a little more than sixty-five years since April 15, 1947, when Jackie Robinson shattered the color barrier on the field forever as he jogged out of the dugout at Ebbets Field to play first base for the Brooklyn Dodgers. "Jackie Robinson probably opened the door to a lot of guys, too—and me," said Johnson in April 2013 as the new ownership held its first Jackie Robinson Day ceremony at Dodger Stadium. "If Jackie hadn't played for the Dodgers, I don't think I'd be an owner of the Dodgers. Look, the man had to endure a lot. Imagine how tough it was for him to focus on baseball when he was getting death threats and everything else. But you know what? He maintained his focus, his discipline. The strength that this guy had to have was amazing."

"Trailblazing owner and tireless crusader in the civil rights movement, who earned the respect of her players and fellow owners...."

Effa Manley, owner of the Negro League Newark Eagles, at Ruppert Stadium, Newark, New Jersey, 1948

In 1997, under Selig's direction and in an unprecedented tribute, Robinson's number, 42, was retired across all of baseball on the occasion of the fiftieth anniversary of that long-fought-for day, which couldn't have happened without the foresight of Branch Rickey, at the time a minority Dodgers partner and general manager, and then commissioner Happy Chandler.

At the same time that Robinson joined the Dodgers farm system, Manley and her husband Abe ran the Eagles, who had moved from Brooklyn to Newark. In what was then baseball's alternate universe, the Eagles glimmered as a sterling business and baseball franchise in a league that was rife with hucksters and fly-by-night operators. Manley, a light-skinned African American woman of uncertain origin, was the rare exception. She co-owned the team from her marriage to the older Abe Manley in 1935 until 1948, two years after his death.

In 1946, the same year Rickey tested Robinson with the Triple-A Montreal Royals, the Eagles won the Negro League World Series with Larry Doby, Don Newcombe, and Monte Irvin, who all eventually ascended to the Majors, on the roster. Bucking all convention, Manley, as business manager, was an essential component of the organization. As the great integration began, a process that led to the destruction of her own business, she bluntly criticized any major league club stealing a Negro League player without compensation. Because of her complaints, the practice ended. In 2006, Manley was elected to Cooperstown, where a plaque describes her as a "trailblazing owner and tireless crusader in the civil rights movement, who earned the respect of her players and fellow owners.... She integrated her players into the community and fielded consistently competitive teams."

Manley was a force in the Major Leagues, where female ownership has been limited. Joan Kroc of the Padres, Jean Yawkey of the Red Sox, and Marge Schott of the Reds all inherited either their respective fortunes or clubs when their husbands died. Selig's daughter Wendy Selig-Prieb ran the Brewers until the franchise was sold in 2005.

But it took decades until a minority would hold that key position of authority with a major league team. Arte Moreno, a marketing and advertising genius from Tucson, grew the Phoenix billboard company Outdoor Systems from a $500,000 business in 1984 to one worth more than $90 million ten years later. A partner in the minor league Salt Lake Trappers, Moreno ultimately purchased the Angels from Disney for $180 million and took control of the club on May 15, 2003, becoming the first Mexican American owner of a U.S.-based major league sports team.

Under Moreno's watch, the Angels have become one of the most solvent teams in Major League Baseball. "[Los Angeles] is a huge area," he told me in the summer of 2013. "There are eighteen million people in the metroplex. There are plenty of people to draw from. The economy is still in transition. I would say that from the economic side, we have no debt. We have a really good long-term television agreement. We own our own radio, and we don't lose money. We may not always make the right decisions, but we try to stay competitive. When I look at it from a macro side, I think the health of the organization is good."

ABOVE

Allan "Bud" Selig, former owner of the Milwaukee Brewers and commissioner of Major League Baseball since 1992, ca. 1973

LEFT

Arte Moreno, owner of the Los Angeles Angels of Anaheim, December 15, 2012

Magic Johnson at the Los Angeles
Dodgers season opener, April 1, 2013

Selig has said the same thing about Major League Baseball. When he
replaced Fay Vincent as interim commissioner in 1992, baseball was a
$1.2 billion-a-year business, and it is now generating in excess of $8 billion
a season. Unlike the other three North American-based sports leagues,
baseball has enjoyed an extended and once-unheard-of era of labor peace
since Selig was formally awarded the job on July 9, 1998.

Baseball is a social institution, Selig often says. And he has supported
that talk with his actions regarding wide-ranging diversity issues. Millions
of dollars have been spent building and staffing baseball academies in
various areas of the country, growing the RBI (Reviving Baseball in Inner
Cities) program that provides baseball support to two hundred thousand
kids in two hundred U.S. communities each year and awarding college
scholarships to minority students through the Jackie Robinson Foundation,
which has a nearly one-hundred-percent graduation rate among its granted
students. Beginning with an equipment truck stop in Las Vegas, the changes
to the game under Selig's watch are too numerous to list, but it's safe to say
that baseball's diversity will be a big part of his enduring legacy.

Mel Allen calls the game
from Yankee Stadium,
May 11, 1956

MEL ALLEN

―

THE VOICE

CURT
SMITH

Billy Gomez, who played bass with pianist Billy Evans, once stated that the jazz musician aims "to make music that balance[s] passion and intellect." For almost a century, announcers have used radio, then television, to carry baseball's music to millions of people.

Baseball aired its first game on the radio over America's first commercial station, KDKA, from Pittsburgh's Forbes Field on August 5, 1921. The first televised major league game was in 1939 at Brooklyn's Ebbets Field. Ultimately, from distant sites—Fenway Park, Crosley Field, Briggs Stadium—the media ferried big league prose. Hank Greenwald, one among numerous Jewish Americans to cover baseball, said, "Football and basketball carry the announcer. The announcer carries baseball." We see or hear them everywhere—the car, backyard, even the Internet. A three-hour game may put the ball in play for only ten minutes, while the broadcaster navigates a sea of dead air, using persona as a paddle. Bob Costas has covered ten Olympic Games. "Despite that, I'm linked to baseball," he mused. "Its pace lets you reveal your personality."

Melvin Allen Israel, a.k.a. Mel Allen, became baseball's most famed announcer. He was also a man who had all, lost all, and against all likelihood came back. In 1955, *Variety* magazine named him "one of the world's 25 most recognizable voices," akin to Churchill or Sinatra. A bystander could walk down the street, a hundred windows open, Allen's voice wafting out, and not miss a pitch. As the 1939–64 voice of the New York Yankees, Mel began each game with his trademark phrase, "Hello there, everybody!" A home run hailed a Yankees sponsor—a "White Owl Wallop" or "Ballantine Blast." When Hank Bauer doubled, or "bad ball" Yogi Berra begot good, "How about that!" followed. You felt the fielder crouched, batter cocked, and pitcher draped against the seats—above all, that there was no place on earth you would rather be. Once, in Omaha, hailing a cab at night, Mel said simply, "Sheraton, please." The cabby, having not recognized him in the dark, nearly drove off the road.

Many found it ironic that the voice of the Yankees was born in Birmingham, Alabama, on February 14, 1913, to Russian émigrés Anna Leibovitz and Julius Allen Israel. Julius's father had reached America at thirty-five, settled in West Blockton, Alabama, and built a dry goods store. Anna left Leningrad at nine. She married Julius in February 1912.

Inheriting, then selling, the store, Julius carted his family across Alabama, settling in Bessemer, a steel-producing city. When its economy tanked, he sold that store, moving to rural Walker County. "Some folks boycotted our *new* store," said Mel. "The Ku Klux Klan had a blacklist." One night the sheets rode. Recognizing a doctor's shoes, Anna twitted him the next day, "My, didn't you look wonderful sitting so straight in your saddle?"

When a hernia and bleeding ulcer put Julius in a hospital, several Klansmen visited, with a bouquet. "Isn't this a great sight?" Anna said. "We have a Jewish intern, a Presbyterian minister, in a Catholic hospital—and the Ku Klux Klan." Shopping for Passover while Julius was hospitalized, she entered a store around whose stove sat a mayor, preacher, and lawyer.

"How's Mr. Israel?" one inquired.

"He's fine," she said.

"You expecting some company?"

"Yes."

"With Mr. Israel in the hospital, is it a man?"

"Indeed it is," she said. "I am told it's Jesus Christ, and there's only one house in town noble enough for him to stay."

Mel's family was his cocoon. At fifteen, he entered the University of Alabama. He earned a law degree by twenty-two and at twenty-three joined CBS Radio in New York, "[S]ens[ing] that his name was more redolent of the CCNY gym than the outfields of mid-America," wrote J. Anthony Lukas, Mel took his father's middle name as a surname, Melvin Israel becoming Mel Allen.

In 1939, at age twenty-six, Mel became a Yankees announcer, wedding irony, fluency, and a graceful front when under pressure. According to *Sports Illustrated,* by 1964 he had become "the most successful, best-known, highest-paid, most voluble figure in sportscasting, and one of the biggest names in broadcasting generally." At high tide, Mel did twenty-four NBC All-Star Games; fourteen Rose Bowl, Army-Navy, East-West, and Blue-Gray football games; horse racing's Triple Crown; CBS TV's *Mel Allen Sports Spot*; NBC Radio's *Monitor*; nearly four thousand Yankees games; and three thousand Twentieth Century Fox film newsreels. Estimates suggest that nearly eighty million people heard him weekly.

Allen aired twenty-one World Series as the whole country, wrote Heywood Broun, "stopped and paid attention." Before his last, in 1963, Mel took his parents to Israel for their fifty-first wedding anniversary, returning via the Vatican. At St. Peter's Basilica, the Archdiocese of New York's Cardinal Spellman had arranged seats near where the pope entered the room. Anna later told the cardinal, "Your Excellency, thank you for those wonderful seats. They were right behind home plate." Yearly, Allen took the annual World Series film to Rome's North American College. When Cardinal Spellman found out, he had him talk to the seminarians in Rome.

"Only in America," Allen said of his career (the same thing, by the way, that Yogi Berra said when he learned that the mayor of Dublin,

Once, in Omaha, hailing a cab at night, Mel said simply, "Sheraton, please." The cabby, having not recognized him in the dark, nearly drove off the road.

Ireland, was Jewish). Mel's life seemed to ratify the American Dream...until, out of nowhere, without even a news release, Allen was fired by NBC at age fifty-one in the fall of 1964. Movietone followed suit and, most stunningly, the Yankees too, after he had served for a quarter century as their voice. People gasped, then mourned. Associated Press baseball editor Joe Reichler recalled that "overnight Mel went from the world's most famous sportscaster to falling off the cliff." He was ignored, even blackballed, vanishing until the mid-1970s. Announcer Red Barber said, "He gave the Yankees his life, and they broke his heart." It mended, but never healed.

Why was Allen, to paraphrase Ring Lardner, suddenly treated like a side dish that his craft declined to order? One rumor whispered that Mel, unmarried, was gay—then a career ender. Other hearsay named heroin, disease, and alcohol. All false. His doctor had misprescribed medicine, clouding Allen's thought and delivery. Although others sensed that something was wrong, Mel was never aware of how the drugs were affecting him. For a decade Allen did commercial bric-a-brac. He had nowhere to hide; no one to halt rumor; no one to help him except his brother Larry and sister Esther. Yet he refused to blame or rage.

Then, in 1977, baseball's first highlights series began: *This Week in Baseball* (*TWIB*). "Growing up [outside Detroit]," said the Yankees' Derek Jeter, "it was our only chance to see other players besides our home team." Allen became *TWIB*'s host and voice-over, helping it become TV's highest-rated sports serial. Allen was "our soul," according to executive producer Geoff Belinfante. The reaction was shock at the very fact of his return. In upstate New York, a casual fan, my mother, entered her living room. She could not have listened to Mel since 1964. "I can't believe it," she exclaimed. "Is *that* Mel Allen?"

To Belinfante, Allen was "eternally grateful to be recognized again." Once, John Candy, not recognizing Allen, asked for directions in a hotel lobby. As Mel replied, a gleam filled the actor's eyes. "You're Mel Allen!" he roared. *TWIB*'s staff was young, and regarded Mel with awe. Their children hugged "Uncle Mel" as he recalled Ruth and Mantle. He was "our Jewish godfather," producer Mike Kostel said. They became *en famille*, and Allen embraced them, as colleagues Barber and Vin Scully and Joe Garagiola did: all telling stories about The Game.

"If baseball is back, Mel Allen must be, too," announced *Sports Illustrated*. In the 1980s, he was crucial to the Yankees' first foray into cable. "The voice is rich, thick, and southern, to many the most recognizable in baseball.... For years he was a forgotten man, but it has all come back to him in abundance. Like the game itself, Allen is timeless." A story of rise, near ruin, and revival, not unlike his faith.

Leo "the Lip" Durocher, manager of the Dodgers, is interviewed by Red Barber prior to the first telecast of a major league baseball game, Ebbets Field, Brooklyn, August 26, 1939

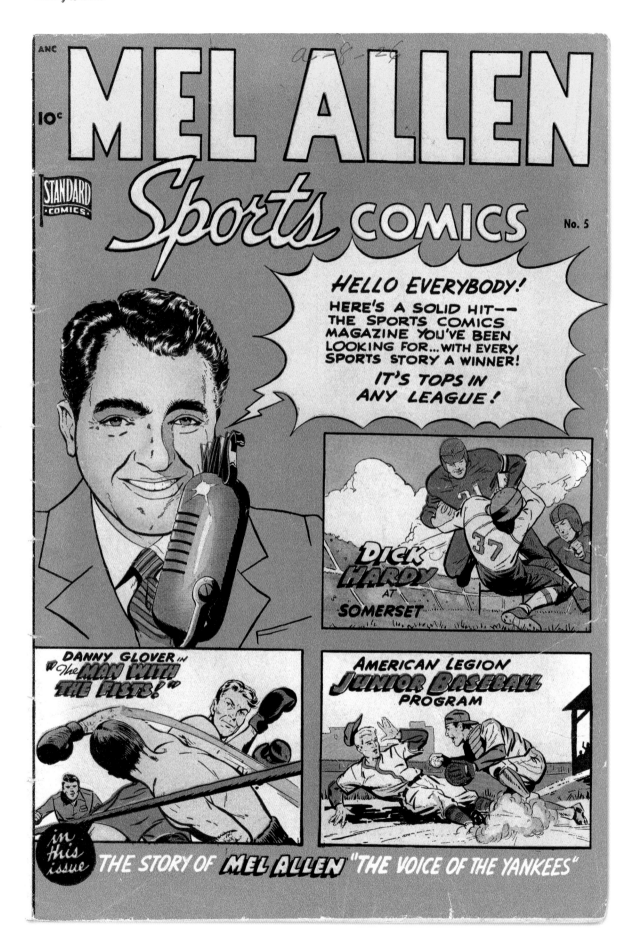

Mel Allen Sports Comics, Issue 1, No. 5, 1949

Allen's mentorship helped the number of Jewish Major League Baseball announcers rise. The Mets' Howie Rose recalled that, as a boy, he had his mom take a Polaroid camera's empty spool, attach it to string, and tie it around his neck to imitate a microphone, allowing Howie to walk around hollering "How about that!"

In 1991, Mel was to be inducted into B'nai B'rith's Sports Hall of Fame at the Grand Hyatt Hotel in Washington, and he kindly asked me to introduce him. Mel included in his remarks a story about the Yankees' Tommy Henrich, who, in 1942, was about to enter World War II:

> Detroit's Dizzy Trout was pitching at Yankee Stadium. Out of the blue the P.A. blared: "Ladies and gentlemen, this is the last time that you will see Tommy Henrich in a Yankee uniform for the duration...."
> The crowd burst a lung. Henrich stepped into the box, yelling, "Come on, Dizzy, throw the ball."
> Trout cupped his hands: "Stand there and listen to it, you SOB. You'll remember it as long as you live."
> Allen paused. "That's how I feel tonight. I'll remember it as long as I live."

On June 16, 1996, the voice of the Yankees died at age eighty-three. That November, the Center for Christian-Jewish Understanding at Sacred Heart University held a memorial service at the place Mel called the Yankee Stadium of cathedrals, St. Patrick's Cathedral. "Why a Mel Allen tribute at St. Patrick's Cathedral?" asked center associate director Rabbi Joseph H. Ehrenkranz. "He was an ambassador of goodwill."

"Why a Mel Allen tribute at St. Patrick's Cathedral?" asked center associate director Rabbi Joseph H. Ehrenkranz. "He was an ambassador of goodwill."

Larry Allen told how his brother often spoke the same weekend at both church and temple. Curt Gowdy, Mel's aide in 1949–50 and later a network superstar, spoke personally about Allen, who had been best man at his wedding. "Where would I be without Mel Allen? Maybe a fishing guide in Wyoming"—his native state. Mel's former neighbor Bill Ries made the chapel smile, recalling one night when Allen came to dinner. "He talked so long the turkey burned."

When Lyndon Johnson died in 1973, a eulogy recalled his "child's dreams [that] could be as wide as the sky and his future as green as winter oats, because this, after all, was America." Dreaming, Allen, like other great baseball announcers, reached families in cities and suburbia and gentle small towns, turning us to wonderment like a heliotrope toward the sun.

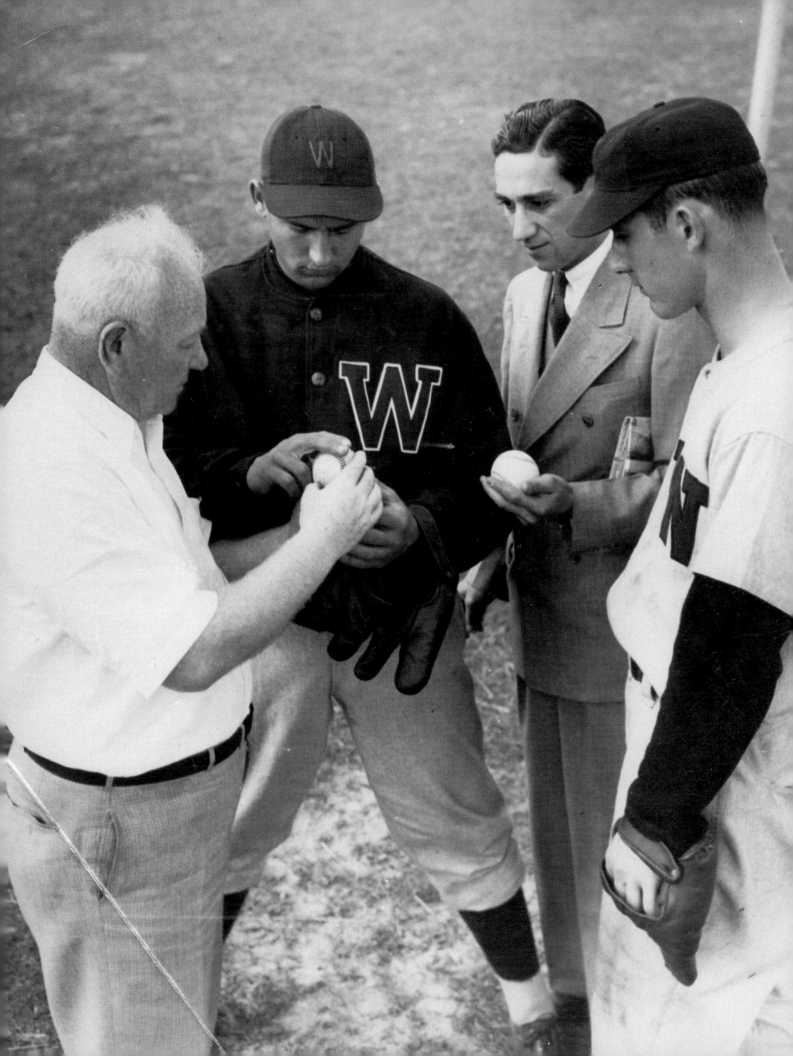

STEVE WULF

A MINYAN:
SPORTS JOURNALISTS

Into the World Series opening, Koufax had taken his glittering 24–5 pitching record in the National League, and, at game's end, this was the item that caused one Yankee to give tongue to the Yankees reaction in the clubhouse. "I wonder," he said, "how come he had lost five games this year."
—Shirley Povich, *Washington Post*, October 3, 1963

The cream of sports journalism sat in the press box of Yankee Stadium for Game 1 of the 1963 World Series, a duel between two storied franchises, two coasts, and two future Hall of Fame left-handers, Whitey Ford and Sandy Koufax. Even though sportswriters are trained to be objective, many of them couldn't help but pull for Koufax. After all, he was a *landsman*.

The first professional baseball player in the nineteenth century, Lipman Pike, was Jewish, but there had only been a smattering of notable Jews in baseball before Koufax: Harry Danning, Buddy Myer, Hank Greenberg, Al Rosen, to name a few of the chosen few. The game was not considered a proper career option in Jewish households, and even if a boy was athletic enough to garner attention from scouts, the sport neither welcomed nor encouraged him.

But journalism was a slightly different story. Newspapers provided a respectable world in which smart, dedicated, and talented scribes could thrive, and the sports pages offered opportunities that were fun, creative, and decidedly American.

One of the people in that press box was a twenty-three-year-old Columbia grad, new to *The New York Times*, Robert Lipsyte. "Over the years, I have thought a lot about why there were so many Jewish sportswriters, particularly baseball writers," says Lipsyte, now seventy-three and widely considered to be among the best in the profession. "The desire to assimilate is certainly part of it, and baseball was the national pastime. There may have been a subliminal desire to get into locker rooms otherwise denied to us. But the overriding reason is the Jewish respect and admiration for laws. Don't forget—Howard Cosell started out as a lawyer. When you think about it, sports has a Talmudic sense of right and wrong. It represents the ultimate meritocracy."

That combination of meritocracies, journalism and sports, could be seen in that long-ago press box, where a s*hul*-ful of Jewish baseball writers sat typing away about

Shirley Povich talking baseball on the field

Koufax's dominant, fifteen-strikeout performance. Space prevents naming them all, but their number is not nearly as impressive as their variety.

Yes, they were all Jewish Americans, but this minyan included a wise man and a wiseass, the pugnacious and the gracious, the inventor of the "save" and the godfather of baseball analytics. Two of them would write classic books of baseball nonfiction. Another would pass on his talents to a daughter who helped open major league clubhouses to women. And another would make his way from Pittsburgh to Cooperstown by writing about what nobody else wanted to write about. Indeed, six of these men won the Baseball Hall of Fame's J. G. Taylor Spinks Award—putting them in the so-called Writer's Wing in Cooperstown.

With the proper Jewish respect for elders, first homage must be paid to Dan Daniel (1890–1981). By 1963, he was thought of as an *alter kocker*, but there was a time when he was the most powerful of all baseball writers. Born Daniel Margowitz, he got his start at the *New York Herald* in 1909, using the byline "By Daniel" to throw off antisemitic readers. In 1930 he convinced Babe Ruth to accept an $80,000 offer from the Yankees by reminding him of all the fans who were out of work during the Depression. Daniel was a prolific contributor to *The Sporting News*, but he wasn't just a baseball writer. He founded *Ring* magazine with Nat Fleischer and collected rare books. With his raspy voice and colorful writing style ("No, for the 4,678th time, nobody has ever hit a fair ball out of Yankee Stadium"), he spun tales that stretched from McGraw to Mantle. In his 1972 Hall of Fame acceptance speech, he said that had it not been for sports, he would have gone into medicine, but he assured the audience, "Had I been a doctor, I would have made house calls."

There is a kind of sportswriter akin to the town crier, and among the best of the breed was another Hall of Famer, Shirley Povich (1905–98) of the *Washington Post*. Povich got his start in the newspaper business on the golf course: he caddied in his native Maine for *Post* publisher Ned McLean, and McLean hired him as a copyboy. This was in 1923; by 1926, Povich was the *Post*'s sports editor. If Povich had not seen it all, he came damn close, from Lou Gehrig's farewell address to Cal Ripken's breaking of Gehrig's consecutive-game-streak record. Perhaps the best way to sum up Povich is to quote Tony Kornheiser, his disciple at the *Post*: "Shirley Povich was forever young."

The man in the press box who looked, and wrote, most like a psychologist was Milton Gross (1912–73) of the *New York Post*. After winning a contest to fill the spot as the second sports columnist for the paper, Gross became one of the first sportswriters to escape the sanctity of the press box to find out what made athletes tick. He did just that before the end of Game 7 of the 1956 World Series, when he rode home with losing Dodger pitcher, Don Newcombe, and his father, creating a classic scene that brought readers to tears.

Of Gross's columns, Dick Young wrote, "They had meat, the raw, red meat. Not the sizzle that substitutes too often for the steak these days. To him, each column was a mission, a crusade." Gross died far too young, at sixty-one, but his children, Jane and Michael, both became prominent writers. It was Jane, working for *Newsday* as a Knicks writer in 1975, who became the first woman to enter a pro locker room.

The writer most likely to be mistaken for a boxer was that very Dick Young (1917–1987). He began as a messenger boy at the *New York Daily News* in 1937, and, until his death, he never tired of writing witty, sometimes acerbic, columns. Of the Dodgers'

Sandy Koufax pitches to Harry Bright during the first game of the World Series, October 2, 1963

epic collapse in 1951, he wrote, "The tree that grows in Brooklyn is an apple tree." He may have been the best writer of leads—ever. When his colleague Joe Trimble froze at the typewriter after Don Larsen's perfect game in the '56 Series, Young pounded out this sentence on his typewriter and handed the copy to Trimble: "The imperfect man pitched a perfect game."

Young could show a softer side and often helped out younger writers. But pity the people who crossed him. In his later years, Young became self-important and scolding. "I remember once being on the Mets' team plane," says Lipsyte, "and Young told Richie Ashburn, 'I am the conscience of baseball.' Ashburn literally started rolling in the aisles, and Dick took great offense. But you had to respect his passion for the game." That passion was acknowledged by Cooperstown in 1978.

The roly-poly gentleman with the large black satchel was Leonard Koppett (1923–2003). Born in Russia, Koppett came to the *New York Herald Tribune* in 1948 after serving in the army and graduating from Columbia. He brought a scholarly approach to his baseball writing—his satchel was mostly filled with reference materials. His *The Thinking Man's Guide to Baseball*, first published in 1967, presaged the sabermetrics that have become essential to understanding baseball. He was honored by the Hall in 1992.

"Sitting next to him in the press box was an experience," says Lipsyte. "He was always pointing things out that should have been done differently. One time, he invited me to a concert with the Philharmonic. We sit down, and as soon as the music starts, he points out that the strings came in a little late."

The scribe with the eyebrows and mien of an owl was Jerome Holtzman (1926–2008). Holtzman, who served in the Marines for two years during World War II, embodied Chicago baseball, covering the Cubs and the White Sox for the *Sun-Times* (twenty-two years) and

When you think about it, sports has a Talmudic sense of right and wrong. It represents the ultimate meritocracy.

Tribune (forty years). In 1959, he came up with a formula for evaluating relief pitchers that evolved into the official "save" statistic.

In recognizing him in 1989, the Hall of Fame noted both his contribution to the statistical side of baseball as well as his classic collection of interviews with pioneering sportswriters, *No Cheering in the Press Box*. A young writer once sat next to Holtzman during a White Sox game and noticed that Holtzman was openly rooting for the home team to win. "Jerome," said the writer, "you wrote the book. No cheering in the press box."

"Screw that," said Holtzman. "I already wrote my lead."

Then there was the group of young writers at the time of the '63 Series known as "The Chipmunks," named by legendary columnist Jimmy Cannon because they were always chattering away and scavenging for offbeat stories. One of them was Leonard Shecter (1926–1974), who would team with Jim Bouton to write the controversial *Ball Four* in 1970. Shecter delighted in thumbing his nose at the powers that be. Fellow "Chipmunk" Larry Merchant, who succeeded Shecter as a *New York Post* columnist, wrote upon Shecter's death from leukemia at the age of forty-seven, "[He] believed that the truth was ultimately more rewarding and entertaining than the fiction of pablum we were fed by the sports establishment."

Fortunately, Shecter lived to see the 1969 Mets win the World Series. And that caused him to lament the bad old days when the Mets were lovably incompetent: "Now it is different...when the Mets lose, there is nothing funny about it at all."

Another future best-seller author was Roger Kahn (1927–), who covered the Series as editor at large for *The Saturday Evening Post*. That was midway through his years covering the Brooklyn Dodgers for the *New York Herald-Tribune* and the publication of his book about them, *The Boys of Summer*. Of that particular Series, Kahn made particular note of the way Koufax stared into the Yankee dugout after striking out the side in the first inning of Game 1.

Kahn has written twenty books and hundreds of magazine articles, but it is worth revisiting *The Boys of Summer* for his evocative style and the humanity of his cast of characters. Here's Kahn quoting Carl Erskine as he opened a scrapbook to a page recounting his fourteen strikeouts in the 1953 World Series: "A great thing about our family comes ten years later. It's 1963. Sandy Koufax goes out and strikes out fifteen Yankees. We're living here [in Indiana] then, but we see it on television. And one of the boys, looking real blue, says, 'Don't feel, sad Dad. You still hold the record for *right-handers*.'"

The writer second most likely to be mistaken for a boxer was Larry Merchant (1931–). Long before he became the feisty old man in the ring for HBO, he was a feisty

> "Jerome," said the writer, "you wrote the book. No cheering in the press box."

Sandy Koufax meets with the media after winning Game 1 of the 1963 World Series, October 2, 1963

wunderkind, the sports editor of the *Philadelphia Daily News* at the age of twenty-six. When Phillies catcher Sammy White threw Merchant's typewriter down the aisle of the team plane, Merchant wrote, "It was the best throw Sammy White made all season."

If you were to look at Merchant's entry in Wikipedia, you would see it was all about his career as a boxing announcer. But whether he was explaining the intricacies of gambling, recounting Abbie Hoffman's days as a Brandeis tennis player, or skewering television broadcasters, Merchant was a sensational friend to have in the sports section. As Marv Albert once said, "I thought Larry Merchant was one of the greatest sports columnists of all time."

There was another Pennsylvania writer at the Series, an Associated Press correspondent from Pittsburgh named Murray Chass (1938–). Chass, who graduated from the University of Pittsburgh with a degree in political science, covered the Yankees for *The New York Times* before becoming the paper's national baseball writer in 1989.

While other writers contented themselves with baseball on the field, Chass saw the importance of the business and labor sides of the game. A mean softball pitcher in his spare time, Chass held accountable players and owners, writers and the commissioner. His doggedness led Dave Anderson, his Pulitzer Prize-winning *Times* colleague, to write, "I'd hate to be the President of the United States if Murray were covering the White House." It also earned him a spot in the Hall of Fame in 2003.

Why stop at a minyan? One other occupant of that October 1963 press box is worth noting, a young reporter for the *Long Beach Independent Press Telegram*, whose own career would earn him a spot in Cooperstown (2000). Thirty-six years after Ross Newhan watched Koufax beat the Yankees twice in a four-game sweep, he saw his own son, David, make his Major League debut with the San Diego Padres.

As it turns out, David was part of a welcome, if unexpected, influx of American Jewish ballplayers that included Shawn Green, Brad Ausmus, Kevin Youkilis, Ian Kinsler, Ryan Braun, and Craig Breslow. Such a wave was something I never could have envisioned back in October 1963, when I interrupted my bar mitzvah studies to watch Koufax in the World Series.

In later years, I devoured *The Thinking Man's Guide to Baseball*, *Ball Four*, and *The Boys of Summer* and lapped up everything Young and Holtzman wrote in *The Sporting News*. Even after I became a baseball writer for *Sports Illustrated*, I marveled at the intelligence and passion that Lipsyte and Chass brought to the sports section.

If you were to ask me why I became a sportswriter, and a baseball writer at that, my answer would be simple. It was because of them.

BASEBALL FICTION

ERIC ROLFE
GREENBERG

A writer of my generation attempting serious baseball fiction could look to a holy trinity of novelists as exemplars: Bernard Malamud, Mark Harris, and Philip Roth. That all three were Jewish at first seemed coincidental (or, as a trinity, ironic); but further reading sharpened the critical eye and taught that writing about baseball, like playing it, watching it, dreaming and fantasizing about it—not to mention organizing, merchandizing, and broadcasting it—all are pathways into an adopted American culture, pursued by many Jews.

Along with language and entertainment, baseball was the great assimilative factor for the native-born sons and daughters of the Great Immigration of 1880–1920 and for their urban and suburban children. So forceful was this drive for integration that each member of the trinity, in their baseball fictions—Malamud's *The Natural* (1952), Harris's *The Southpaw* (1953) and *Bang the Drum Slowly* (1956), and Roth's *The Great American Novel* (1973)—chose narrative voices that are specifically not Jewish, and only Harris included Jews among his fictional characters. This narrowing is all the more remarkable in that the greater share of Malamud's and Roth's works are surveys of contemporary American Jewry.

Malamud's *The Natural* is the Ur-novel of literary baseball fiction. Inspired in part by an actual event, the 1949 shooting of Phillies first baseman Eddie Waitkus, and woven around the legend of Sir Percival and the Fisher King (the manager of the New York Knights is named Pop Fisher), the novel takes on the stylistic conventions of boys' books of the '30s and '40s and, magically, transforms them into language that dances across its two hundred-plus pages. It is a book of eternal themes, its Christian symbolism reworked into a modern idiom. If Jews are missing from Malamud's cast, so also are any references to the wider world outside the game. Baseball in *The Natural* is a world unto itself: Depression and war surround the events but are never mentioned. Malamud was not writing about baseball so much as the corruption of souls, and his baseball world is as insular as a Dantean circle of Hell.

Jews are likewise absent from Roth's *The Great American Novel*, which can be read as a satire not only of baseball and its standing in American culture but also of Malamud's novel itself. What references it contains to Jews are derogatory: the owner of the Tri-City Greenbacks is "a fat little Jew

Bernard Malamud, 1957

101

with an accent you could cut with a knife," and there is a one-eyed pitcher named Seymour Clops, "a Jew on top of it!" Although a basic Jewish theme underlies the work—it has not escaped commentary that the Ruppert Mundys, condemned to play the 1943 season as perpetual visitors when their home stadium is turned into military barracks, are analogous to the wandering tribes of Israel—Jews as such play no part in Roth's story. "Baseball," says the Mundys' manager, "is this country's religion." And the players, each and every one carrying the name of an ancient god or hero—a satiric extension of Malamud's Fisher King theme—are dazzling in their imperfections. If Malamud wrote of the corruption of souls, Roth writes of the corruption of an entire nation's socioeconomic foundation, and chooses baseball as the epitome of that corruption.

Mark Harris foregoes the mythic in his paired novels, and his baseball world breaks out of the insularity that encloses those of Malamud and Roth. Left-handed pitcher Henry Wiggen narrates the tale in the deliciously tangled language of a nonwriter attempting to be literary. He explains his style to his father:

> "Say it out loud first," I said, "and remember it and write it down,and then get up and walk around and say some more, and quick run and write that down, too. Write it like you speak it and then knock out the apostrophes."
> "Why?" he said. "What have you got against apostrophes?"
> "Nothing," I said. "They do it in the paper, so I do it."

And so for print, contractions are out—"it's" obediently becomes "it is" and "doesn't" is "does not"; mix in certain antique or archaic constructions—using "wish" rather than "want," or "for" instead of "because"—and the literary Wiggen sings from the page. It is wonderful music. Harris is so much his character that his character has created Harris's narrative voice.

Jewish characters are scattered through the books—a high school teacher named Epstein and an amateur team organizer named Goldenberg; and Doc Solomon, team psychiatrist, whose function includes being abused by Bruce Pearson, the reserve catcher doomed by Hodgkin's disease in the second novel. In a drunken rage, Pearson "lace[s] into Doc Solomon, calling him a Jew and what not else."

The most fully realized of Harris's Jewish characters is Sid Goldman, slugging first baseman, who is on the club but not truly of the club. Moody and inward looking, a nonparticipant in the horseplay and badinage of the clubhouse who fiercely resents the newspaper and magazine coverage that spotlights him as he challenges Babe Ruth's sixty-home-run record, he is eternally an outsider, however brilliant his contributions to winning.

Another writer who chronicles the Jewish experience is Chaim Potok, whose *The Chosen* (1967) begins on a ball field. The book was the first to depict the insular world of the Hasidim for a wider reading public; and beginning with so familiar a feature of American life as a high school nine was a brilliant way to draw readers into a story about the more mysterious Hasidic community, a minority of a minority. A line drive off the bat of Danny Saunders, son and heir presumptive to the revered

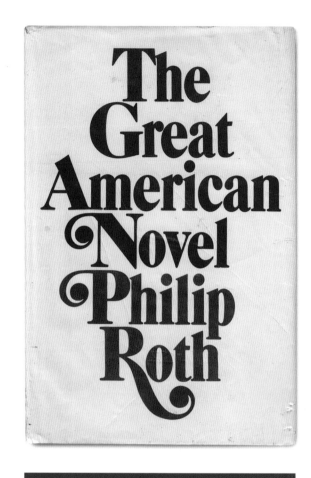

Roth writes of the corruption of an entire nation's socioeconomic foundation, and chooses baseball as the epitome of that corruption.

The Great American Novel
by Philip Roth, 1973

leader of a Russian Hasidic sect in Brooklyn, very nearly blinds the opposing pitcher, Reuven Malter, himself the son of an Orthodox (but not Hasidic) rabbi. Their friendship begins when Danny visits Reuven in the hospital's ophthalmological ward.

Deep into the story, Danny recalls "what torture it was to talk to [his father] about organizing a ballclub." Reuven understands: "To the rabbis who taught in the Jewish parochial schools, baseball was an evil waste of time…. But to the students…an inter-league baseball victory had come to take on only a shade less significance that a top grade in Talmud, for it was an unquestioned mark of one's Americanism." Baseball soon disappears from the story, which plays out in a variety of generational and theological conflicts, but baseball has set the scene and laid down the themes that the novel pursues.

> ## It wasn't until I brought it home to the familiar role of a boyhood player grown to a man in the ballpark crowd that the narration began to ring true in my own ear.

And from all this, what could an aspiring novelist take, and what must he bring to his own work? None of these stories were about baseball per se; each uses baseball as a setting for larger themes. I have always thought of *The Celebrant* (1983) not as a baseball novel but a religious one, its themes being hero worship, its effect upon both hero and worshipper, the Judeo-Christian conflict, and the immigrant experience. The first thought I had for the novel occurred when I read Eliot Asinoff's *Eight Men Out*, a report of the 1919 Black Sox Scandal. There was Christy Mathewson, dying of his war wounds, sitting on high in the Comiskey Park press box in judgment of the players, making marks in his scorecard against their names at any dubious play. The religious symbolism seemed obvious: Christy as Christ. Malamud had shown me the way to turn such elements into baseball fiction.

In Roth I took the purest delight; I read as if Roth had written just for me. The more deeply one knows baseball's history and legends, the more joy there is in reading Roth's inversions and extrapolations. His knowledge of the game makes him a deadly parodist, and a parody of baseball is a parody of America. A Jewish author, already infamous for *Portnoy's Complaint* (1969), takes on the voice of an arch-WASP, a Smith, a Word Smith. I find more in *The Great American Novel* with each reading, which is the mark of—well, a great American novel. In Harris I found a ball club that has become as familiar to me as the Brooklyn Dodgers I rooted for in my boyhood. His players are entirely human; his themes are no less compelling for being common and everyday. Baseball fiction need not be mythic, but it needs to be about more than winning or losing a ballgame.

And in Potok, the narrative voice was entirely Jewish. Early on, I attempted *The Celebrant* with any number of narrative voices; it wasn't until I brought it home to the familiar role of a boyhood player grown to a man in the ballpark crowd that the narration began to ring true in my own ear.

Baseball continues to offer to all novelists a familiar and reader-friendly milieu, a built-in structure (Malamud, Roth, and each Harris book cover a single season), and a language rich with metaphor and symbolism. And of course, like Hebrew, the bases are run right to left.

BERNARD MALAMUD

The Natural

AS ROY fingered the ball for the last throw the Whammer came by holding over his shoulder a Louisville Slugger that he had won for himself in the batting cage down a way. Harriet, her pretty face flushed, had a kewpie doll, and Max Mercy carried a box of cigars. The Whammer had discarded his sun glasses and all but strutted over his performance and the prizes he had won.

Roy raised his arm to throw for the fifth kiss and a clean sweep when the Whammer called out to him in a loud voice, "Pitch it here, busher, and I will knock it into the moon."

Roy shot for the last kiss and missed. He missed with the second and third balls. The crowd oohed its disappointment.

"Only four," said the girl in yellow as if she mourned the fifth.

Angered at what had happened, Sam hoarsely piped, "I got ten dollars that says he can strike you out with three pitched balls, Wambold."

The Whammer looked at Sam with contempt.

"What d'ye say, Max?" he said.

Mercy shrugged.

"Oh, I love contests of skill," Harriet said excitedly. Roy's face went pale.

"What's the matter, hayfoot, you scared?" the Whammer taunted.

"Not of you," Roy said.

"Let's go across the tracks where nobody'll get hurt," Mercy suggested.

"Nobody but the busher and his bazooka. What's in it, busher?"

"None of your business." Roy picked up the bassoon case.

The crowd moved in a body across the tracks, the kids circling around to get a good view, and the engineer and fireman watching from their cab window.

Sam cornered one of the kids who lived nearby and sent him home for a fielder's glove and his friend's catcher's mitt. While they were waiting, for protection he buttoned underneath his coat the washboard Roy had won. Max drew a batter's box alongside a piece of slate. He said he would call the throws and they would count as one of the three pitches only if they were over or if the Whammer swung and missed.

When the boy returned with the gloves, the sun was going down, and though the sky was aflame with light all the way to the snowy mountain peak, it was chilly on the ground.

Breaking the seal, Sam squeezed the baseball box and the pill shot up like a greased egg. He tossed it to Mercy, who inspected the hide and stitches, then rubbed the shine off and flipped it to Roy.

"Better throw a couple of warm-ups."

"My arm is loose," said Roy.

"It's your funeral."

Placing his bassoon case out of the way in the grass, Roy shed his coat. One of the boys came forth to hold it.

"Be careful you don't spill the pockets," Roy told him.

Sam came forward with the catcher's glove on. It was too small for his big hand but he said it would do all right.

"Sam, I wish you hadn't bet that money on me," Roy said.

"I won't take it if we win, kiddo, but just let it stand if we lose," Sam said, embarrassed.

"We came by it too hard."

"Just let it stand so."

He cautioned Roy to keep his pitches inside, for the Whammer was known to gobble them on the outside corner.

Sam returned to the plate and crouched behind the batter, his knees spread wide because of the washboard. Roy drew on his glove and palmed the ball behind it. Mercy, rubbing his hands to warm them, edged back about six feet behind Sam.

The onlookers retreated to the other side of the tracks, except Harriet, who stood without fear of fouls up close. Her eyes shone at the sight of the two men facing one another.

Mercy called, "Batter up."

The Whammer crowded the left side of the plate, gripping the heavy bat low on the neck, his hands jammed together and legs plunked evenly apart. He hadn't bothered to take off his coat. His eye on Roy said it spied a left-handed monkey.

"Throw it, Rube, it won't get no lighter."

Though he stood about sixty feet away, he loomed up gigantic to Roy, with the wood held like a caveman's ax on his shoulder. His rocklike frame was motionless, his face impassive, unsmiling, dark.

Roy's heart skipped a beat. He turned to gaze at the mountain.

Sam whacked the leather with his fist. "Come on, kiddo, wham it down his whammy."

The Whammer out of the corner of his mouth told the drunk to keep his mouth shut.

"Burn it across his button."

"Close your trap," Mercy said.

"Cut his throat with it."

"If he tries to dust me, so help me I will smash his skull," the Whammer threatened.

Roy stretched loosely, rocked back on his left leg, twirling the right a little like a dancer, then strode forward and threw with such force his knuckles all but scraped the ground on the follow-through.

At thirty-three the Whammer still enjoyed exceptional eyesight. He saw the ball spin off Roy's fingertips and it reminded him of a white pigeon he had kept as a boy, that he would send into flight by flipping it into the air. The ball flew at him and he was conscious of its bird-form and white flapping wings, until it suddenly disappeared from view. He heard a noise like the bang of a firecracker at his feet and Sam had the ball in his mitt. Unable to believe his ears he heard Mercy intone a reluctant strike.

Sam flung off the glove and was wringing his hand.

"Hurt you, Sam?" Roy called.

"No, it's this dang glove."

Though he did not show it, the pitch had bothered the Whammer no end. Not just the speed of it but the sensation of surprise and strangeness that went with it—him batting here on the railroad tracks, the crazy carnival, the drunk catching and a clown pitching, and that queer dame Harriet, who had five minutes ago been patting him on the back for his skill in the batting cage, now eyeing him coldly for letting one pitch go by.

He noticed Max had moved farther back.

"How the hell you expect to call them out there?"

"He looks wild to me." Max moved in.

"Your knees are knockin'," Sam tittered.

"Mind your business, rednose," Max said.

"You better watch your talk, mister," Roy called to Mercy.

"Pitch it, greenhorn," warned the Whammer.

Sam crouched with his glove on. "Do it again, Roy. Give him something simular."

"Do it again," mimicked the Whammer. To the crowd, maybe to Harriet, he held up a vaunting finger showing there were other pitches to come.

Roy pumped, reared and flung.

The ball appeared to the batter to be a slow spinning planet looming toward the earth. For a long light-year he waited for this globe to whirl into the orbit of his swing so he could bust it to smithereens that would settle with dust and dead leaves into some distant cosmos. At last the unseeing eye, maybe a fortuneteller's lit crystal ball—anyway, a curious combination of circles—drifted within range of his weapon, or so he

> # The ball flew at him and he was conscious of its bird-form and white flapping wings, until it suddenly disappeared from view.

thought, because he lunged at it ferociously, twisting round like a top. He landed on both knees as the world floated by over his head and hit with a whup into the cave of Sam's glove.

"Hey, Max," Sam said, as he chased the ball after it had bounced out of the glove, "how do they pernounce Whammer if you leave out the W?"

"Strike," Mercy called long after a cheer (was it a jeer?) had burst from the crowd.

"What's he throwing," the Whammer howled, "spitters?"

"In the pig's poop." Sam thrust the ball at him. "It's drier than your granddaddy's scalp."

"I'm warning him not to try any dirty business."

Yet the Whammer felt oddly relieved. He liked to have his back crowding the wall, when there was a single pitch to worry about and a single pitch to hit. Then the sweat began to leak out of his pores as he stared at the hard, lanky figure of the pitiless pitcher, moving, despite his years and a few waste motions, like a veteran undertaker of the diamond, and he experienced a moment of depression.

Sam must have sensed it, because he discovered an unexpected pity in his heart and even for a split second hoped the idol would not be tumbled. But only for a second, for the Whammer had regained confidence in his known talent and experience and was taunting the greenhorn to throw.

Someone in the crowd hooted and the Whammer raised aloft two fat fingers and pointed where he would murder the ball, where the gleaming rails converged on the horizon and beyond was invisible.

Roy raised his leg. He smelled the Whammer's blood and wanted it, and through him the worm's he had with him, for the way he had insulted Sam.

The third ball slithered at the batter like a meteor, the flame swallowing itself. He lifted his club to crush it into a universe of sparks but the heavy wood dragged, and though he willed to destroy the sound he heard a gong bong and realized with sadness that the ball he had expected to hit had long since been part of the past; and though Max could not cough the fatal word out of his throat, the Whammer understood he was, in the truest sense of it, out.

The crowd was silent as the violet evening fell on their shoulders.

TIMELINE

A CENTURY AND A HALF OF BATS AND BALLS

From a scrappy amateur game, baseball grew into our national pastime and a multibillion-dollar industry. It continues to evolve as our country changes.

Trace the sport's major milestones, as well as events and characters both legendary and little known.

1800 – 1919

1845 On October 6, in the first recorded game, the Knickerbocker Base Ball Club plays...the Knickerbocker Base Ball Club. It's an intramural affair at Hoboken's Elysian Fields.

1846 David D. Hart umpires a game for the Knickerbocker Base Ball Club.

1866 Lipman Pike, of Dutch-Jewish heritage, hits 6 home runs (5 in succession) for the Philadelphia Athletics, who win 67–25 against the Alert Club of Philadelphia (which apparently wasn't quite so alert after all).

1871 The 9-team National Association of Professional Base Ball Players, America's first professional league, plays its first game on May 4.

1879 William Edward White becomes the first African American to play in the Majors...for just one game with the Providence Grays.

1882 Louis Kramer, Aaron Stern, and others organize a second major league: the American Association. Kramer and Stern, with the Cincinnati Reds, are the first Jews with ownership stakes in a major league club.

1900 Barney Dreyfuss buys the Pittsburgh Pirates, which he owns until his death 32 years later. In 1903, Dreyfuss coinvents the World Series, where the Boston Pilgrims sink his Pirates.

1909 Former St. Louis Cardinals manager Louis Heilbroner creates baseball's first statistical bureau. Four years later, brothers Al Munro and Walter Elias found the Elias Sports Bureau—still official statistician of Major League Baseball

1919 Eight Chicago White Sox players conspire with gamblers to throw the World Series. Reeling from the scandal, MLB places its bet on Judge Kenesaw Mountain Landis, hiring him for the brand new office of Commissioner.

1920
-
1957

1920   The New York Yankees buy Babe Ruth from the Boston Red Sox. Rube Foster founds the Negro National League.

1926–
1927   Abe Povich (brother of Shirley, uncle of Maury) plays for the Hebrew All-Stars, who face off against the Knights of the Ku Klux Klan and split two contests.

1931   Syd Cohen joins the Mexican-based Nogales Internationals of the Arizona-Texas League. Amid complaints that Nogales relies too heavily on US players, its manager introduces the Spanish-speaking Cohen as "Pablo Garcia."

1934   A Florida hotel bars Jewish players Harry Danning and Phil Weintraub, in town for spring training with the Giants. The management relents only after Giants manager Bill Terry threatens to move the entire team to another hotel.

"THE HORSE" DANNING

1935   Babe Ruth retires. The American League names Hank Greenberg its Most Valuable Player. He is the first Jewish player awarded this title.

1938   Abram J. Shorin and his three brothers found the Topps Chewing Gum Company—and in 1951 hit a homer with a line of baseball cards. Topps still produces its famed collectibles.

1942   Play ball! FDR gives the green light to let professional baseball continue during World War II.

1947   Jackie Robinson plays for Brooklyn on April 15. When the Cleveland Indians sign Larry Doby— followed in 1948 by Satchel Paige and Minnie Miñoso—both leagues are racially integrated.

1953   Al Rosen is unanimously voted the American League's Most Valuable Player—the first player since Hank Greenberg (1935) to receive all first-place votes.

1958
-
1994

1959   Relief pitcher Larry Sherry wins two World Series games for the Los Angeles Dodgers and saves their other two victories, an unparalleled feat.

1962   Jackie Robinson is the first African American player inducted into the Baseball Hall of Fame.

1966   Marvin Miller becomes executive director of the Major League Baseball Players Association. He improves the bargaining rights of MLB players, securing their economic standing for decades and creating one of America's strongest labor unions.

1971   On June 3, Ken Holtzman becomes the first Cub since Larry Corcoran to pitch two no-hitters (Corcoran had three, from 1880 to 1884).

OAKLAND   PITCHER

KEN HOLTZMAN   A's

1973 Ron Blomberg of the New York Yankees becomes MLB's first regular-season designated hitter when he faces right-hander Luis Tiant at Fenway Park on April 6.

1967 Minnesota's Carleton College introduces Rotblatt, an annual one-day, nine-hour, 100+ inning softball match reputedly named by a student with a vintage trading card of White Sox pitcher Marv Rotblatt. Carleton still hosts the merry marathon event.

1979 Daniel Okrent and friends, while dining at La Rotisserie restaurant in New York City, invent Rotisserie baseball, forerunner of the fantasy sports leagues.

1988 In a nod to noshers, the Baltimore Orioles offer kosher food at Memorial Stadium in the year before Camden Yards opens.

1993 In February, Cincinnati Reds owner Marge Schott is fined $25,000 and banned from operating her team for a year, resulting from her use of ethnic and racial slurs.

1995
-
PRESENT

1995 Los Angeles Dodgers pitcher Hideo Nomo is named National League Rookie of the Year, the first Japanese player to win a Major League Baseball award.

1997 On the 50th anniversary of Jackie Robinson's first Dodgers game, all Major League play stops for fans nationwide to watch a special presentation at Shea Stadium. Acting Commissioner Bud Selig retires Robinson's #42 in perpetuity, except for players currently wearing that number.

2000 Ichiro Suzuki is the first Japanese-born position player to sign with a major league team, the Seattle Mariners. Concession stands at Seattle's Safeco Field introduce "Ichiroll" sushi in his honor.

2002 Theo Epstein becomes general manager of the Boston Red Sox. At age 28, becomes the youngest GM in major league history

2002 On May 23, Los Angeles Dodger Shawn Green hits four home runs in one game against the Milwaukee Brewers, joining only 15 others (in both leagues) who had achieved that feat. Green also sets a new MLB mark, going 6 for 6, with 19 total bases.

2007 Ryan Braun of the Milwaukee Brewers is the first Jewish player named Rookie of the Year.

2010 The Chico Outlaws of the Golden Baseball League draft female pitcher Eri Yoshida, formerly of Japan's Kansai Independent Baseball League—the first woman to play professionally alongside men in America since Ila Borders, and the first to play professional baseball in two countries.

2011 Justine Siegal is the first woman to pitch batting practice for a major league team, the Cleveland Indians. She later repeats that role for the A's, Rays, Cardinals, Mets, and Astros.

2013 Ryan Braun receives a 65-game suspension for violating MLB's antidrug policy.

JOHN THORN

OVERCOMING
Adversity

Fight or Flight

New York Female Giants
captain Ida Schnall at bat, 1913

OFFICIAL RECORD

Vol. 2. No. 109.   NEW YORK, MONDAY, AUGUST 23, 1886.   Price, One Cent.

YESTERDAY'S GAMES.

LICKED IN AN INNING.

SIX THOUSAND PEOPDE SAW THE GAME.

The Brooklyns played pretty good ball in the game yesterday at Ridgewood, Long Island, and did up the Mets in great shape. It was by no means a brilliant game, as the errors were so numerous that not a single run scored by either club was earned. The Metropolitans opened the game by scoring two runs in the first inning on a base on balls, a wild pitch, a base hit and two fielding errors. The next display of scoring was in the third inning, when the Brooklyns got in three runs on two bases on called balls, two wild throws and two base hits. All interest in the game was destroyed in the sixth inning, when the Brooklyns scored six unearned runs. The score:

METROPOLITAN.

	AB	R	1B	PO	A	E
Forster, 2d b.	5	1	0	4	5	0
Roseman, l. f.	4	1	1	0	0	0
Orr, 1st b.	5	0	1	11	0	0
Behel, c. f.	4	2	2	1	0	0
Hankinson, 3d b.	4	0	1	4	3	1
Brady, r. f.	4	0	0	3	0	0
McLaughlin, s. s.	4	0	0	1	3	0
Holbert, c.	4	0	1	2	1	4
Cashman, p.	4	0	0	0	1	3
Totals	38	3	5	27	14	8

BROOKLYN.

	AB	R	1B	PO	A	E
Pinkney, 3d b.	5	1	1	0	2	1
McClellan, 2d b.	5	1	1	3	5	1
Phillips, 1st b.	3	1	1	13	0	0
Swartwood, r. f.	4	1	1	3	1	0
Smith, s. s.	4	1	1	2	5	3
Clark, l. f.	5	0	1	0	0	2
Peoples, c.	4	2	1	6	0	1
Kennedy, c. f.	3	0	1	0	0	0
Henderson, p.	3	2	1	0	0	0
Totals	35	4	6	29	12	2

SCORE BY INNINGS.

Brooklyn	0	0	3	0	0	6	0	0	0	—9
Metropolitan	2	0	2	0	0	0	0	0	0	—4

RAH! FOR THE FLIP FLOPS.

There are two social clubs located in the Ninth and Sixteenth Wards, this city, which contain some pretty jolly boys. They are all great baseball enthusiasts, and some of thine are pretty fair players. The respective names of the clubs are the Flip Flops and Our Own. There has been a doubt between them as to which contained the most expert ball tossers, so the matter was finally settled yesterday by each club selecting nine of their best men and competing for the diamond honors at New Dorp, Staten Island.

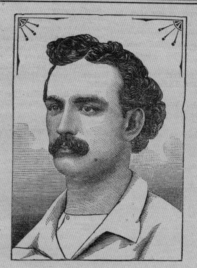

Only five innings were played, but that proved a delicate sufficiency, as the Flip Flops had knocked Our Own clean out of the lot by that time. Following is the score:

Flip Flops	1	3	4	17	9	—34
Our Own	7	0	2	0	1	—10

HOW THEY STAND.

The championship record to date stands as follows:

NATIONAL LEAGUE.

	Won.	Lost.	Per Ct.		Won.	Lost.	Per Ct.
Detroit	63	22	.741	Boston	39	44	.470
Chicago	60	24	.714	St. Louis	29	57	.337
New York	58	27	.682	Kansas C.	19	60	.241
Philadel'a	50	30	.625	Washing'n	13	67	.162

AMERICAN ASSOCIATION.

	Won.	Lost.	Per Ct.		Won.	Lost.	Per Ct.
St. Louis	67	32	.673	Cincinnati	51	51	.510
Louisville	60	40	.592	Athletic	37	55	.396
Pittsburgh	53	44	.552	Metro'litan	34	57	.371
Brooklyn	49	46	.516	Baltimore	33	59	.360

The mistakes of umpires, if honest ones, ought to go all the same, and kickers should be set down upon very decidedly. If an umpire is honest his mistakes will not be frequent, and if a kick is tolerated at all there will never be an end to it. The rules make the dictum of the umpire final, and he ought to see that the rules are executed.

DIAMOND WAFTINGS.

Great-head Galvin.

Barkley makes a good left-fielder.

T. Griffin leads the Uticas at the bat.

Nicol, of St. Louis, is still on the sick list.

Mays owes much of his success to Holbert.

It's a very cold day when Dave Orr strikes out.

Poorman has one of the best records in the country for right field.

In three games Ryan, of the Chicagos, made two singles, a double, two triples and a home run.

Charlie Fulmer thinks that it is not necessary for him to wear a mask, as his face is good enough to stop a ball as it is.

When Murphy, of the Blues, fails to make a hit, there is little wonder that his companions cannot do more than keep him company.

Billy Purcell is doing his best to win the championship for the Atlantas. That club and the Savannahs are very close to one another.

Barnie released Trott because he made only one error in nineteen games, and hired another fellow that makes nineteen errors in one game.

LIPMAN PIKE,

Whose portrait is given above, was born in this city May 25, 1849, and has had a long and successful career on the ballfield. He played several seasons with the junior clubs of Brooklyn, and on July 14, 1865, made his first appearance with a senior organization—the Atlantics of that city—in a game with the Gothams, of Hoboken, N. J. His professional career commenced in 1866, when he was engaged by the Athletic, of Philadelphia, acting as their third baseman. During the seasons of 1867-68 he played with the Mutuals, of this city, filling various positions in the infield, and in 1869 and 1870 he was connected with the Atlantics, of Brooklyn. In 1871 he was one of the Haymakers, of Troy, and from there he went to Baltimore, where he played during the following two seasons with the professional club of that city. He played centre-field for the Hartfords, and has since occupied that position in a majority of games. In 1875-76 he played with the St. Louis club; in 1877-78 with the Cincinnatis, and in 1879 with the Springfield, Mass., Club until it disbanded, when he joined the Albanys. He continued with the Albanys until they disbanded, in July, 1880, and finished the season with the Metropolitans of this city. At the commencement of the season of 1881 he announced his determination, to retire from professional playing, and engage in mercantile business. He has, however, lent a helping hand to his first love, the Atlantics, of Brooklyn, and figured in their home game in 1881. As a batsman he has ranked high during his twenty-one season's career, being, like all left-handed men, a very hard hitter, and he has accomplished many brilliant feats as a fielder, being a sure catch, a remarkably fast runner, and singularly graceful in all his movements.

Roseman looks like a "scrapper."

Detroit has released Sam Crane. Dunlap's engagement was the cause.

Thompson has been off in his batting for some time past, and Conway was unfortunate enough to get way when big Sam got his eye on the ball again.

New Orleans is busy figuring for a place in the Southern League next year, and should have it, as the New Orleaners are great people for sport.

FIGHT OR FLIGHT.
That is how a Jew, like anyone else, deals with adversity in life or in that charmed realm that is our present subject, baseball. Contemplating prejudice, one may perceive a rich range of responses—modulated, grayed, complex—hardly binary, it would appear. A plausible, if unsustainable, third alternative may also exist: sitting on the fence in hope that the threat will pass. In real time, though, it all boils down to fight or flight.

Both are honorable choices. Neither victory nor defeat will confirm character; one does what seems possible in the moment. When a Jewish baseball player changed his name in 1905, it was a sensible response to a rabidly antisemitic fan base, especially in the rural minor leagues. So was, in later years, challenging a dugout heckler to a fistfight, declining to play on Yom Kippur, or, most potently, letting results talk.

Ostracized over centuries, Europe's Jews gravitated to the occupations permitted to them. As immigrants to these shores, they at first did the same. How could they know that in America, as in baseball, anything—yes, anything—was possible?

Like other minorities, Jews turned adversity on its head, making of it a fuel for performance and the glue of a faith and a people. As Jews ventured into mainstream culture, perhaps from a "disreputable" profession like theater or sports—in both of which they were "players," that is, not themselves—they might be forgiven if they forgot for a moment that they were Jewish. Until the very recent past, however, they could be certain that the world would remind them.

Chasing Dreams—the title of the exhibition that inspired this book—is in large measure a Jewish tale, but it is also the story of all the outsiders who struggled to claim a rightful share of the American Dream, only to find their grip slipping on a traditional, distinct identity. As an immigrant boy myself, born in a displaced persons camp in 1947 to Holocaust survivors, I wished for nothing more fervently than to be one of the gang. Still, I was unwilling to let go entirely of that feeling of being odd, singular, special. Baseball eased the transition, permitting me to be that contradiction in terms describing each member of an American minority: the same but different. As a game emphasizing individual accomplishment within the context of unified effort, baseball offered a model of how one might become part of the team...how an outsider might be an American. To the tempest-tost of Europe like me, baseball seemed fair: accomplishment would be rewarded no matter where you came from.

What goals were sought by Lipman Pike and Andy Cohen? Barney Pelty and Erskine Mayer? Hank Greenberg and Sandy Koufax? The very same ones pursued by Jackie Robinson and Minnie Miñoso, Hank Aaron and Ichiro Suzuki, Roberto Clemente and Shin-Soo Choo. A level playing field, with respect on and off it.

Issues of inclusion and exclusion plagued baseball from the start: men versus women (in England both had played baseball, separately and together, in the eighteenth century), then gentlemen versus laborers, then native born versus immigrants, then amateurs versus professionals. Later it became a way to discourage women, Jews, and Hispanics of light skin color, and ultimately a door was closed to African Americans after it had, tantalizingly, been left open in the 1870s.

English immigrant Henry Chadwick, the only writer inducted into the Baseball Hall of Fame in Cooperstown (all the other writers are in a separate category) wrote in his introduction to *Spalding's Official Base Ball Guide* for 1884:

> What Cricket is to an Englishman, Base-Ball has become to an American.... On the Cricket-field—and there only—the Peer and the Peasant meet on equal terms; the possession of courage,

Official [Baseball] Record with engraving of Lipman Pike, August 23, 1886

nerve, judgment, skill, endurance and activity alone giving the palm of superiority. In fact, a more democratic institution does not exist in Europe than this self-same Cricket; and as regards its popularity, the records of the thousands of Commoners, Divines and Lawyers, Legislators and Artisans, and Litterateurs as well as Mechanics and Laborers, show how great a hold it has on the people. If this is the characteristic of Cricket in aristocratic and monarchical England, how much more will the same characteristics mark Base-Ball in democratic and republican America.

Chadwick's vision of baseball as a model democratic institution would have to wait for the turn of the century to be fully articulated, and for Jackie Robinson and Branch Rickey to be fully realized. But his belief that baseball could be more than a game—could become a model of and for American

Spalding's Official Base Ball Guide, 1884
A.G. Spalding & Bros.

life—has proven true. As Robinson ringingly titled his 1964 book, *Baseball Has Done It*.

The outsider experience as it has played out on the ball field and in the stands has been a great experiment in equality, the goal of the continuing great experiment that is America itself. Like liberty, baseball lifts a lamp to the entire world. It is a meritocracy more nearly perfect than the nation whose pastime it is, and as such can be both inspiration and scold. "Second only to death as a leveler," wrote Alan Sangree of baseball in 1907, forty years before Jackie Robinson set foot on a major league field.

After a brief era of good feeling in the 1870s and 1880s, when African Americans and a single Cuban-born American played alongside whites at the highest levels of baseball, people of color were explicitly barred. Irish immigrants had had a relatively easy progress through the baseball ranks, for while they regularly endured attacks on their faith and their allegiance, they at least could sidestep the American obsession with skin color.

The outsider experience as it has played out on the ball field and in the stands has been a great experiment in equality, the goal of the continuing great experiment that is America itself.

So too with the Jews, who, while they participated in baseball to no great extent in the nineteenth century, were never barred or banned. Indeed, Jews began to play the game quite early on (Seaman Lichtenstein, with the New York Base Ball Club of 1845); act as umpire (David D. Hart, with the Knickerbocker Club one year later); lead the first professional league in home runs (Lipman Pike each year from 1871 through 1873); and own a major league club (Aaron S. Stern of the Cincinnati Reds, beginning in 1883). And yet, by 1905 only ten Jews had played in any of the major leagues.

Unflattering explanations were offered. The *Indianapolis News* noted under a November 2, 1903, headline: "Few Hebrews, Sport Loving Though They Are, Play Base Ball."

MEMBERS OF THE LORD BALTIMORE BASE BALL CLUB OF BALTIMORE, MARYLAND.

DRAMATIC NEWS AND SPORTING JOURNAL.

JUNE 1, 1872

EVERETT MILLS.   GEORGE W. HALL.   JOTY RADCLIFFE.   ROBERT MATTHEWS.   THOMAS CAREY.
LYMAN PIKE.   THOMAS YORK.   H. BIGHAM.   WILLIAM FISHER.   W. H. CRAVER.

The "Lord Baltimores," a Baltimore Base Ball Club, featured Lipman Pike (lower left corner), 1872

"One thing that puzzles me," says Barry McCormick [infielder with the Chicago Cubs], "is why Jews don't play base ball. The only Jew in the game today, as near as I can recollect, is Kane, the pitcher, whose right name is Cohen. Back in the '70s there was a crack Jewish player, Lipman Pike, and Ed. Stein, Anson's pitcher, was a Hebrew, I believe. Somehow or other, the Jew does not play ball. He is athletic enough, and the great number of Jewish boxers shows that he is an adept at one kind of sport, at least. I see Jewish names in the foot ball elevens and Jewish boys making good in track teams. Jewish gentlemen of means back the ball clubs, and are good, game backers too. Yet the athletic Hebrew does not play ball. Why is it?"

In the month before McCormick's remarks, the Pittsburgh Pirates, owned by Barney Dreyfuss, a Jew, had been defeated in the first World Series of the modern era. That Dreyfuss had been the driving force behind the institution of a championship series between the National League and its upstart rival, the American League, has been monumentally important and won for him a plaque in the Baseball Hall of Fame.

Another Jewish owner of the same period, Andrew Freedman of the Giants, was infamous for his high-handed treatment of players, issuing fines that the other owners had to make good so as to avoid lawsuits against the National League. Indeed, Freedman was so roundly hated that his fellow owners responded only halfheartedly to an antisemitic remark hurled his way by Baltimore Orioles outfielder Ducky Holmes, who had formerly played for Freedman in New York. (Before a July 25, 1898, game, Holmes, responding to razzing from his former teammates, shouted across the diamond, "Well, I'm—glad I don't have to work for a *sheeny* no more.") Freedman ordered his men off the field, forfeiting the game to Baltimore, despite his own players' sympathy with Holmes (or antipathy toward Freedman). Holmes was suspended; Freedman was fined. When the suspension was rescinded, but the fine was left to stand, intramural conflict followed, boiling over into a war that gave birth to a rival, and saved baseball from destroying itself.

So if they were not barred from the field or the front office—or the press box or the radio booth—what has been the Jews' particular adversity in baseball, the special obstacle with which they had to contend? Hatred. Jews were distrusted or despised not merely because they were different but also because they seemed recalcitrant about giving up their identity. In *The Century*'s September 1921 issue, Herbert Adams Gibbons offered:

> This clannishness would eventually break down were it not for the deliberate efforts of Jewish leaders who are determined that Israel shall remain an *imperium in imperio.* If the Jews persist in maintaining a distinct ethnic consciousness and an exclusive community life, anti-Semitism will thrive in America as it has thrived in Europe. The American nation, itself the result of fusion, will not tolerate without protest a foreign element in it.

New York *Daily News* sports editor Paul Gallico wrote a decade later regarding basketball, a game Jews then dominated, that it "appeals to the Hebrew with his Oriental background [because] the game places a premium on an alert, scheming mind and flashy trickiness, artful dodging, and general smartaleckness."

These Jews were crafty, and they were obdurate. No matter how they may have longed for inclusion, exclusion was what bound them together. They would not cease to be Jewish any more than African Americans would cease to be themselves. And that is why Jews were hated, I believe, more than any alternative explanation residing in the thousands of academic studies on the subject of antisemitism.

As an overserious boy, I had asked myself, in the 1950s, that if the slaughter in Europe could happen and be permitted to happen, what made them hate us so much? Must it not be in some measure our fault? It is in a Jew's nature to look in the mirror when trouble comes, but this was introspection beyond all reason. Though I ceased to ponder this question long ago, when I gave up boyish musings, I have taken comfort recently in discovering—at a sports auction site, no less!—an offering of a letter in German from Albert Einstein to a Mr. Braunstein,

who had extended help to a Jewish refugee. On September 4, 1938, during his time at the Institute for Advanced Study in Princeton, New Jersey, Einstein wrote:

> Dear Mr. Braunstein, I feel I must thank you especially for the important help that you were willing to lend your namesake. The person is well worth it in every regard, as I have come to learn through reliable information. Judging by our enemies, we Jews must be a very remarkable little people. That is not usually so obvious! I send you my friendly greetings, Yours, A. Einstein.

Chosen. Distinct. Exclusive. Scheming. Flashy. Smart-alecky. At least others were worse. And with each insult or assault came affirmation that we were indeed a very remarkable little people.

So if we were so sure of ourselves, so cocky, why did five ballplayers named Cohen change their names before entering the major leagues? Blacks certainly could not routinely change their names to avoid detection. As David Spaner wrote in the eighth edition of *Total Baseball* in 2004:

> In 1980, Dorothy Corey Pinzger, the widow of Edward Corey, who pitched for the White Sox in 1918, explained her husband's decision. "The name was changed from Cohen to Corey due to the ethnic slurs.... We have a clipping in the scrapbook which noted that in his appearance in one of the Midwest League games, Ed was loudly and continuously derided about his ethnic background from a few of the unintelligent fans. The clipping further noted that the greatest majority of the fans were 'good sports,' but just those few harassed him. The name was changed by this method: The H in COHEN was dropped and the R inserted; likewise the N was dropped, and the Y inserted, and the name became COREY."

Sammy Bohne and Phil Cooney were also born as Cohen, as were Harry Kane and Reuben Ewing. Jesse Baker was born Michael Silverman. Henry Lifschutz became Henry Bostick. Joe Rosenblum became Joe Bennett. James Herman Soloman became Jimmie Reese. "There must have been at least half a hundred Jews in the game but we'll never

COONEY, SPOKANE, N.W.L.

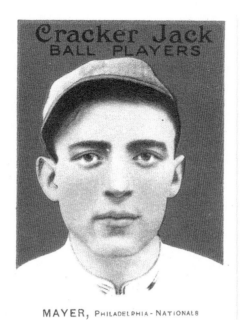

Cracker Jack
BALL PLAYERS

MAYER, PHILADELPHIA - NATIONALS

JAMES REESE
NEW YORK A.L.

PELTY-ST.LOUIS-AMER.

SAMMY BOHNE
SECOND BASE, CINCINNATI NATIONALS

So if they were not barred from the field or the front office – or the press box or the radio booth – what has been the Jews' particular adversity in baseball, the special obstacle with which they had to contend? Hatred.

CLOCKWISE FROM TOP LEFT

Phil Cooney played one game as shortstop for the New York Highlanders in 1905; Jacob Erskine Mayer, pitcher for the Philadelphia Nationals, 1912, Cracker Jack series; James "Jimmie" Reese, born James Herman Solomon, shown here playing for the New York Yankees, 1931; Barney Pelty, pitcher for St. Louis, 1912; Sammy Bohne, born Samuel Cohen, second baseman for the Cincinnati Reds, 1922

The Dauvray Cup, silver, Gorham Manufacturing Co., 1887

know their real names," Ford Frick surmised in 1925. "During the early days of this century the Jewish boys had tough sledding in the majors and many of them changed their name."

Around the time of Frick's observation, something clicked—perhaps the prevalence of Jewish stars in vaudeville and film intersecting with the advent of radio—and Jews began to be courted as box-office draws. Mose Hirsch Solomon—dubbed the Rabbi of Swat after hitting .421 with forty-nine homers for the Hutchinson Wheat Shockers of the Southwestern League—proved a short-term project for John McGraw's Giants, washing out after only two games. Andy Cohen enjoyed more success playing The Great Jewish Hope in the late 1920s, lasting two seasons as the Giants' regular second baseman. The Yankees, desperate to please their Jewish fans in the 1940s—their first Jewish player had been the one-gamer Phil Cooney—even persuaded Ed Whitner to use his stepfather's name of Levy. "You may be Whitner to the rest of the world," said general manager Ed Barrow, "but if you are going to play with the Yankees you'll be Ed Levy, understand."

Women had been courted as fans (even nonpaying ones) ever since the game's dawn. Baseball management hoped that their presence would lend "tone" to the proceedings and keep a lid on the rowdies, in the stands and on the field.

In fact, women played the game and were involved in management, beginning with St. Louis Cardinals owner Helene Britton. Jewish women, too, from a surprisingly early onset.

Women entered the playing arena at the Seven Sisters schools of the Northeast, at which Jews were less than welcome. In 1866 Annie Glidden, a student at Vassar College, wrote home describing campus life: "They are getting up various clubs now for out-of-door exercise…. They have a floral society, boat clubs and base-ball clubs. I belong to one of the latter, and enjoy it highly, I can assure you." Ultimately, women's baseball largely devolved from such high-toned clubs to novelty acts with a girlie-show air, generally in the form of scantily clad Blondes versus Brunettes, with exotic geographic locators applied to each.

Pulchritudinous Broadway stars like Helen Dauvray would be seen at the Polo Grounds simply to be seen, though they exhibited some interest in baseball and its handsome practitioners. Miss Dauvray went so far as to marry one of them, Giants shortstop John Ward. In 1887 she funded the first World Series trophy (the "Dauvray Cup") and ornate gold pins for each member of the winning Detroit Wolverines. Born Ida Gibson, Miss Dauvray was half-Jewish, her mother having been born Louisa De Young, brother of M. H. De Young, future editor of the *San Francisco Chronicle*. Though nonobservant in her practice of the faith, she gave benefit performances in San Francisco for Congregation Shaari Zedeck on March 25, 1875, and Congregation B'nai Israel on July 15, 1875.

The first woman to play in organized baseball was not Jewish. On July 5, 1898, Lizzie (Stroud) Arlington, with the blessings of the president of the Atlantic League (a Class B minor league) Ed Barrow, later famous as the man who made pitcher Babe Ruth an everyday player, threw an inning for the Reading Coal Heavers against the Allentown Peanuts. She gave up two hits but no runs.

Women also played with professional traveling teams like the Boston Bloomer Girls (based in Kansas City, actually). Ida Schnall, a Jewish immigrant from Austria and famous swimmer, started up the New York Female Giants, and her two squads, composed of Jewish and gentile young women, played exhibition contests in 1913. Ida invariably pitched. In later years she would make an "aquacade" movie (*Undine*, 1916) that exploited her curves.

Women were never formally barred from playing in the big leagues (three women played in the Negro

New York Female Giants, 1913, team captain Ida Schnall is standing with crossed bats

Women were never formally barred from playing in the big leagues (three women played in the Negro Leagues), any more than Jews were. The presumption may well have been that they wouldn't be good enough, so why bother?

Leagues), any more than Jews were. The presumption may well have been that they wouldn't be good enough, so why bother? Women still await their Lipman Pike, Hank Greenberg, and Sandy Koufax.

Fight or flight? Evading confrontation, eluding adversity—these were the tactics that made sense all the way up to World War II.

There was a memorable fight in 1933 between second baseman Buddy Myer of the Washington Senators and the Yankees' Ben Chapman, who, in 1947 as manager of the Philadelphia Phillies, gained infamy for his taunting of Jackie Robinson. Chapman spiked Myer and then hurled a number of antisemitic epithets at him. Chapman and Myer's fight spread to the dugouts and the stands. Myer's father was Jewish and his mother Christian, and he never considered himself a Jew, but he never felt the need to correct press accounts of his Judaism, and, anyway, he took offense at Chapman's slurs. Only years after his retirement did Myer bother to state publicly that he had always felt he was German rather than Jewish.

Hank Greenberg fought in his own way. A formidable figure who could challenge an entire dugout, the Detroit Tigers' slugger did his best work in overcoming adversity by letting his bat speak for him. Cleveland's Al Rosen followed Greenberg's path—though not averse to using his fists, he spoke loudest through his accomplishments. In 1953 he fell one thousandth of a point shy of winning the batting title that would have given him the American League Triple Crown.

Greenberg's experience of dealing with prejudice intersected with Jackie Robinson's struggles as a Brooklyn Dodger rookie on May 17, 1947. Robinson collided with Greenberg, finishing up his career

as the Pittsburgh Pirates' first baseman, on a close play and heard the catcalls from the stands. When Robinson reached first base again later in the game, Greenberg reportedly complimented him on his stoic demeanor: "Stick in there. You're doing fine. Keep your chin up."

I was a month old, not yet an American, when this now legendary moment occurred. But by 1952, only five years later, I had become strongly attached to Robinson—he was still a big-league star, with a dazzling baseball card. Greenberg, meanwhile, had moved off center stage though still, unbeknownst to me then, a major figure in the game. Jews tend to go with the underdog for obvious historical reasons, and Robinson seemed to me a real hero. He was hated for no good reason. Jews know something about that.

My parents and the Polish immigrants in their New York City social circle, unlike so many Holocaust survivors, told their grisly tales with an unnerving gusto: Max Linden, the jeweler, never tired of telling, over dinner, how he had lain overnight under a pile of corpses, waiting for the propitious moment to act upon the surprising intelligence that he, unlike everyone else who had been shot, was not dead. Thrilling as the story was to me as a very young boy, I soon could not bear to hear it, for all its undertones of dread, helplessness, and dumb luck.

This age of horrors and heroes, ended before I was born, shaped my parents so indelibly that it inevitably shaped me too, fostering fear, shame, and, most damaging to a creative soul, a sense of overriding caution. Baseball became my real visa

This was Sandy's success, and Jackie's, and Hank's. In the end the only question to be asked of those who followed was "Can you play?"

to America and to becoming (almost) one of the guys. Like the American West, with its cowboys and Indians, baseball provided an institution with legends that could stand up to Nazis and Jews. And unlike America's western frontier, closed since 1890, in baseball heroism still seemed possible.

By my teen years Sandy Koufax had come into his own and, as Greenberg had done, made Jews proud to see one of their own proclaimed as the best. It is now hard to imagine, but when Koufax and the Dodgers left Brooklyn for California in 1958, the Holocaust was thirteen years past, not yet safely distant in the rearview mirror. Looking back now, nearly sixty years later, it may be hard for young Americans to grasp the resonance of a Jewish baseball hero at that time. No similar emotion attached to Ryan Braun when he won the National League's Most Valuable Player award in 2011; let us hope that America's Jews never have reason to need a new hero as they needed Koufax.

When the Los Angeles Dodgers' rookie relief pitcher Larry Sherry became the hero of the 1959 World Series, winning two games and saving the

team's other two victories, I was keenly aware that he—like Koufax, who had lost a 1–0 thriller in Game 5—was Jewish. By the time of Koufax's sudden retirement after the 1966 World Series, it seemed no longer important that he was a Jew; the principal story line attaching to him was that he was a great athlete whose time in the sun had sadly been cut short.

This was Sandy's success, and Jackie's, and Hank's. In the end the only question to be asked of those who followed was "Can you play?"

And then came the murders at the 1972 Olympics in Munich. In case we had forgotten, we were Jews. Mike Epstein, the massive slugger of the Oakland A's who had won the good-natured nickname "SuperJew"—in itself a sign of our people's rising acceptance—donned an armband in remembrance of the slain Israeli athletes. So did Jewish teammate, Ken Holtzman, and outfield star Reggie Jackson, an African American. When the A's squared off against the Cincinnati Reds in the World Series a month later, Jackie Robinson was honored for the twenty-fifth anniversary of his breaking the color barrier. Nine days later he died.

With Branch Rickey, Jackie Robinson had forced America to confront the falsehood that baseball could truly be a national pastime while intentionally excluding anyone. Although the baseball-playing population of African Americans in the major leagues has diminished from a high of, in some published estimates, twenty-eight percent in the late 1960s—actually it peaked near twenty percent in 1975—to perhaps eight percent today, more people of color play the game in the major leagues than

have ever done so before. If you count all the people of color in baseball—whatever their nation of origin—the number is over forty percent today, and the upward trend is inexorable. America is a nation of nations, and its emblematic game is enriched by reflecting that truth.

Recent years have seemed a golden age for Jewish players in Major League Baseball, with sixteen in 2013 alone. Beyond Greenberg and Koufax, Steve Stone won a Cy Young Award and Ryan Braun became an MVP. On May 23, 2002, Shawn Green established a single-game record for the ages, with nineteen total bases on four home runs, a double, and a single, scoring five times. Kevin Youkilis became a Moneyball hero. It is today routine, rather than remarkable, for Jews to be baseball players—with stars and supernumeraries just like every nationality or creed.

Is that a triumph? Yes, but it is also a challenge. What are those things that make Jews special—chosen, even—if not their outsider status? What will drive us to prove our people's individual excellence, by ourselves or through our heroes? As a people forged in adversity, America's Jews will have to find something else to supply the tie that binds. As in the past, baseball will be a help.

Jackie Robinson slides safely into home despite the best efforts of Yankee catcher Yogi Berra during Game 1 of the World Series, Yankee Stadium, 1955

SCOTT SIMON

Hero

AS I began this book, many Americans were beginning to be cautious about whom they called a hero. Athletes, actors, entrepreneurs, and celebrities had casually and carelessly been described as such. To do so after September 11, 2001, seemed preposterous. In the weeks following the attacks on New York and Washington, D.C., and the foiled attack that sent a plane crashing into western Pennsylvania, Americans saw the grim and affecting faces of genuine heroes—and they were caked in ash, blood, tears, toil, and sweat.

A man or woman might sink a basketball, strike a baseball, or scintillate before a camera lens. Those talents can be worthy. But real heroes risk their lives for others. My wife and I were crossing Midtown Manhattan about three weeks after the attacks and saw an assemblage of broad shoulders in blue uniforms with red patches standing outside the entrance to a church. The men and women talked softly; anonymous black cars thrummed their motors softly; pink and white flowers were piled softly into the crooks of the concrete stairs. It was the funeral for a New York firefighter. We went inside, impulsively, and then stayed, decisively. Gerard Barbara, who was a fifty-three-year-old assistant chief of the Fire Department of New York, had died risking his life for strangers. It did not seem strange—in fact, it seemed important—to take a seat amid some of the men and women who had loved him. They wore blue uniforms, thick-soled black shoes, and red eyes. Mayor Giuliani got up to speak, a gravelly voiced man in a gray suit, who also had red eyes. It was Mayor Giuliani's fourth funeral service of the day.

"Your father," he said to Gerard Barbara's son and daughter, "used his great gift of courage to serve others. The name he gave you," he continued in the blunt tone of a commandment, "is now a permanent part of the history of this city. And now, I would like everyone here to stand and express their appreciation for your father." We stood, cried, and clapped our hands until our palms burned like our eyes, then we applauded some more. A line of blue shoulders with red patches filed softly out of the church and back onto

Jackie Robinson signing autographs at Ebbets Field four days before his major league debut, April 11, 1947

Fifth Avenue, where, for at least a time, FDNY had replaced DKNY as a signature of distinction.

The following weekend, we watched Cal Ripken, Jr. play his last game of major league baseball—his 3,001st. Over a quarter of a century as a professional athlete, Cal Ripken had become such an insignia of sturdiness and class that the umpires stood in a line to shake his hand. His opponents removed their fielding gloves to applaud him. The signs blooming amid the green seats of Baltimore's Oriole Park at Camden Yards said WE LOVE YOU CAL; THANKS, CAL; and CAL: WE'LL NEVER FORGET YOU.

But the word hero seemed conspicuously, deliberately absent. Events had revised our national vocabulary. At least for the moment—it would be nice to think even for longer—it would be hard for Americans to look out at a mere playing field and see the kind of heroism we had been reminded to revere in men and women in blue uniforms with red patches.

But even by this wiser standard, Jackie Robinson was a hero. The baseball diamond is not simply a playing field in his story. It was the ground on which he was most open and vulnerable to taunts, threats, and sharpened spikes.

The first African American major league ballplayer of the twentieth century routinely took his rolling, pigeon-toed stride out into the infield or batter's box on days and nights when local police had culled the stadium's mail to show him an assortment of explicit and persuasive death threats. It is tempting today, when Jackie Robinson is enshrined in halls of fame, social studies curricula, classroom calendars, songs, and statues, to suppose those threats were empty. But in the late 1940s, beatings, bombings, lynchings, and shootings scarred the landscape of the United States. They could be just as public as—well, as baseball games.

Jackie Robinson gave his life for something great; heroes do. He chose to bear the daily, bloody trial of standing up to beanballs and cleats launched into his shins, chest, and chin, and the race-baiting taunts raining down from the stands, along with trash, tomatoes, rocks, watermelon slices, and Sambo dolls. And then he performed with eloquent achievement and superlative poise. Robinson allowed that hatred to strike him as it would a lightning rod, channeling it down into the rugged earth of himself. All that America saw for many years on the baseball field was that iron as upright as a steeple, never bending. But inside, the strain slowed his body, whitened his hair, thickened his circulation, aggravated his diabetes, and rendered him slow and blind. He was dead by the age of fifty-three—a martyr (a word as deliberately applied as hero) to trying to make America live up to its creed.

Jackie Robinson playing for the Negro League Kansas City Monarchs, 1945

If Jackie Robinson had not been selected to play the role he performed so well, no doubt other superb African American athletes would have soon stepped onto the stage. The skills of Larry Doby, Roy Campanella, Sam Jethroe, Ray Dandridge, Willie Mays, Monte Irvin, Ernie Banks, and an aging Satchel Paige were too great not to tempt major league clubs that were searching for new sources of talent. World War II had moved many Americans to examine their nation's own self-image as a bulwark of freedom. Editorial writers and civic leaders were already clamoring for America to integrate the armed forces, which had just won the world's liberty, the schools, in which children learned about justice, and sports, which purported to epitomize American values. How could a young black man who might be called up to risk his life backing up Pee Wee Reese in Guam, or Yogi Berra in Normandy, not be allowed to earn a living alongside them on the same playing field?

The baseball diamond is not simply a playing field in his story. It was the ground on which he was most open and vulnerable to taunts, threats, and sharpened spikes.

America's modern civil rights revolution was already stirring by the time Jackie Robinson arrived in major league baseball. With Vernon Johns, Thurgood Marshall, A. Philip Randolph, and many more, it had already produced heroes. But Robinson's courage and accomplishment put a familiar face on the kind of bravery that it took for blacks to stand up for their rights. His heroism was no greater than that of millions of others—some achievements simply cannot fit into box scores. But Robinson's renown gave his heroism reach.

It is possible to see, in Robinson's slow, purposeful walk into the face of taunts and threats, some of the same unbowed courage that Americans would later admire in the civil rights marchers who faced down stinging water sprays, sharp rocks, and snapping police dogs. When Robinson joined Dr. Martin Luther King's nonviolent campaign in Birmingham in 1963, marchers called out, "Show us, Jackie!"

Jackie Robinson is so highly esteemed for his Gandhian restraint against the onslaughts of bigotry that it is easy to mistake him for a social activist. He certainly became a militant campaigner for civil rights, an outspoken newspaper columnist, and a combative Republican when that party was more identified among blacks with Lincoln, La Guardia, Rockefeller, and Lindsay, while the Democrats were dishonored by Strom Thurmond, Orville Faubus, and George Wallace.

But first and last, Jackie Robinson was a hard-nosed, hard-assed, brass-balled, fire-breathing athlete. The Jackie Robinson that his old Pasadena and UCLA teammates remembered could be a petulant star. He mocked lesser competitors and came to expect that his regal status on fields of play would excuse him from the need to attend class or complete assignments; and so it did. When, on a couple of occasions, Robinson's high spirits and dark skin brought him into the grasp of the Pasadena police, his case was considered with compassion by a local judge, who was loath to deliver a

penalty that would cause the accused to miss next Saturday's game. Few
other young black men in Southern California could rally so effective a
defense as Robinson's in rushing yards, passes caught, and punts returned.

Jackie Robinson played less than a single season in the Negro Leagues,
for the fabled Kansas City Monarchs. Among a group of gifted professionals
who had to endure all-night rides on bone-clattering buses and blocked
doors at whites-only diners and motels, Jackie Robinson was remembered
more for griping about the league's showboating and lack of training
and discipline. He let his teammates know that he considered the league
beneath his talents (and maybe it was—for all of them).

The Jackie Robinson who stayed on to become a perennial major league
star after he became a hero could be prickly. Another way to say it is: Jackie
Robinson could be a prick. Even after he had become one of the most
admired personalities in America, Robinson could spring up and cry racism
at umpires with the impudence to call him out on a close slide or a strike.
He could crash into an opponent's knees on inconsequential plays, just to

Jackie Robinson celebrates his thirty-
fifth birthday with his wife and children,
St. Albans, New York, 1954

let them know he could hurt them. He harangued opposing players, and sometimes his own teammates, with graphic epithets of the kind that would have once been considered legal provocation for a duel (although the epithets were never racial and rarely sexual—Jackie Robinson was no racist, and he was even a bit of a prude).

But Jackie Robinson was no less a hero for being a full-blooded human being. When he was summoned by history, he risked his safety and sanity to give history the last full measure of his strength, nerve, and perseverance. In the end, real heroes give us stories we use to reinforce our own lives.

Shortly before nine o'clock on the morning of September 11, 2001, Jackie Robinson's widow, Rachel Robinson, and Dorothy and Mark Reese, Pee Wee Reese's widow and son, were in New York's City Hall, along with old Dodgers Ralph Branca and Joe Black. They were there to choose among five sculptor's models arrayed on a conference table, each depicting that fabled moment from the 1947 season in which Pee Wee Reese had crossed the field from his post at shortstop during a downpour of racial taunts to slip his arm encouragingly around Jackie Robinson's shoulders.

Before the group could choose a model to be cast in bronze and put up in Brooklyn, they heard a boom, then a commotion. New York police officers rushed them onto a bus. The bus got blocked and could not move through the tangle in the streets. New police officers sprinted aboard and took the Dodger family members into the bomb shelter of a nearby bank building, which is where they were, huddled and held rapt before a television set, when the first World Trade Center tower fell from the skyline. Dorothy Reese turned to her son, who is a California filmmaker. "I'm just glad," she said in the first gloom of the attack, "that Jackie and your father aren't here to see this." Mark Reese gently, consolingly, disagreed. "I think Pee Wee and Jackie are here," he told his mother. "And we need their courage now." I can't think of a time when we don't.

The story of Jackie Robinson's arrival in the major leagues is a heroic American legend. It is not in the same rank as Valley Forge, Gettysburg, Lincoln's trials, Harriet Tubman's bravery, Chief Joseph's valor, or the gallantry of the police and firefighters who ran willingly into the firestorm of the World Trade Center. But Jackie Robinson's story still testifies to the power of pure personal courage to turn history and transform adversaries into admirers. It is a story that endures all the nicks and nits of revisionism because, when the last page is turned, it plays on in our minds and lives: a bold man, dark-skinned and adorned in Dodger blue, who displays the daring and audacity to stand unflinchingly against taunts, strike back at beanballs, and steal home with fifty thousand people watching and waiting for Jackie Robinson to spring willingly into the path of a pitched ball and slide into the ironbound clench of a catcher protecting home plate. It is a story that still rouses us to shake off dust, blood, and bruises and keep going.

MICHAEL BERENBAUM

JACKIE, THE JEWS, AND ETHNICITY IN POSTWAR AMERICA

Because Jackie was the first, he played for everyone who had been denied a chance, whose future was closed because of racism and segregation; he was the forerunner of the civil rights movement and the struggles by women and gays for equality that would follow. He would do anything to win.

I was but a toddler when Jackie broke in. My mother was often ill and my father, a decorated World War II veteran, struggled to make up for lost time in the postwar years. In 1945, the year I was born, he was thirty-five and just beginning his career, working all hours of the day and night. We had an African American cleaning lady, Minnie — an intelligent, stately woman, who in our era would have gone to school and become a professional, but in those days struggled to survive. Minnie loved me and she loved the Dodgers, and the Dodger she most loved was Jackie. My father loved Jackie too, and their admiration for Robinson was race blind, the great equalizer between men, women, and children of all backgrounds.

Robinson was chosen to overcome the weight of centuries. My father and Minnie understood his struggle. Orthodox Jew and underprivileged black, they saw in his daily battle a mirror of their own lives and the hope for future generations. If he made it, they could; if not them, then their children.

Our loyalty to the Dodgers was ethnic. We Dodger fans never understood how the Yankees could arouse anyone's passion. They were the WASPs, the prep-school kids, corporate types! When the rich get richer, there is no drama and little inspiration. Rooting for the Yankees in the 1950s was like rooting for General Motors. You respected the pinstripers' class, elegance, and talent, but how could you get passionate about them? They were the men in the gray suits — cold, ruthless, efficient. We understood the Bronx Jews who rooted for them; they had to cheer for their neighbors. It was expected that Manhattan Jews from "certain" neighborhoods and the Jews of Westchester and Connecticut would root for their own kind.

But Brooklyn was for those who aspired to greatness and were but one or two games away. The Yankees won five pennants in a row, not once but twice. Brooklyn was two games away from greatness. Had they won the last games of the 1950 and 1951 seasons, they too, like the Yankees, would have won five pennants in a row, but

Roy Campanella, Jackie Robinson, and Gil Hodges congratulate teammate Sandy Koufax after 14 strikeouts against the Cincinnati Redlegs, a National League high for the 1955 season.

they lost the last game of the 1950 season to the Philadelphia Phillies, and Bobby Thompson's hit, the "shot heard round the world," ended the Dodgers' 1951 hopes.

Pee Wee Reese was the Dodger captain. Kentucky-bred and almost a decade older than his teammates, he had come up before World War II and was a star before his career was interrupted by wartime duties. Reese was serving in World War II when he heard that the Dodgers were interested in Robinson as a shortstop, the next choice to replace him, and he was burning. The taunts of his fellow soldiers did not diminish his anger. But he decided then and there that if Robinson could beat him in competition for the job, then he deserved it. Combat, the defining experience of the "Greatest Generation," was also a meritocracy. What you did earned the respect or the scorn of your comrades. So when Reese answered for Robinson, when he braved the taunts of fans and the displeasure of his Southern friends by embracing Robinson as a teammate, America took note.

Roy Campanella, the Dodger catcher, was all heart. In his every move, one experienced the joy of the game, the love of baseball. Stocky and compact, Campy could be surprisingly swift on the base path and a stone wall protecting the plate. Campy would kibitz with the batters and the umpires. He was as masterful at banter as at handling pitchers, speaking to them not just with his mouth, but by pounding his glove, gesturing in every direction. When Campy— three times the National League's Most Valuable Player—played well, the Dodgers would win.

Campanella was formed by his experience in the Negro Leagues. Prior to being signed by the Dodgers, Campy had played baseball year round. He reported to the Negro Leagues each spring, barnstormed in the fall, and went down to Venezuela to play winter ball. Travel was by bus, where players often ate and slept, denied entry into hotels in the segregated South and the inhospitable North. Doubleheaders were routine, and teams often played in two different cities during the same day. Negro Leaguers brought their own lights and poles to play nighttime baseball in unlit stadiums.

By the time he began his ten-year major league career, Campanella had already been playing professional baseball for twelve long years. But until Robinson was signed, Campanella could only dream of a big-league career. He forever remained grateful that he was given his chance.

My father never spoke about his life in combat, never uttered a word about the enemy he faced or the two Bronze Stars and Purple Hearts on his discharge papers. He must have fought the enemy fiercely and directly, and we, his children, and theirs grew up hearing story after story about his pride in being Jewish and his refusal to let an antisemitic comment slide. Like Robinson, or so he taught us, you don't put up with assaults on your pride or attacks on your people.

In my New York yeshiva on the tony Upper East Side, we were taught that a yarmulke was an indoor garment. Hats were to be worn in the street. Rabbi Joseph Lookstein, its formidable founder, wanted to show that Orthodoxy could be first rate,

> So, while my father and Minnie rooted for Jackie, more often than not they played the racial and ethnic game like Campy. Jackie was respected; Campy was loved.

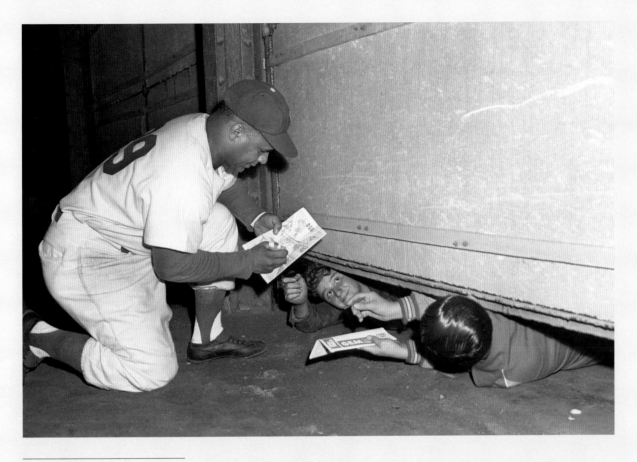

Roy Campanella signing autographs after hitting his thirty-first home run, Brooklyn, September 30, 1950

not only a practice restricted to poor, accented Jews. This was the time when Philip Roth was writing of "Eli the Fanatic," the fearsome Jew who practiced his piety in public and embarrassed his assimilating neighbors. When our fathers also told us not to make waves, but to celebrate how far we had come, to remember with gratitude the opportunities we had been afforded, we thought of Roy Campanella. Ever thankful, he could not be angry. So I did as I was told by my father; we flew the flag on Memorial Day or July 4th so the non-Jewish neighbors would know that Jews are patriotic, and I had to mow the lawn so they could see that Jews are proud of manual labor.

First-generation Jews, Italians, and Irish and other ethnics understood Campy. The talented sons of pushcart peddlers and small merchants, of factory workers, mechanics, and machinists were grateful to get their chance to attend City College, let alone Harvard or Yale. So, while my father and Minnie rooted for Jackie, more often than not they played the racial and ethnic game like Campy. Jackie was respected; Campy was loved.

We learned Jewish theology from the Dodgers. Twice a year, at the end of Yom Kippur and the conclusion of the Passover Seder, Jews chant "Next Year in Jerusalem." Each year — except for that magical year of 1955, pious Dodger rooters called out "wait 'til next year."

We learned tribal loyalty from the Dodgers. Brooklyn Jews thought of the Giants as the primitive *goyim* — not polite gentiles — evil men set for a pogrom. Dodger-rooting blacks thought of the Giants — even with Willie Mays — as "white," ready to dominate, destroy, pillage. Catholics thought of the Giants as Protestants, renegades, rebellious, destructive. The Giants knew no shame. When Walter O'Malley traded Robinson, traded a legend, to the Giants at the end of the 1956 season, Robinson walked away from the game. He retired rather than don the hated uniform — the man would not, could not, convert.

And we learned Jewish history from the Dodgers, who went into exile after the 1957 season. The Dodgers followed the population shift westward and made the national pastime into a coast-to-coast game. Prior to their departure, the farthest west a baseball had to travel was St. Louis, Chicago, or Cincinnati. The Dodgers were not the first to abandon their city: the Boston Braves had moved to Milwaukee, the St. Louis Browns had gone to Baltimore, where they became Orioles, but the Dodgers were different. They had been making money. The team had enjoyed fan support, and, above all, the Dodgers were Brooklyn, inexplicably linked to the borough and its citizens. It was betrayal, abandonment of the faithful.

Some transferred allegiance more easily. Not I.

When the Mets debuted in 1962, they deliberately wore the combined colors of the Dodgers and the Giants. They were created to fill the void, much as parents who lose their child will often conceive another child as consolation. The second child is deeply loved for who he or she is, but cannot take the place of the first child. The loss is still there; the scar remains.

The Mets repeated the early days of the Brooklyn Dodgers. They were lovable losers, entertaining, pathetic, interesting, but essentially hopeless. Former Dodger greats came back to New York, Snider and Hodges among them, but were a shadow of their former selves, like seeing your high school sweetheart as an overweight, middle-aged woman. You can remember the face and even the figure that once made her so attractive, but still something is missing. When the Dodgers played the Mets, we were forced to choose between old loyalties that ran deep and the new interest being developed.

But life continues. Yavne, the Torah academy founded by Yochanan ben Zakkai, followed the Second Temple's destruction in 70 CE. Jews remember the pain of exile, but still they found another way to seek holiness. They mourned, they remembered, they endured, they rent their clothes when they saw the Temple in ruins, yet they built new shrines, synagogues, and study halls.

"I'm Rooting for Jackie Robinson" pin-back button sold at Ebbets Field during Jackie Robinson's 1947 rookie season

THE NEGRO LEAGUES

SHIRLEY
POVICH

"This Morning with Shirley Povich" from the *Washington Post,*
April 7, 1939

Orlando, April 6—

There's a couple of million dollars worth of baseball talent on the
loose, ready for the big leagues yet unsigned by any major league clubs.
There are pitchers who would win 20 games this season for any big
league club that offered them contracts, and there are outfielders who
could hit .350, infielders who could win quick recognition as stars, and
there is at least one catcher who at this writing is probably superior to
Bill Dickey.

Only one thing is keeping them out of the big leagues—the
pigmentation of their skin. They happen to be colored. That's their crime
in the eyes of big league club owners.

Their talents are being wasted in the rickety parks in the Negro
sections of Pittsburgh, Philadelphia, New York, Chicago and four other
cities that comprise the major league of Negro baseball. They haven't got

Shirley Povich in
the press box

a chance to get into the big leagues of the white folks. It's a tight little boycott that the majors have set up against colored players.

It's a sort of gentlemen's agreement among the club owners that is keeping Negroes out of big league baseball. There's nothing in the rules that forbids a club from signing a colored player. It's not down in black and white, so to speak. But it's definitely understood that no team will attempt to sign a colored player. And, in fact, no club could do that, because the elasticity of Judge Landis' authority would forbid it. And the judge can rule out of baseball any character whose presence he may deem "detrimental" to the game.

Just how a colored player would be detrimental to the game has never been fully explained, but that seems to be the light in which they are regarded by the baseball brass hats. Perhaps it is because there is such an overwhelming majority of Southern boys in big league baseball who would not take kindly to the presence of colored athletes and would flash a menacing spike, or so. Perhaps it's because baseball has done well enough without colored players. It's a smug, conservative business not given to very great enterprise and the introduction of new and novel features.

There have been campaigns aimed at smashing the boycott. One New York newspaper openly advocated the signing of Negro players, and Heywood Broun has often berated the baseball magnates for drawing the color line. But despite the presence of thousands of colored customers in the stands, the club owners have blithely hewed to the color line. They are content, seemingly, to leave well enough alone and make no concerted play for Negro patronage.

A $200,000 CATCHER

But in its restricted localities, Negro baseball has flowered. There are Negro teams which now might do very well in big league competition even if they played as a Negro entity. The Homesteads of Pittsburgh are probably the best colored team. They train in Florida each spring, even as do the American and National League teams. The other evening at Tinker Field, the Homesteads met the Newark Eagles of the same colored league. Curious Washington players flocked to the game and went away with deep respect for colored baseball.

Walter Johnson sat in a box at the game, profoundly impressed with the talents of the colored players. "There," he said, "is a catcher that any big league club would like to buy for $200,000. His name is Gibson. They call him 'Hoot' Gibson, and he can do everything. He hits that ball a mile. And he catches so easy he might just as well be in a rocking chair. Throws like a rifle. Bill Dickey isn't as good a catcher. Too bad this Gibson is a colored fellow."

That was the general impression among the Nats who saw the game. They liked the Homestead catcher, and they liked the big, lanky Negro pitcher for the Homesteads who struck out 12 Newark players in five innings. They liked the center fielder who can go a country mile for the ball, and they liked the shortstop, who came up with fancy, one-handed

> **Just how a colored player would be detrimental to the game has never been fully explained, but that seems to be the light in which they are regarded by the baseball brass hats.**

Leroy "Satchel" Paige, pitcher for the Kansas City Monarchs, 1939

plays all night. They had to like 'em. They were swell ball players.

Until last season there was a colored pitcher around named "Satchel" Paige. The colored folks have a penchant for picturesque names for their idols and "Satchel Paige" was so-called because of the size of his feet. He was 6 feet 3, a left hander and a whale of a pitcher. "He retired last year at the age of 44," said Jimmy Wasdell, "and he was still a great pitcher. I've been on clubs that barnstormed against Negro teams and in a dozen games against the Paige we never beat him. He beat Paul and Dizzy Dean one night, 1–0, and we only got one hit off him. I was the only minor leaguer on our club."

JOHNSON WAS MISTAKEN

Negro baseball is now a flourishing game, but as long as 30 years ago, the colored folks had their swell ball teams. Walter Johnson on a barn-storming trip in 1909 went to Harlem to pitch for a colored team against the Lincoln Giants.

"I didn't know it was to be a colored team," Johnson was saying, "but they were paying me $600 for the day's work and that was big money. I went up there with my catcher, Gabby Street. Gabby was from Huntsville, Ala., and he didn't like the idea of playing colored baseball, but that $300 he got was too much to overlook.

"It was the only time in my life that I was 2-to-1 to lose. Those were the odds they were offering against me. I'll never forget the first hitter I faced. He was an outfielder they called Home Run Johnson. Up at the plate he says to me, 'Come on, Mr. Johnson, throw that fast one in here and I'll knock it over the fence.' That's what he did, too. But that was the only run they got off me and I won the game, 2–1.

"I didn't like the way this Home Run Johnson was crowing about his hit, so the next few times up there I buzzed a couple close to his head just to scare him. He was hitting the dirt all day. Then in the last inning he didn't even wait for me to cut loose. He ducked before I let the ball go. Then he got up off the ground to see what happened and struck his head in the way of a slow curve I had just cut loose."

BASEBALL CIRCUS

FUN - LAUGHS - THRILLS

The GLOBETROTTERS of BASEBALL

BASEBALL'S NUMBER ONE SHOW TEAM

SUPER STAR HANK AARON STARTED HIS BASEBALL CAREER WITH THE CLOWNS

44th SEASON

BOBO SMALL
Bobo Small, versatile comedy star of the Indianapolis Clowns. Small, the showboat of comedy will be seen in action when the Clowns play.

——— *ALWAYS A CROWD PLEASER* ———

INDIANAPOLIS CLOWNS

- VS -

Kingston Braves
WED., AUG. 15
Dietz Stadium
8:00 P.M.

STEVE ANDERSEN
Famous One Armed First Baseman who reminds Fans of Former Major League Star One Armed Pete Gray.

Ioway-Record — Muscatine, Ia.

CHANGING THE LANDSCAPE OF AMERICA'S GAME

―――

JEWISH ENTREPRENEURS AND BLACK BASEBALL

ADRIAN BURGOS JR.

Jewish impact in black baseball came from beyond the playing field through team owners, league executives, booking agents, and journalists. In these roles Jews created opportunities for African American and Latino players to exhibit their skills during baseball's racially segregated era and, later, aided pioneering black players to gain entry into organized baseball. The multiple roles filled by Jewish men like Ed Gottlieb, Abe Saperstein, and Syd Pollock nevertheless caused concerns for many Negro League officials, serving as a constant reminder to black baseball's African American and Latino team executives that countless whites did not want to do business with them directly.

The outsider status of Jewish entrepreneurs, as neither African American nor black Latino, complicated their participation in black baseball.[1] Typically starting out as operators of "barnstorming" teams, which competed with Negro League teams on the field and at the gate, Jewish owners often vied for talent with their black baseball colleagues, such as when Syd Pollock stocked his 1928 Havana Red Sox roster with Latino players recruited from Alex Pompez's Negro League team. Pollock's poaching of talent upset Pompez, who in turn convinced his fellow American Negro League (ANL) owners not to schedule exhibition games versus the Red Sox. A year later Pompez blocked Pollock's application to officially join the ANL. Pollock defended his business practices in a letter to the *Amsterdam News*, proclaiming, "our record is clean, our business methods held in high esteem, by managers throughout the country."[2] The public defense had no effect. ANL executives continued to spurn Pollock and his team.

Jews also played a significant role as booking agents. As agents, for instance, Ed Gottlieb and Abe Saperstein scheduled Negro League teams at available ballparks, determining which teams would play, where, and at what price. Marquee events at Yankee Stadium, the Polo Grounds, and other major league parks were vital to the financial success of black baseball teams. For much of the 1940s, Ed Gottlieb Sporting Enterprises handled all aspects of hosting such affairs at Yankee Stadium as well as at a variety of Philadelphia venues. In return for a percentage of the gate, his outfit handled publicity, printed game tickets, distributed flyers to local

Baseball Circus with the Indianapolis Clowns, Poster, 1973

stores, and advertised the events in newspapers. These activities caused some to wonder if Jewish entrepreneurs placed their financial self-interest above the Negro Leagues' economic and social aims as a race enterprise.

Style, substance, and stereotypes were all factored into the 1936 debut of Pollock and Saperstein's Ethiopian Clowns. Showmanship had always been an element of black baseball. However, Negro League executives believed that to thrive as a professional business, baseball skills had to be emphasized over entertainment. The Ethiopian Clowns, however, openly combined athletics and entertainment in an effort to attract crowds. That Pollock and Saperstein had a controlling stake in the Ethiopian Clowns exacerbated tensions over the brand of comedic baseball they promoted. Once again, the involvement of Jews in these "performances" led African American team officials and sportswriters to worry that black respectability and race pride were not the primary motivators of the Ethiopian Clowns' Jewish operators. Controversy over the Ethiopian Clowns' comedic routines and face painting prompted Negro League owners to pass a resolution that labeled the team's practices a "detriment" to black baseball. Face painting together with the comedic routines

These activities caused some to wonder if Jewish entrepreneurs placed their financial self-interest above the Negro Leagues' economic and social aims as a race enterprise.

signified not only clowning; more worrisome was its association with blackface minstrelsy. In blackface minstrelsy white entertainers (and in rare cases black performers) painted their faces black and performed stereotypical black characters while singing plantation melodies that portrayed harmonious race relations during America's slave era. That the white owners of a Negro League team allowed for these practices to become a defining part of a professional team's brand offended African Americans pressing for racial equality. The team and its owners, the *Chicago Defender* contended, had been "capitalizing on slap-stick comedy and the kind of nonsense which many white people like to believe is typical and characteristic of all Negroes."[3] The following year Syd Pollock took sole control of the team and gained admission into the Negro American League after agreeing to drop "Ethiopian" from the team's name and to have the Clowns play "straight ball"—players used their real names and no longer painted their faces.

Pollock continued to field African American teams with his characteristic promotional flamboyance long after the integration of baseball. In 1951 he signed Toni Stone as the first woman to play in the Negro Leagues. Mamie "Peanut" Johnson and Connie Morgan soon followed Stone and, despite the upset over their inclusion, performed alongside men on the Clowns roster. Given their brand of entertainment and Pollock's marketing flair, it is unsurprising that Pollock's Clowns outlasted the formal Negro Leagues, barnstorming into the 1980s.

BROKERING WIDER INCLUSION

Integration forever altered professional baseball. While Gottlieb, Pollock, and Saperstein would, with the dismantling of baseball's racial barrier, work with major league officials on scouting and acquiring black talent, Jewish sportswriters Lester Rodney, Bill Mardo, and Nat Low had earlier joined African American journalists in campaigning for the inclusion of Negro League talent in organized baseball. Their columns rallied integration's supporters, suggested Negro League stars who deserved a close look, pressured major league teams to host tryouts, and organized a letter-writing campaign to Major League Baseball commissioner Judge Kenesaw Mountain Landis supporting integration.

These efforts produced tangible results. Boston city councilman Isadore Muchnick joined forces with African American sportswriter Wendell Smith to secure an April 1945 tryout with the Red Sox for three Negro Leaguers: Sam Jethroe, Marvin Williams, and a relatively unknown Jackie Robinson. The Red Sox declined to sign any of the three. Defenders of Red Sox owner Tom Yawkey claimed politics had motivated the Jewish councilman and accused him of seeking to influence black voters—although Muchnick's Mattapan district was less than one percent black in 1945. Revealingly, the Red Sox became baseball's last holdout to integration. The team's first black player, Pumpsie Green, debuted in July 1959.

In contrast to the articles openly advocating integration penned by Rodney, Mardo, and other Jewish sportswriters, the involvement of Jewish entrepreneurs in baseball's racial integration occurred primarily behind the scenes. In 1948 Cleveland Indians owner, Bill Veeck, hired Abe Saperstein to scout the black baseball circuit. Baseball historians debate whether Veeck had previously collaborated with Saperstein in an effort to purchase the Philadelphia Phillies in 1943 and to surreptitiously stock the team with Negro League stars.[4] Whatever their intention, Major League Baseball's owners approved the sale of the Philadelphia franchise to another bidder. Veeck's hiring of Saperstein, a black baseball insider, suggested a different approach than the one taken by Branch Rickey and the Brooklyn Dodgers, who incorporated no Negro League front-office talent during the initial years of baseball's integration. Saperstein's recommendations influenced Cleveland's acquisition of Satchel Paige, Orestes "Minnie" Miñoso, and other talented Negro Leaguers, making Cleveland the American League's most racially diverse organization.

Ed Gottlieb ranked among the early critics of Branch Rickey's method for integrating baseball. Evidence indicates that Rickey originally planned to sign three (not one) Negro Leaguers in 1945.[5] Pitcher Roy Partlow of Gottlieb's Philadelphia Stars was considered a strong candidate, but Gottlieb insisted on compensation for Partlow. That Negro League owners requested payment for the loss of talent may have led Rickey to scuttle his original plan. In the August 1945 press conference that launched baseball's "great experiment," Rickey announced the signing of Jackie Robinson as a free agent, paying nothing to the Kansas City Monarchs and declaring the Negro Leagues a racket. Rickey presented himself as rescuing Robinson from an illegitimate enterprise as a justification for the uncompensated acquisition of the talented ballplayer.

Veeck's hiring of Saperstein, a black baseball insider, suggested a different approach than the one taken by Branch Rickey and the Brooklyn Dodgers, who incorporated no Negro League front-office talent during the initial years of baseball's integration.

Notes

1 For a full treatment of this issue, see Rebecca T. Alpert, *Out of Left Field: Jews and Black Baseball* (New York: Oxford UP, 2011).
2 *New York Amsterdam News*, 31 July 1929: 8.
3 *Chicago Defender*, 3 Jan. 1942: 24; Neil Lanctot, *Negro League Baseball: The Rise and Fall of a Black Institution* (Philadelphia: U of Pennsylvania P, 2004), 108, 227.
4 David M. Jordan, Larry R. Gerlach, and John Rossi, "A Baseball Myth Exploded: Bill Veeck and the 1943 Sale of the Phillies," *The National Pastime* 18 (SABR, 1998): 3–13; Jules Tygiel, "Revisiting Bill Veeck and the 1943 Phillies," *Baseball Research Journal* 35: 109–15.
5 John Thorn, "Jackie Robinson's Signing: The Real Story," Web, 23 Nov. 2013, http://ourgame.mlblogs.com/2012/04/15/jackie-robinsons-signing-the-real-story/. This is an updated version of the article he coauthored with Jules Tygiel, "The Signing of Jackie Robinson: The Untold Story," *Sport,* June 1988: 65–66.
6 *Baltimore Sun,* 4 Feb. 1971: C1.

A PLACE AT THE TABLE

At a February 3, 1971, press conference, commissioner Bowie Kuhn and Hall of Fame president Paul Kerr announced that Major League Baseball and the National Baseball Hall of Fame would form a special election committee to correct the exclusion of black baseball players who had been barred from organized baseball during the era of segregation. The commission included former Negro League players Monte Irvin and Roy Campanella, black sportswriters Sam Lacy and Wendell Smith, and former Negro League owners Ed Gottlieb and Alex Pompez.

Over the course of his career in black baseball and sports promotion, Gottlieb had witnessed some of black baseball's greatest players: Satchel Paige, Josh Gibson, "Cool Papa" Bell, and Martin Dihigo, among others. He told journalists that Negro League players "would have been of major league caliber if there had been no color line at the time they were playing."[6] From 1971 through 1977, Gottlieb and his fellow committee members used their prominent seats at the table to elect nine Negro Leaguers into the Hall of Fame: Satchel Paige (1971), Josh Gibson and Buck Leonard (1972), Monte Irvin (1973), James "Cool Papa" Bell (1974), Judy Johnson and Oscar Charleston (1976), and Martin Dihigo and John Henry "Pop" Lloyd (1977). Gottlieb's participation on this committee completed an important cycle. Jewish entrepreneurs had created opportunities for African American and Latino ballplayers to play in the Negro Leagues, provided them greater exposure through showcase games at major league stadiums, and brokered access for their entry into organized baseball following the launch of racial integration. Now they had voted on the enshrinement of Negro League players into the Hall of Fame, ensuring that this hallowed space of commemoration of baseball's greats acknowledged those who came before the changing of America's game.

HARRY PASSON'S CONTRIBUTION TO BLACK BASEBALL IN PHILADELPHIA

REBECCA
T.
ALPERT

In 1953, the businesses on the 500 block of Market Street (across from where the National Museum of American Jewish History stands today) were purchased by the city of Philadelphia to create a new home for the Liberty Bell. Among the stores that had to be relocated was one that was itself a Philadelphia landmark, Passon's Sporting Goods. The store, which opened for business at 507 Market Street in 1920, had during the following three decades served as a hub of Philadelphia sports life and a critical meeting place for Jews and African Americans involved in semi-professional baseball.

Harry Passon (1897–1954), who owned the eponymous store, had been an athlete and coach in his youth. He played first base on a variety of local baseball teams and was a founding member of the famous SPHAs, the South Philadelphia Hebrew Association basketball team. But Passon knew at an early age that his talents were on the business side of sports, and the store originated when Passon and two of his SPHA teammates, Eddie Gottlieb and Hughie Black, founded PGB Sports (named after the trio). Black and Gottlieb soon left the business to Harry, who invited his four brothers to join him in a family enterprise.

Passon's Sporting Goods sold equipment and uniforms like most sporting goods retailers, but it also served as the offices for two organizations at the heart of Philadelphia's sporting scene: the Passon Athletic Association and Ed Gottlieb's Sports Enterprise. Moreover, in the days before sports radio, Passon's served as a social center where Philadelphia fans could meet athletes and talk about sports, or anything else that was on their minds. Most important, Passon's served as the hub for "booking games," where teams went to find opponents and rent venues.

Harry Passon used the store as a "home base" from which to extend his connections deeply into the world of Philadelphia baseball. In 1929 he rented a popular ballpark in West Philadelphia (at 48th and Spruce Streets) that he renamed Passon Field, where he became among the first in baseball history to install lights for evening games. He also took an active role in challenging Pennsylvania's Blue Laws, which outlawed charging admission for Sunday contests. Recognized as a leader in semiprofessional baseball, Passon was named state commissioner in 1936. But his most

Passon's Sport Center, 507 Market
Street, Philadelphia, 1952

Passon was part of a complicated history of Jewish ownership of baseball teams, white and black.

significant contribution to baseball in Philadelphia was as the owner of his own teams: the Passons, a white team often referred to in newspapers as the "storeboys" and the Bacharach Giants, a black team that he organized in 1931.

Passon was part of a complicated history of Jewish ownership of baseball teams, white and black. In the early years of professional baseball, several wealthy German Jewish men owned white professional teams, including the Cincinnati Reds, Pittsburgh Pirates, New York Giants, and Boston Braves. But by the 1920s only one of these, Barney Dreyfuss of the Pittsburgh Pirates, remained. The next generation of Eastern European immigrant Jews felt unwelcome in the world of professional baseball, and, had they been welcome, most lacked the necessary capital to own a professional sports team. In semiprofessional sports, however, where the ownership ranks were more diverse and capital requirements less significant, many Jews played roles in the business of baseball as owners of the white (and sometimes Jewish) semiprofessional teams common in that era.

Developing side by side with the white teams were black teams, which started to form in the late nineteenth century when white players and owners demanded that blacks be excluded from the racially mixed but predominantly white teams on which they had played until then. Many of these newly formed black teams had white owners, although early on none were Jewish. Whereas black baseball is commonly referred to as "the Negro Leagues," the term does not do justice to the breadth of the segregated game that began in the 1880s. Hundreds of black baseball teams sprang up, although many were not organized into leagues because owners and players did not have the financial resources to sustain them. Most commonly, black teams (even those affiliated with the official Negro Leagues) "barnstormed" to make ends meet, traveling around the country to find opponents wherever they could, sometimes playing four games in one day. By the 1920s these black baseball teams were predominantly owned and operated by African Americans.

Several Jews became involved in the business of black baseball during the 1930s, including Syd Pollock, Abe Saperstein, Ed Gottlieb, and Harry Passon. Although less well-known than his peers, Passon played an important role in the sport during his short-lived ownership of a Negro League team. Passon's experiences, and the reasons for the brevity of his ownership, together illustrate some of the more difficult problems facing black baseball, and Jewish ownership, in segregated America.

Although the teams themselves were segregated, black teams often played against white teams and relied on white businesses for equipment, booking venues, scheduling, and advertising. The relationships were sometimes friendly, but sometimes fraught, as Harry Passon would discover. His first contacts with black baseball took place at his sporting goods store, where leading black baseball entrepreneur Ed Bolden, a middle-class black man who worked at the post office, purchased equipment for his renowned team, the Hilldale Daisies. In fact, Bolden was one of Passon's first customers. Because of the relationship they developed, Bolden turned to Passon for assistance in 1931, when the Depression and business problems with other owners were making it difficult for him to keep the Daisies going. Rumors reported in the black press suggested that Bolden had moved his equipment to Passon Field and had plans to start a new team in partnership with Passon. Soon it became apparent that Bolden intended instead to start his new team, the Philadelphia Stars, in partnership with Ed Gottlieb. In response, Passon decided to organize his own black baseball team, perhaps in the spirit of competition with Gottlieb, his friend and rival.

Passon set his sights on the Bacharach Giants, a formerly successful franchise that also found itself in financial straits. Ironically, the team was named in honor of a white Jew, Harry Bacharach, the mayor of Atlantic City. Bacharach had welcomed the team to play there in the 1920s after they had moved up from Jacksonville, Florida, and although he had no official involvement with the team, the name stuck.

Passon devoted quite a bit of money, time, and energy to making the Bacharach Giants successful; for example, he added seats and lighting to Passon Field to accommodate the large numbers of African American fans that he expected to attend night games. The Bacharachs, who were managed by Otto Briggs, a former star on Bolden's Hilldale Daisies, began in 1932 to play as an independent team at Passon Field every Monday night, and they traveled on Wednesdays and Saturdays. Passon hired high-quality players, and scheduled games

The team played an important role by offering opportunities for African American youth in Philadelphia to get their start in the game; a noteworthy player for the reorganized Bacharachs was Roy Campanella, one of the first players to break the color barrier in the major leagues.

Harry Passon

against strong opponents, including the Pittsburgh Crawfords, Homestead Grays, and New York Black Yankees. The Bacharachs also played against the white Passons, Gottlieb's Jewish SPHAs baseball team, and the popular religious Christian team from the House of David, a midwestern barnstorming outfit whose players sported long beards.

After the 1933 season Passon learned that a new league was forming, and Pittsburgh team owners Cumberland Posey of the Homestead Grays and Gus Greenlee of the Pittsburgh Crawfords invited the Bacharachs to join. But Bolden and Gottlieb objected—their team, the Philadelphia Stars, was already part of the league, and they did not want another Philadelphia team to join. Passon withdrew his application, but he made it clear that neither he nor Posey understood the objection. They both considered the Bacharachs to be a strong attraction and thought the local competition would draw fans. Eventually, a compromise was reached, and the Bacharachs played the first half of the 1934 season as associate members, winning twenty-two of twenty-seven games. They were awarded full membership in July, over Bolden's objections, but the team did not fare well through the rest of the season. Poor play and several episodes of violence (including a player assaulting an umpire and a detective being injured while arresting some men accused of beating a park attendant) that alarmed those living near Passon Field gave the impression that Passon was not managing the team or the ballpark well.

Although Chester Washington in the *Pittsburgh Courier* (March 9, 1935) praised the Bacharachs' owner as a man who "caught the vision and pledged unstinted efforts toward making a permanent and abiding organization for Negro baseball," Passon was nevertheless ready to quit. After selling the players' contracts to the Negro National League for $400, he reorganized the Bacharachs as an independent team with new players who played locally through the mid-1940s. The team played an important role by offering opportunities for African American youth in Philadelphia to get their start in the game; a noteworthy player for the reorganized Bacharachs was Roy Campanella, one of the first players to break the color barrier in the major leagues.

In 1954, one year after Passon Sporting Goods moved from Market Street, Passon was found dead in the store's new location a few blocks away, an apparent suicide. Although his time in black baseball was brief, he should be remembered, in the words of the commissioner of the Negro National League and sportswriter Rollo Wilson in the *Pittsburgh Courier* (October 13, 1934), as a "big hearted" sportsman who did all he could to advance the game.

Today

One Happy Man.
Is the Elephant Dull?
Borneo Head Hunters.
Savings Banks Warned.

By ARTHUR BRISBANE

(Copyright, 1920.)

Jacob Schiff spent part of his life making money, part giving it away. He was a banker, but his work was not mere handling of money, watching it grow. His firm backed E. H. Harriman, the railroad genius. And that backing by the Schiff firm made it possible for Harriman to make of a run-down, typically inefficient American railroad a splendid system needed by the country.

The Jews of the world may well praise Jacob Schiff and mourn for him. Such work as his, such a life ceaseless, useful labor, with wise philanthropy its chief purpose, answers ignorant, vicious, and jealous libels upon the Jewish people.

Happy the man who, like Mr. Schiff, can forbid any praise at his funeral. He needs none.

A writer expresses contempt for the elephant's intelligence because natives "fasten a little wooden bell on a small dog, and the dog, without even barking, drives the elephant before him." The little wooden bell keeps ringing and the hunter knows where the elephant is.

"Great lack of intelligence," thinks the learned writer. You would not chase a gorilla or lion in that fashion. Possibly not, but the elephant's intelligence may account for its superstitious fear of the little wooden bell. It is not long since intelligent man, king of the primate tribe, used to ring bells to scare away thunderstorms and witches and evils supposed to be riding in the air. When it comes to a fear of the bells, the elephant is not much inferior to man.

In Borneo they hunt heads. They kill the owner, save the head, dry it with the hair on and the teeth showing, and keep it as an interesting curio. That is considered all right. For a Borneo man must have heads to ornament his home, and he can't get them unless he kills somebody.

But, in that same Borneo, if you steal one of these dried heads from the owner the penalty is death. This, you say, is barbarous. How horrible to permit the collecting of human heads, then punish with death the stealing of one of those heads. You see a sad imitation of that in our civilization. Men that like to collect gold are allowed to work children to death in factories, mills, and mines to get the gold. That is all right, quite legal.

WEATHER:
Partly cloudy and cooler tonight; Wednesday fair and cooler; moderate southwest and west winds. Temperature at 8 o'clock, 70 degrees.

NUMBER 11,639.

Published every evening (including Sunday) Entered as second class matter at the postoffice at Washington, D. C.

The Wash

WASHINGTON, TUE

EIGHT WHITE SOX

CHARGE STARS THREW GAMES

Chicago Jury Will Prosecute Ball Players for Series Plot.

TWO PITCHERS ARE NAMED

Gandil, McMullin, Felsch, Risberg, Cicotte, Williams, Jackson Weaver Accused.

CHICAGO, Sept. 28.—Indictments against eight members of the Chicago White Sox for alleged crookedness in the 1919 world series were voted this afternoon by the Cook county grand jury, which has been probing conditions in organized baseball. The men indicted are:

Chick Gandil, former first baseman; Fred McMullin, utility infielder; Happy Felsch, center fielder; "Swede" Risberg, shortstop; Eddie Cicotte, pitcher; Claude Williams, pitcher; Joe Jackson, left field, and Buck Weaver, third baseman.

The true bills charge conspiracy to commit an illegal act.

MAHARG MAY TESTIFY.

One of the witnesses likely to be subpoenaed today is William Maharg, former prizefighter, whose reported confession at Philadelphia that he and Bill Burns, former White Sox pitcher, were involved in the "fixing" of the 1919 world series constitutes the latest sensation of the probe. Mrs. Henrietta B. Kelly, owner of an apartment building in which several White Sox players lived; "Kid" Gleason, manager of the White Sox, and Ray Schalk, star catcher, are witnesses

President Wilson

Pitcher's Wife Who Will Be Quizzed in Ball Scandal

Mrs. Claude Williams, wife of the star pitcher of the Chicago White Sox. She is to be called as a witness by the Cook County (Ill.) Grand Jury, and quizzed in connection with the baseball scandal now being probed.

gton Times

FINAL EDITION

NING, SEPTEMBER 28, 1920. [Closing Wall Street Prices]   THREE CENTS EVERYWHERE.

ALL PLAYERS INDICTED

eclares League Can Aid Ireland

ES GIVEN NT BOOST

Also Will Benefit, commendations, of ion's Committee.

cents a quart for win- the price recommended committee of the Fed- tizens' Association, ap- ntly to investigate the tion in Washington. and 20-cent milk was by producers.

imous report, the com- recommended that the st of milk to the local ould not exceed 42 cents The committee declared e producer and dairymen in the effort to prevent milk price increase.

RS ARE WARNED.

ttee in suggesting the intimates that the pro- d a fight on their hands gnore the 17-cent recom- The committee points out available from the North- In event the producers and Virginia insist on milk price higher than united effort probably to buy milk elsewhere. ttee believes, that the prices has been passed trend and tendency is

---

BELFAST RIOT INJURES SCORE

Soldiers Clear Streets At Point of Bayonet, But Disorders Soon Resume.

"I FEEL USED UP," WHISPERS McSWINEY

LONDON, Sept. 28.—"I feel quite used up," Terence McSwiney, hunger striking lord mayor of Cork, said in a half whisper to his sister Mary this morning, as he started his forty-seventh day of self-imposed starvation.

The lord mayor of London was informed by the prison authorities, in answer to a telephone inquiry, that McSwiney was "weakening perceptibly," and that the prisoner had lost weight during the night.

BELFAST, Sept. 28.—More than a score of persons were injured in a great outbreak of rioting here today. Following a series of clashes early in the day, during which seven persons were hurt, the soldiers cleared the streets at the point of the bayo- net.

The violence was renewed later, rioting extending into Earl street. Reinforcements of soldiers were rush- ed to the scene and the streets were patrolled by troops in armored cars

---

BAVARIAN TROOPS IN DEFIANCE PLEDGE FEALTY TO KING

BERLIN, Sept. 28.—Forty thou- sand completely equipped home guard troops in Bavaria are defy- ing the demobilization order and have renewed their oath of alle- giance to "the Kingdom of Ba- varia and the German Empire," said a Munich dispatch to the Lokal Anzeiger today.

The troops paraded at Munich Sunday and the streets of the city were gay with flags. The con- centration of more than two di- visions in Bavaria, recruited to more than war strength, is arous- ing fears among the socialists that there may be a repetition of the von Kapp uprising of last March.

FRANCE TAKES WORLD AIR CUP

Lecointe, Flying a Nieuport, Wins Bennett Trophy After Americans Quit.

ETAMPES, France, Sept. 28.— Sadi Lecointe, flying in a Nieuport Gordon

---

TAKES HAND IN COX CAMPAIGN

President Writes Letter to Cali- fornian on Irish Issue As Opening Gun.

ERIN NEEDS WORLD FORUM

Points Out League Would Be Ideal Place for Her to Submit Claims.

President Wilson today took his first active step in the campaign to aid Governor Cox by issuing a state- ment on the League of Nations as affecting the Irish question.

The statement, issued through Secretary Tumulty at the direction of the President, took the form of an answer to a letter from Edwin M. Swartz, of Los Angeles, who wrote asking what could be done about the Irish situation.

WORLD FORUM NEEDED.

"It seems to me that it is necessary for the peace and freedom of the world that a forum be created to which all peoples can bring other matters which are likely to affect the peace and freedom of the world," says the statement.

President Wilson's letter to Mr. Swartz, signed by Secretary Tumulty, follows:

"Mr. Edwin M. Swartz,

THE BLACK SOX SCANDAL REVISITED

"A SENSATIONAL TRIAL ABOUT IRISH PLAYERS AND JEWISH GAMBLERS"

"A SENSATIONAL TRIAL ABOUT IRISH PLAYERS AND JEWISH GAMBLERS."[1] So announced the *Forverts* in July 1921 when eight members of the White Sox sat on trial in Chicago for fixing the World Series of two years before. The players had all-American nicknames like "Buck" and "Chick," "Happy" and "Lefty," "Swede" and, of course, "Shoeless Joe," but to the Yiddish press they were all Irish because the mind of Yiddish Jewry followed an irrefutable (if incorrect) ethnic logic:

MICHAEL SCOTT ALEXANDER

(1) the *goyim* run everything in America;
(2) judging by New York City, the *goyim* are Irish; therefore
(3) baseball is Irish.

Incidentally, Jews also thought boxing and basketball were Irish games, even if those sports did have Jewish superstars, including Benny Leonard in the ring and Nat Holman on the court (as a member of the Original Celtics, no less). But baseball had not yet been cracked significantly, and would not be until 1926, when the New York Giants purchased Andy Cohen's contract in the hope of drawing Jewish fans to the Polo Grounds. Until then, Jews participated in America's game vicariously, often through gambling.

New York's biggest bookmaker, Arnold Rothstein, shared a box seat at the Polo Grounds with Giants owner Charles A. Stoneham, for whom Rothstein had mediated the purchase of the team in 1919. Though Stoneham was a Wall Street broker, Rothstein knew him better as the owner of the Oriental Park Racetrack and the Havana Casino of Havana, Cuba. Rothstein had also for some time been in the pool-hall business with the Giants' general manager John McGraw. To sportsmen like these, gambling and sports were simply inextricable, especially gambling on baseball.

From its very beginning, baseball had been conjoined with wagering. A score was initially called an "ace" and a team's turn at bat was called a "hand." Not surprisingly, suspicions concerning gambling and fixes recurred throughout the history of the game, though these do seem to have increased during the years of World War I. Concerns were raised about the World Series of 1914 and also of 1917, and rather serious allegations were

Baseball fans were quick to locate tragic heroes and swarthy villains along ethnic and antisemitic lines instead of doing the more difficult work of untangling the thicket of wagering, corruption, and greed that crossed all ethnic borders and permeated all aspects of the game.

made regarding the World Series of 1918. Finally, in 1920, when White Sox pitcher Eddie Cicotte confessed to organizing the fix of the 1919 World Series, a collective gasp was heard across America. The baseball scandal coincided with a more general burst of xenophobia that had been ignited by the war and the Russian Revolution and was directed in particular toward Southern and Eastern European immigrants. Baseball fans were quick to locate tragic heroes and swarthy villains along ethnic and antisemitic lines instead of doing the more difficult work of untangling the thicket of wagering, corruption, and greed that crossed all ethnic borders and permeated all aspects of the game.

Historians are still divided as to who actually fixed the Series and whether Arnold Rothstein himself had much to do with it. Based on available evidence, I conjecture that the underpaid players of Chicago contacted Abe "The Little Hebrew" Attell, a former featherweight boxing champion (and an associate of Rothstein, as well as of every other serious gambler in America). They asked Attell if he knew anyone interested in financing a fix. The players probably also contacted another known gambler by the name of John J. "Sport" Sullivan of Boston, since both gamblers independently turned to Rothstein for financial backing within days of one another, and I find it hard to believe that each independently came up with the same scheme. It seems far more likely that the players themselves were out fishing for a financial backer. In my opinion, Rothstein himself did not come up with the scheme, nor did he hand

Brooklyn Fans Hold Pennant Jubilation---First World's Series Game Shifted to Ebbets Field

DODGERS RECEIVE GIFTS FROM FANS

New National League Champions Are Cheered by 5,000 Brooklyn Enthusiasts.

Grants Permission for Shortstop Sewell to Play

PERMISSION for the Cleveland Americans to use their Shortstop Sewell, successor of the late Ray Chapman, in the world's series, of the Indians win the American League Pennant, was granted last night by Charles H. Ebbets, president of the Brooklyn National League champions. Sewell joined the Cleveland team after Chapman's death and his contract was promulgated after the time limit of August 20, making him ineligible for the inter-league series.

Mr. Ebbets's announcement was made in reply to a telegram from President J. Dunn of Cleveland, in which he made a request to use Sewell. The Brooklyn president said he hoped Cleveland is successful in the American race in view of the decision of the Chicago American players.

The jubilation of Brooklyn fans over the triumph that brought the National League championship home centred chiefly last night about the pavement of the club and the figure of Charles Ebbets. More than 5,000 people packed the Harrison Place Y. M. C. A. auditorium. Borough President Edward Reigelmann took charge of the ceremonies and said he was positive Brooklyn would take the world's series. Charles Ebbets made a speech announcing that he was retiring from baseball—when he had rounded out forty years of management—which he computed would be ten years hence.

CLAUDE WILLIAMS, PITCHER.   JOE JACKSON, OUTFIELDER.   EDDIE CICOTTE, PITCHER.   "BUCK" WEAVER, THIRD BASE.

White Sox Players Who Have Been Indicted by Chicago Grand Jury.

FRED McMULLIN, UTILITY INFIELDER.   "CHICK" GANDIL, FIRST BASE.   CHARLES RISBERG, SHORTSTOP.   OSCAR FELSCH, CENTRE FIELD.

PENNANT NOT YET WON, SAYS GLEASON

Probable Make Up of White Sox Team for Rest of Season.

White Sox Riddled Race Virtually Over

BY winning yesterday's game while the White Sox were idle the Clevelands made a slight mathematical increase in their chances of capturing the American League pennant, but a factor of vastly more importance in their favor was the suspension by Owner Comiskey of the seven active members of the Chicago team who were indicted by the Grand Jury.

Nothing original about the exposure of our business insides in the papers yesterday and day before.

A Boston house charges us with stealing its thunder. It did the same thing last Spring—merely following the Packers.

No patent infringement; just a little daylight let into the public mind, usually muddled over the difference between profit on cost and profit on sales.

Offer the next man you meet 100% profit on the cost of his goods, provided he allows you 75% discount from his bill! See if he doesn't snap at an imaginary 25% profit.

Unless percentage of profit as well as percentage of expense is based upon sales, a merchant is apt to come out at the "little end of the horn."

It is well not to have a distorted vision about these matters.

When ready for Fall clothes, just come along and see our good stuff, with no tricks except a "come back" if you want your money.

ROGERS PEET COMPANY
Broadway   Broadway
at 13th St.   at 34th St.
"Four Convenient Corners"
Broadway   Fifth Ave.
at Warren   at 41st St.

CLEANUP OF GAME IS NOT TOO LATE

Baseball People Should Be Thankful for Revelations
—Sport Gossip.

By WILLIAM B. HANNA.

Careers of the Indicted World's Series Players

Yankee Players Are Offered to Comiskey

INDIANS INCREASE LEAD TO A GAME

Sisler Makes His 250th Hit, Breaking Record Made by Cobb in 1911.

National and American League Records.

over any money to pay the players. On the other hand, David Pietrusza, a meticulous historian whom I respect a great deal, believes otherwise, and I encourage interested readers to consult his work as well as my own.[2]

Many American Jews, when asked directly, can point to a bookmaker on their family trees. Along with the clothing and entertainment industries, gambling can be considered the third great Jewish American business, and it's still going strong (now mostly legally, of course). In fact, over the past hundred years Jews have been the most active participants in American sports betting, as compared to other religious and ethnic groups.[3] The Jewish fascination with what was once known as "the sporting life" did not begin with the fix of 1919, and it certainly did not end with it. Jews were involved in famous college basketball scandals in 1951 and then again in the 1970s. They have been the oddsmakers of record for the sports-betting industry at least since Walter Annenberg began to publish his first newspaper, *The Racing Form*, in 1922 and then bought the Nationwide News Service ("The Racing Wire") in 1927. In the 1940s, after GIs invented the point spread and thereby opened up head-to-head sports for bookmaking, Leo Hirschfield, a Jew from Minneapolis, became the first major handicapper to recommend odds for sports other than horse racing. His telephone service for bookmakers became known as "the Minneapolis line," which in my own youth I remember my Uncle Seymour referring to (by then anachronistically) when I sometimes went with him to meet his bookmaker (e.g., "What's the Minneapolis line on the Cowboys tonight?").

I don't remember my uncle ever watching a sporting event through to its completion. To him, a game ended when the spread was beat; that's when the television channel got flicked over to the next game. I imagine Arnold Rothstein in his day shared the same restless energy as he paced through the stands of the Polo Grounds looking to make a quick wager on the outcome of the next pitch. For these Jewish Americans, and I suspect for a great many like them, America itself was not a spectator sport where a Jew had to settle for fawning over the prowess of *goyishe* athletes or Irish politicians from the sidelines. In America, anyone could get in on the game. It just took a little chutzpah.

OPPOSITE
_____
"White Sox Players Who Have Been Indicted by Chicago Grand Jury," *Sun and New York Herald*, September 29, 1920

ABOVE
_____
Arnold Rothstein, ca. 1910

Notes

1   *Forverts*, 22 July 1921, 5.
2   David Pietrusza, *Rothstein: The Life, Times, and Murder of the Criminal Genius Who Fixed the 1919 World Series* (New York: Carroll, 2003); Michael Alexander, *Jazz Age Jews* (Princeton: Princeton UP, 2001).
3   See Maureen Kaillick, Daniel Suits, Ted Dielman, and Judith Hybels, "Survey of American Gambling Attitudes and Behavior," in *Gambling in America*, app. 2 (Washington, D.C.: 1976), 297–334, esp. 300; see also Mark H. Haller, "The Changing Structure of American Gambling in the Twentieth Century," *Journal of Social Issues* 35 (1979), 93–97.

MARTY APPEL

THE YANKEES FRONT OFFICE

In 1967, I wrote a letter to the New York Yankees' public relations director, looking for summer employment. My credentials were modest: I was a knowledgeable baseball fan who was editor of my high school and college newspapers. I assumed mine would be one of hundreds of similar letters and I would not hear back. But I did! To my amazement, Bob Fishel, the team's veteran PR man, needed someone to take on the chore of responding to Mickey Mantle's fan mail. Unanswered mail, he knew, was not good public relations. I was invited to an interview with Bob and impressed him sufficiently that I was up to the task of addressing envelopes and stuffing in a photo of The Mick.

What I later learned was that mine was the only such letter Fishel received, and that he was perhaps more delighted than I to make the connection. I was going to work for the NEW YORK YANKEES!

I remember reactions from friends and family, ranging from relative indifference to some concern about the team's essence.

My friends had minimal enthusiasm. This was, after all, the late 1960s, and America's teens were preoccupied with more meaningful interests—the Vietnam War, civil rights, assassinations, and a bitter presidential election. Baseball, alas, had become rather passé among young people. Many baby boomers found football to be more exciting, more relevant, and better on television. Those were, in fact, baseball's toughest days. Attendance was flat, marketing barely existed, and fans clung to long-dead heroes instead of current players.

Older acquaintances, especially those who were Jewish, looked at my choice of employer with skepticism.

"The Yankees?" they said. "Not a very Jewish organization."

To tell the truth, I had never thought about that. I had never felt discriminated against when attending a game and was barely aware of any player's religion. The Yankees seemed perfectly happy to take my $2.50 for a reserved seat, and sell me a scorecard and a hot dog. Was there a Jewish player in the team's history? I hadn't really thought about it.

In fact, I was even a member of the Bobby Richardson Fan Club. Bobby stood out as a rare evangelical in the game, and he took advantage of his fan club mailing list to send periodic religious tracts extolling the teachings of Christ. Did I care? Not a bit.

154

I'd toss aside the religious tract, renew my annual membership, and root my heart out for the little second baseman. I wore his number one in Little League and eventually had the chance to meet Bobby; and we continue to be friends to this day.

Some older fans made a point of studying a team's demographics over the years. The rival New York Giants had periodically featured Jewish players like Andy Cohen or Sid Gordon, both for their skills and as a way to draw "the Broadway crowd," a veiled reference to the Jewish presence in show business. Over in Brooklyn, the Dodgers had Cal Abrams and coach Jake Pitler, and a promising local pitcher named Sandy Koufax, who had joined the team in 1955; as such, they were the team of the people in a heavily Jewish borough. And they integrated baseball with Jackie Robinson, all of which made the Dodgers the team where race, religion, and creed mattered not.

Marty Appel, at age nineteen, standing with thirty-six-year-old Mickey Mantle, whose fan mail Marty processed. It was Mantle's final season with the team

The Yankees, though, were the "Wall Street" team. The first Jewish Yankee (actually, they were the Highlanders then) was a pitcher named Phil Cooney, who joined the team in 1905, although no one seemed to know that he was actually Phil Cohen. He didn't last very long, and then in 1930 came Jimmie Reese, who roomed with Babe Ruth (or with Babe's suitcase, as he liked to say). Jimmie's real name was Hymie Solomon, but again, few seemed to know that. And many New York Jews still remember a 1933 game that featured a fight between Yankees outfielder Ben Chapman and Washington's Jewish infielder, Buddy Myer, where Chapman reputedly made a number of antisemitic comments to Myer. Chapman later earned notoriety as the race-baiting Phillies manager who hurled epithets at Jackie Robinson.

The Yankees were considered very blue blood, very corporate, very conservative, and, in the days when ad agencies and brokerage houses would seldom hire Jews, the Yankees of Jacob Ruppert, Ed Barrow, Dan Topping, Del Webb, Larry MacPhail, and George Weiss seemed equally content to follow along.

The 1939 hiring of a young broadcaster named Mel Allen could have had an impact in the Jewish community had it been better known that he was in fact Melvin Allen Israel. But Mel never took off for a Jewish holiday, and most were unaware of his ethnicity. Indeed Barrow, the general manager, may have been unaware of it when he hired him; he would likely have been shocked to attend Mel's 1996 funeral and find Joe DiMaggio, Yogi Berra, and Phil Rizzuto seated at the service wearing yarmulkes.

There was, however, a strong Jewish presence among the newspapermen covering the team that could not be ignored, especially in the days when the writers traveled as part of "the family." The most respected scribe on the Yankees beat was Dan Daniel, born Dan Markowitz, and his successors included Milton Gross, Leonard Shecter, Leonard Koppett, Leonard Cohen, Stan Isaacs, Steve Jacobson, Maury Allen, Max Kase, Ben Epstein, Bert Gumpert, Milton and Arthur Richman, Dick Young, Joe Reichler, Hal Bock, Hy Goldberg, Harold Rosenthal, Larry Merchant, Bob Lipsyte, Vic Ziegel, Ira Berkow, Murray Chass, and Moss Klein, plus the occasional presence of Roger Kahn, Dick Schaap, and broadcaster Howard Cosell (born Cohen). The city's newspapers were not discriminatory when it came to putting men (although never women) on the coveted Yankee beat.

And so, when I was hired in 1967, I was probably one of only a few Jewish employees in the team's history.

Fishel, hired as PR director in 1954, didn't change his name, but didn't take off for the holidays either. George Weiss, who hired Fishel because he thought his Jewishness would play well with the writers, may have been presumed Jewish by some, but he wasn't. And so, when I was hired in 1967, I was probably one of only a few Jewish employees in the team's history.

One might say that the more liberal-minded president of the team, Michael Burke (these were the days of CBS ownership), created an atmosphere more conducive to diversity, but just a couple of years later he passed on hiring the very popular Marv Albert as a broadcaster, and Marv confided to some that he felt the "Jewish" issue may have been a factor.

As for players, Ron Blomberg was the team's top draft choice in 1967, and no secret was made of his ethnicity. The "great Jewish hope" never quite panned out, but his presence on the roster spoke volumes about a new openness on the team.

When George Steinbrenner bought the club in 1973, he brought in Gabe Paul as team president, and he was followed by Cleveland legend Al Rosen. Steinbrenner's last hire as team president was Randy Levine. Gabe did not emphasize his religion, but when he was hired as the first president of the Houston Colt .45s in 1961, the fact that he was not allowed to join the elite country clubs to woo season-ticket subscribers and sponsors cost him his job.

In my long tenure in the Yankee front office and as TV producer (I succeeded Fishel in 1973), I must have had five hundred meetings with Mr. Steinbrenner and never once heard him utter an insensitive racial or religious remark. But his five-term manager, Billy Martin, reputedly harbored such prejudices, which some believe led to his denying Ken Holtzman a logical start in the 1976 World Series. After Holtzman left in 1977, it took thirty-six more years until Kevin Youkilis came along as the next Jewish Yankee.

So, while I never felt personally singled out or discriminated against in my years in and around the team, I came to be sensitive to the team's checkered history on the subject of religion, and hope that my presence may have contributed in a small way to a more enlightened time in Yankee history, at least in terms of its front-office operation. If nothing else, it gave me an appreciation for the feelings of minorities in the workplace.

Let me conclude with this story. After engaging in yet another fight, this time against Boston catcher Birdie Tebbetts, Ben Chapman was suspended. Under the stands some days later, in a place where players could sneak a smoke, Tebbetts ran into Lou Gehrig.

"Did you land a good punch?" Gehrig asked Tebbetts.

"Yes sir," said the awestruck catcher.

"Would you fight him again?"

"Yes, sir."

"Well," said the Yankees' captain, "if you ever do and you land two good punches, I'll buy you the best suit you ever owned."

DIAMONDS ARE A GIRL'S BEST FRIEND

PAMELA
S.
NADELL

"A kiss on the hand may quite continental, but diamonds are a girl's best friend," cooed Marilyn Monroe in *Some Like It Hot* (1953). Yet millions of women hanker not after a rock that is "square-cut or pear shaped," but a diamond on a field of green pointed by three bases and home plate.[1] Was cultural historian Jacques Barzun thinking of women too when he wrote: "Whoever wants to know the heart and mind of America had better learn baseball"?[2] If not, he should have, for women's infatuation with our national pastime dates to its invention. Already in 1866, Vassar, then a women's college, fielded a team.[3] Women's professional barnstorming and Bloomer Girl teams followed. In 1875, the Blondes (nine blondes) faced off against the Brunettes (what else but nine brunettes) in the first game "ever played in public for gate money between feminine ball-tossers."[4] Thanks to the smash-hit film *A League of Our Own* (1992), fans around the world know that from 1943 to 1954 the All-American Girls Professional Baseball League (AAGPBL) took to the field.[5]

Of course, far more American women "root, root, root for the home team" from the stands than have ever played on baseball's diamonds.[6] In 1883 the Athletics and the Orioles proclaimed Thursday Ladies' Day, expecting the presence of females to "eliminate foul language, and make the game cleaner in every way."[7] From then until now, countless numbers of American women—and America's Jewish women—have been among baseball's most ardent fans.

For new Americans, baseball was their ticket into this land. Two days after landing in New York in 1979, the British-born journalist Lesley Hazleton found herself at Yankee Stadium. After "three hot dogs, two bags of peanuts, three glasses of beer and nine innings," she glimpsed "a mythical place called America." The writer, who had learned the language of curveballs and hardballs from the Americans she met while living in Israel, grasped instantly that baseball was the "code to understanding this culture, the key to the continent."[8]

That code proclaimed baseball "our national religion and ballparks our green cathedrals."[9] Growing up in the Bronx in the 1950s, Laura Cunningham, an orphan raised by her eccentric, unmarried Jewish uncles, awaited the "annual visitation of the godlike Yankees" alighting

Thelma "Tiby" Eisen
swings a baseball bat

159

upon Yankee Stadium, which, she was convinced, "had been standing...on 161st Street since before Christ."[10] Chicago's Lil Levant knew just what Cunningham meant. Coming out of the shadows of the gate into the sparkling sun of the "shrine" (Wrigley Field), she felt what others feel "when they go to church."[11]

Fathers, brothers, and boy cousins introduced daughters, sisters, and girl cousins to the game. Letty Cottin Pogrebin, author of *Deborah, Golda, and Me,* learned baseball's catechism from her cousin Danny. He not only taught her how to keep an official scorecard but sometimes, "when the planets were in perfect alignment," gave her a turn at bat.[12]

In some families baseball follows the patriarchal line; in others love for the game passes from mother to daughter. Lil Levant's household was parted not by a sea, but by baseball. Her father rooted for the White Sox, while her mother, Rhoda Levant, a Cubs fan, made sure her three daughters were on her team.[13]

Still, little girls did not just want to cheer on their team; they wanted to play. In Jane Leavy's autobiographical novel *Squeeze Play,* the narrator's grandmother Delia Bloom Berkowitz takes her granddaughter A.B. to Saks Fifth Avenue to buy a baseball glove. On the High Holidays, A.B. smuggles that glove alongside a transistor radio into her temple. While A.B. listens to the 1964 World Series, her grandmother "prayed and sang" for her future. *Squeeze Play* may be fiction, but the grandmother of *The New York Times* best-selling author of *Sandy Koufax: A Lefty's Legacy* did indeed buy her granddaughter that glove at Saks's flagship store on Fifth Avenue.[14]

Even if as girls they threw balls against a wall for hours on end and practiced batting at the sandlots with their brothers, by the time girls became teens, most had left playing the game behind. Some were sidelined to softball—the "she-sport" to baseball's "he-sport." Originating in late nineteenth-century Chicago's crowded urban spaces, softball's smaller diamond and larger ball were commended as a less strenuous alternative to baseball, ideal for teaching girls and young women the teamwork and sportsmanship their brothers were learning from baseball.[15]

Nevertheless, as the more than four hundred pages of the *Encyclopedia of Women and Baseball* make abundantly clear, some women continued to chase their dreams to play the game; and outside forces sometimes converged to make those dreams come true.[16]

In 1943, with minor league farm teams largely wiped out by the draft and major leaguers, like Hank Greenberg and Joe DiMaggio, trading in their baseball jerseys for Army uniforms, the Office of War Information threatened to cancel the season. Instead, major league owners organized a women's professional league.[17] One of its stars was Thelma "Tiby" Eisen.

For nine seasons, Eisen, an outstanding center fielder, showed "the guys that women could do this too." In 1946, her best season, she made the All-Star team, led the league in triples, and stole 128 bases. The *Total Baseball* encyclopedia names her one of the league's twenty greatest players.[18]

Eisen was not the only Jewish woman to make it to the professional side of the game. Despite filmmaker Nora Ephron's quip after interviewing "Bernice Gera, First Lady Umpire" that "I am utterly baffled as to why any woman would want to get into professional baseball," other Jewish women did.[19] Anita Foss joined the AAGPBL after her husband was killed in the Navy.[20] Later Justine Siegal, the first woman to coach men's professional baseball and to throw batting practice to a major league team, founded Baseball for All.[21]

But Jewish women did not have to play the game to be part of it. In the 1940s Esther Schimmel sold all-beef hot dogs—no pork for her—across the street from the Cardinals' Sportsman's Park. Other Jewish women discovered even better seats in the owner's box.

Even though the Yankees' Charlotte Lazarus Witkind cracked that "there is nothing in the world quite so limited as being a limited partner of George Steinbrenner's," she still had had a "ball." Her 1998 World Series championship ring—everyone from owners to locker-room attendants got one—held twenty-four chip diamonds, one for each Series the Yankees had won.[22]

Witkind was in the major leagues, but Phyllis Getzler was in the minors, where she, husband Stanley, and son Josh were the majority owners of the Staten Island Yankees. What made their partnership unique was that the Getzlers are Orthodox Jews. The Staten Island

In some families baseball follows the patriarchal line; in others love for the game passes from mother to daughter.

Yankees sold *glatt* kosher hot dogs and before every evening game held a minyan, where women, as well as men, said Kaddish.[23]

Yet praying at ballparks was not the only way Jewish women challenged boundaries through baseball. They also wanted to topple baseball's barriers for others. The writer Hilma Wolitzer's "first subversive act" was signing a petition on the playground to "allow Negroes to play in organized baseball." A few years later, when Jackie Robinson came up to bat, she "experienced something like anxious pride.... Hadn't I put him there practically by myself?"[24] Of course she hadn't, but she mirrored the pride so many Americans and American Jews felt when, for the first time, a black man claimed his place on a white team.[25]

Using baseball to right American wrongs, two Jewish women helped smash Little League's gender barrier. In 1971 Rutgers University professor Judith Weis, organizer of the Essex County, New Jersey, chapter of the National Organization for Women (NOW), read in the papers about how "Little League Libber" Maria Pepe had had to quit her team after the national organization threatened to revoke its charter because the rule book said little girls weren't allowed to play. Weis led NOW up to bat for Pepe and filed a sex-discrimination suit with the New Jersey Division of Civil Rights.[26]

Esther Schimmel's hot dog stand at Spring and Dodier Streets, across from Sportsman's Park, St. Louis, ca. 1948

In 1973 Judge Sylvia Pressler, then a civil-rights hearing examiner, not only ruled for Pepe, she recommended that national Little League change its "boys only" policy. Countering one psychiatrist who had testified that forcing teams to integrate would be bad for children's mental development, she argued that even if "whites like to be with whites, blacks like to be with blacks, and Jews like to be with Jews," when it comes to Little League, this violated the law. "We must start somewhere in reversing the trends in this society.... The sooner that little boys realize that little girls are equal," the better. Pressler appreciated that "[t]he institution of Little League is as American as the hot dog and apple pie. There is no reason why that part of Americana should be withheld from girls." A year later the New Jersey Appellate Court agreed, but, by then, Maria Pepe, aged fourteen, was too old to play.

Jewish women's love affair with this "part of Americana" endures. Aviva Kempner spent more than a decade making the film *The Life and Times of Hank Greenberg*.[27] Rabbi Mindy Portnoy's children's book *Matzah Ball: A Passover Story* takes place at the Orioles' Camden Yards.[28]

Even Marilyn Monroe came to adore those green diamonds. Her lipstick—and the autographs of the 1952 World Champion Yankees—grazes "the world's most expensive baseball."[29] Monroe converted to Judaism before marrying her third husband, the playwright Arthur Miller.[30] After their divorce she returned to Yankee Stadium alongside husband number two, baseball giant Joe DiMaggio. Because, as long as Americans have played baseball, women—including America's Jewish women as fans and players, owners, and hot dog vendors—have been in the game.

Maria Pepe in Hoboken Young Dems
Little League team uniform, 1972

Notes

1   Jule Styne and Leo Robin, "Diamonds Are a Girl's Best Friend," 1949. A number of books about women and baseball use this title; see, e.g, Elinor Nauen, ed., *Diamonds Are a Girl's Best Friend: Women Writers on Baseball* (Boston: Faber, 1994).

2   Jacques Barzun, *God's Country and Mine: A Declaration of Love Spiced with a Few Harsh Words* (Boston: Little, Brown, 1954), 159.

3   Gai Ingham Berlage, *Women in Baseball: The Forgotten History* (Westport: Praeger, 1994), xii.

4   Ibid., 29.

5   The league was originally the All-American Girls Baseball League; the word "Professional" was added in the 1980s; Grant Provance, "All-American Girls Professional Baseball League," in *Encyclopedia of Women and Baseball*, ed. Leslie A. Heaphy and Mel Anthony May (Jefferson: McFarland., 2006), 9–16.

6   Jack Norworth and Albert von Tilzer, "Take Me Out to the Ball Game," 1908.

7   Berlage, *Women in Baseball*, 4.

8   Lesley Hazleton, "First Game," in Nauen, *Diamonds Are a Girl's Best Friend*, 6–8. For Hazleton's autobiographical sketch, see "The Accidental Theologist," Web, 10 Nov. 2013, http://accidentaltheologist.com/about/.

9   Jean Hastings Ardell, *Breaking into Baseball: Women and the National Pastime* (Carbondale: Southern Illinois UP, 2005), 136.

10 Laura Cunningham, *Sleeping Arrangements* (New York: Plume, 1989; rpt. 1991), 11, 22–23.

11 Quoted in Ardell, *Breaking into Baseball*, 45–46.

12 Letty Cottin Pogrebin, *Deborah, Golda, and Me: Being Female and Jewish in America* (New York: Crown, 1991), 37–38.

13 Ardell, *Breaking into Baseball*, 43–46.

14 Jane Leavy, *Squeeze Play* (New York: Doubleday, 1990), 3–4, 20–21.

15 Marilyn Cohen, *No Girls in the Clubhouse* (Jefferson: McFarland, 2009), 129–31.

16 Heaphy and May, *Encyclopedia of Women and Baseball*.

17 Provance, *Encyclopedia of Women and Baseball*.

18 Larry Ruttman, *American Jews & America's Game: Voices of a Growing Legacy in Baseball* (Lincoln: U of Nebraska P, 2013), 35–46, quotation, 39; David Spaner, "Thelma Eisen," in *Jewish Women: A Comprehensive Historical Encyclopedia* (Jewish Women's Archive, 2009).

19 Nora Ephron, *Crazy Salad: Some Things about Women* (New York: Knopf, 1975), 54.

20 Ruttman, *American Jews & America's Game*, 35–46; Heaphy and May, *Encyclopedia of Women and Baseball*, 106.

21 Heaphy and May, *Encyclopedia of Women and Baseball*, 267.

22 Charlotte Witkind and Naomi Schottenstein, "Charlotte Witkind (Interviewed by Naomi Schottenstein)," Columbus Jewish Hist. Soc., Web, 6 Nov. 2013, http://columbusjewishhistory. org/?post_type=oral_histories&p=536.

23 Pamela S. Nadell and Phyllis Getlzer, "Interview with Phyllis Getlzer," (5 November 2013). *Baseball America 2007 Directory: Your Definitive Guide to the Game* (New York: Simon & Schuster, 2007), 187.

24 Hilma Wolitzer, "Jackie Robinson," in Nauen, *Diamonds Are a Girl's Best Friend*, 232–34.

25 See, e.g., "Hank Greenberg A Hero to Dodgers' Negro Star," *The New York Times*, 18 May 1947: S5.

26 This and the following paragraphs are based on Schlesinger Library, Radcliffe Institute, Harvard University. NOW (National Organization of Women), MC 496, folder #31.10 PIO. Task forces: Sports, 1974–1975, n.d., State of New Jersey, Department of Law and Public Safety, Division on Civil Rights, 8 Nov. 1973. This is also discussed in *No Girls*, 142-152. The headline "Little League Libber" appears in *Makers Profile: Maria Pepe, Little League's First Girl*, Web, 10 Nov. 2013, http://www.makers.com/ maria-pepe. Pamela S. Nadell interview with Judith Weis, 5 Nov. 2013. *National Organization for Women, Essex County Chapter, Division on Civil Rights v Little League Baseball, Inc.*, 127 N.J. Super. 522; 318 A.2d 33; 1974 N.J. Super. LEXIS 756; 66 A.L.R. 3d 1247 (1974). "Little League in Jersey Ordered to Allow Girls to Play on Teams," *The New York Times*, 8 Nov. 1973: 99. Dan Lewerenz, "Little League to Honor Girls' Pioneer," *Chicago Tribune*, 12 Nov. 2003: 3B.

27 Aviva Kempner, *The Life and Times of Hank Greenberg* (2000).

28 Minda Avra Portnoy, *Matzah Ball: A Passover Story* (Rockville: Kar-Ben, 1994).

29 "Kissed by Marilyn and Signed by DiMaggio...The World's Most Expensive Baseball," *Mail Online*, 27 July 2011.

30 Lila Corwin Berman, *Speaking of Jews: Rabbis, Intellectuals, and the Creation of an American Public Identity* (Berkeley: U of California P, 2009), 145–51; "When Marilyn Monroe Became a Jew," *Reform Judaism* (Spring 2010).

IT STARTS WITH A GIRL AND A BASEBALL

As a blonde-haired Jew, I didn't always fit in at Hebrew school. It didn't help that I also looked like a boy with my short hair and tomboyish style. My Hebrew name is *Yahfah,* meaning "beautiful." It was a nice gesture, given to me by a thoughtful Hebrew teacher, but I never felt the name really fit me. What I was more accustomed to was when a substitute teacher would ask me in front of the whole class where my *yarmulke* was. The other bad thing about Hebrew school was that it forced me to miss after-school sports every Tuesday and Thursday. To me, going to school again, after seven hours of regular school, was torture. Truthfully, I hated Hebrew school.

When I was younger, I felt Judaism was there to limit me. It just didn't seem to me that girls got equal billing. I remember feeling a great injustice when I had my bat mitzvah at the Wailing Wall and I had to stay in the "girl" area. Or when I would go to temple with my grandpa Alvin and he, my dad, Michael, and brother, Lindsey, had the good seats in the center of the sanctuary, while my sister, Cathryn, my grandma, Laura, and I had to view the service from the side as we tried to peek through the latticed barrier that separated us. How could I connect with a Jewish God when it didn't even seem like he cared about girls like me?

It was my dad who first introduced me to baseball. He signed me up for T-ball just like my brother. I loved playing. I'll never forget, at age six or seven, when my dad took me to my first Cleveland Indians game. We lived in Los Angeles, and the Indians were playing the Angels. My father was so excited when the Indians won. I had never seen him cheer so loud, and I felt that, like my dad, I would always be a Cleveland Indians fan. When we moved to Cleveland in fourth grade, my grandfather began taking my brother and me regularly to Indians games. He would buy us all the cotton candy and hotdogs we could manage to eat, and at the end of the game we would choose a souvenir. Going to those games are some of my fondest childhood memories.

Beyond the obligatory Jewish family get-togethers, I put being Jewish on the back burner as I got older. I didn't really see how it mattered to me. That was until I had my daughter, Jasmine. And then I knew I was Jewish. It came to me as a feeling, as a connection both to my family and to a greater understanding of how my new daughter and I related to the overarching Jewish story. But I had decided this renewed Jewish connection would be on my terms, based on my own spiritual

Justine Siegal throws batting practice to the Cleveland Indians during spring training, February 21, 2011

beliefs. Those beliefs supported my notion of an empowered Jewish woman, even if that meant stepping outside the box of tradition.

In 2009, I became the first-base coach for the Brockton Rox of the Can-Am League. Being the first woman to coach men's professional baseball was not always easy. Not everyone thought I should be there. Sometimes I would forget that I was a woman in a traditionally man's world, and I would have a great time interacting with players and fans. But other times I would have to fight those who wanted me to quit. I was called "useless," pushed out of team meetings and meals, and constantly told I was doing things wrong. I lived in a teetering state of baseball bliss and discrimination.

One long night in New Jersey, when I was coaching first base, I began to hear the jeers of a couple of drunk male fans sitting close to the fence near first base. They were shouting things like "What's your bra size?" and other demeaning comments. I was a bit embarrassed because I saw kids sitting around the two men; and I felt this was not the kind of behavior kids should see at a ballpark. I wondered why no parent stood up to them. The jeers then turned to criticisms of how I had positioned myself. As the first base coach, I was standing just outside the coaching box, an insider trick I had learned from the Rox coaching staff: standing a bit farther from home plate gives coaches more time to react to line-drive foul balls. Unfortunately, as the game went on, these two men began shouting at me to "Get in the box!" Admittedly, this was a better jeer than a public discussion of my bra size. However, these men had somehow recruited lots of kids to start chanting "Get in the box!" The fans were so loud that it was hard to concentrate. It continued for a few innings. When I went back to my dugout, I asked the player next to me if he had heard all the chanting. I was surprised when he said no. I wondered if he really hadn't heard them or if he just didn't want to engage with me. Either way I felt alone—both on the field that day and in my dugout.

> **Sometimes I would forget that I was a woman in a traditionally man's world, and I would have a great time interacting with players and fans. But other times I would have to fight those who wanted me to quit.**

For the next game, I'm not sure if there was a special promotion or if the Orthodox community always came out to this New Jersey team's games, but Jews were everywhere. The drunken men were gone, and I enjoyed the beautiful sunny day at the ballpark. We won, and as the game ended, the seats began to clear. I was walking from the field to the locker room when I heard clapping. I looked up, and I saw a Jewish man clapping for me. His two young children looked on. He had purposefully waited for me to walk through the exit gate so he could show his support. I assumed he knew I was Jewish, perhaps by my last name or more likely from one of the articles circulating in Jewish papers. His gesture of approval filled me. There was just something about him being both Orthodox and a man that made me feel validated in a way I didn't even know I needed. As I walked off the field, I looked up at him with his children and smiled. In that moment I knew I was not alone.

A couple years later, I had the incredible opportunity to throw batting practice to six major league teams: The Indians, A's, Rays, Cardinals, Astros, and Mets. I was living the dream. Not just my dream, but the dream of fans all around the world. I

Justine Siegal at batting practice with Sam Fuld of the Tampa Bay Rays

represented everyone who was told they couldn't do something they loved for some poor reason—such as being too short, not rich enough, having the wrong skin color, or not believing in the right god. I was told I shouldn't play baseball because I was girl. I just didn't think that was a good enough reason. So I set out to prove those naysayers wrong. And that's how in 2011 I found myself wearing a Cleveland Indians jersey.

I was in Goodyear at the Indians' spring training complex. They had set aside the umpire locker room for me to change into my uniform. My daughter, Jasmine, who was now thirteen and the absolute joy of my life, was with me. Together we walked into that locker room, and the first thing we saw was an Indians jersey hanging up for me with the number fifteen on the back. Fifteen had become my new lucky number as that was the day Jasmine was born. My Cleveland cap sat on the shelf right above the jersey. I was breathless with excitement. As I put on my uniform, beginning with the navy socks, following a superstitious order I had begun years ago as a young player, I couldn't help but think about the history of what the Indians had meant to me and my family. All those dinner conversations dedicated to how the Indians would do that season or the countless days at the stadium spent watching games and collecting autographs with my brother, Lindsey. I knew I was living my family's dream too. As I finished getting dressed, I tucked in my jersey, arranged my pigtails, took a deep breath, looked at Jasmine, and together we started toward the baseball field.

I figured that throwing batting practice to a major league baseball team was more of a mental challenge than a physical one. Don't get me wrong, I worked my tail off at the JCC gym, using personal trainer Mike Zollklewicz to help me rebuild my arm after a previous injury. But in the end, I knew I really just needed to throw a four-seam fastball, fifty feet, at about seventy miles per hour, for eight to ten minutes. That I could do. But mentally I knew that if I messed up on that batting practice mound, it could be a long time before an MLB club let another woman throw batting practice to them. And the whole point of my outing was to show how much girls and women love the game of baseball and how they wanted to be a part of it, not just fans watching from the bleachers.

I threw a strike on my first pitch to the Indians. Then I threw another one. I was nervous, my hands were clammy, and I had to continually wipe the sweat from my fingers so I could maintain a good grip on the ball. After a bit, I got into a rhythm and momentarily forgot I was throwing to the team I had longed to be part of since I was a little girl. My relaxed state was slightly rattled when I heard and felt a ball whiz by my head. But I began humming again and continued throwing. As the coach yelled, "Last hitter," I stopped, looked around, and just savored the moment. I then threw my last pitch, picked up the balls with the guys, and gave everyone a huge smile. One hitter smiled in return and asked when I was coming back.

Life as a female baseball player has not always been easy. I was thirteen when my new coach told me he didn't want me on his team. He felt girls should play softball and that baseball was for boys. But I didn't listen to him and I didn't quit. I was twenty-three, a young mom, and still looking for a place to play baseball, when I got tired of waiting for opportunities and decided to create them. I wanted Jasmine to grow up knowing that if she wanted to play baseball she could. Jasmine became a symbol of all the other girls who may one day want to play baseball. I started a women's baseball league in Beachwood, Ohio, and it later turned into what is now Baseball for All.

Baseball for All is a nonprofit organization that provides meaningful opportunities in baseball, especially for girls. My motivation is simple. If you tell a girl she can't play baseball, what else will she believe she can't do? In the same line of thinking, if you tell boys that girls can't play baseball, what else will they think girls can't do? I want to live in a society where both boys and girls grow up believing in themselves and knowing they have the freedom to become who they want to be. Martin Buber wrote: "Play is the exultation of the possible." In baseball, as in life, I believe the boundaries of what is possible can start with a girl and a baseball.

Justine Siegal on the field with Baseball for All player Alyssa Ridinger, age thirteen, at the international female baseball tournament coorganized by Siegal's nonprofit, Mexico, 2012

ROBERTO CLEMENTE

TRANSCENDING NATION

ROB
RUCK

When Roberto Clemente arrived in Pittsburgh in April 1955, he found few African American or Latino teammates to welcome him to the Pirates. Though the city had been black baseball's crossroads during the 1930s and '40s, when the Homestead Grays and Pittsburgh Crawfords dominated the Negro Leagues, the Pirates had been slow to integrate. The city had a substantial black population, but few Latinos lived there and nobody quite knew what to make of Clemente, a twenty-year-old from Carolina, Puerto Rico, who spoke scant English. To white Pittsburghers, he was a black man with an immigrant's accent. To black Pittsburghers, Clemente was a dark-skinned outlier they could not understand.

Although few realized it at the time, Roberto Clemente was the vanguard of a wave of Afro-Caribbean ballplayers who would remake the game. He, his teammates, and the city, however, tried to make sense of the sport's racial and cultural transformation without a road map.

Though he moved in with an African American family in the Hill District, Pittsburgh's principal black neighborhood, Clemente did not fit comfortably into either black or white Pittsburgh. Mocked by sportswriters, who reduced his statements to a demeaning "Spanglish" and portrayed him as a showboating hypochondriac despite the very real damage he had suffered from a car crash, Clemente often felt alone in the clubhouse and in his new hometown.

But he owned Forbes Field. As he racked up four batting titles and began a string of twelve consecutive Gold Glove Awards for his play in right field, as he stood for hours after games signing autographs and chatting with fans, as he played and talked with panache while most ballplayers were tobacco-chewing men of few words, Pittsburgh more than warmed to Roberto Clemente. In 1966, Myron Cope wrote in *Sports Illustrated* that Clemente's relationship with Pittsburgh fans had become "one of the unwavering love stories of the national pastime."[1] This handsome and indomitable man became an outspoken and unwavering advocate for Latin and African American players.

Clemente had never played minor league baseball in the South—if he had, blood might well have been shed. But in spring training one year, when darker-skinned players were refused service at a restaurant in Florida,

Clemente confronted a white teammate: "Look, if you're going to accept anything from anybody from that restaurant then you and me are gonna...have a fight because I think it's not fair.... I don't want you—none of the fellas—to eat anything." He told *Sport* magazine in 1961 that darker-skinned Latinos were treated as badly as African Americans had been when the color line was first breached. "They bear the brunt of the sport's remaining racial prejudices," he insisted.[2]

Roberto took Latin teammates into the Pittsburgh home where he and Vera raised their three children—each born in Puerto Rico at Roberto's insistence. He gave Mateo Alou, Manuel Mota, and other men something he had never enjoyed, a mentor on and off the field. Back in Puerto Rico, he lobbied the government to build Ciudad Deportiva (Sport City) for disadvantaged youth. When Martin Luther King, Jr. toured Puerto Rico, Roberto escorted him around the island. When King was murdered in April 1967, Clemente galvanized ballplayers of all races to postpone the season's opening until after his funeral.

And then came the 1971 World Series. That season, Pittsburgh had fielded the first all black and Latino lineup in major league history. The roster was stacked with African Americans and players from Cuba, Panama, Venezuela, and Puerto Rico. When the Pirates fell behind the Baltimore Orioles two games to none, Roberto told his teammates to climb aboard his back—he would carry them. And he did. In Game 3, Clemente ignited their comeback. Dribbling a ball back to the pitcher in the seventh inning, Clemente bolted pell-mell to first base, startling pitcher Mike Cuellar and beating his throw to first. Rattled, Cuellar walked Willie Stargell and surrendered a three-run home run to Bob Robertson. Pittsburgh won in seven games and Clemente, batting .414 with two home runs and fielding with characteristic verve, was named Series MVP.

When interviewed in the locker room afterward, Clemente spoke in Spanish to a national audience, asking for his parents' blessings "on this, the proudest moment of my life." For many listeners, it was the first time they ever had been addressed on television in their native tongue. "To have someone suddenly speak to you in Spanish," Juan Gonzalez recalled, "reinforced a pride in your own language and culture and in who Roberto was."[3]

Until then, Clemente had played in a small media market at a time when few African Americans and no Latinos received endorsements or much attention from the press unless they were in trouble. Now,

For many listeners, it was the first time they ever had been addressed on television in their native tongue.

Clemente, having become a man of the people both in Pittsburgh and Puerto Rico, was seen as a pan-Caribbean icon—the region's first native son to star in the United States sporting arena.

When Clemente first arrived in Pittsburgh, the Hispanic population of the United States was relatively small. By the 1970s, the nation's foreign-born population had fallen to historic lows, under five percent. But this would soon change significantly. The foreign-born percentage of the country and of professional baseball more than doubled during the next twenty years, with Latinos driving these demographic changes. Latin immigrants often identified with Clemente, who once said: "I grew up with people who really had to struggle to live."[4] He never forgot them, nor did they forget him.

Nowhere was that truer than in Nicaragua. Clemente first played there during the 1962 Caribbean Winter League Championships. He returned in 1972 to manage Puerto Rico's team in the World Amateur Championships. Just months before, he had lashed his 3,000th hit in what became his last regular season at bat. Though the Pirates faltered in the playoffs and did not defend their Series title that fall, Clemente's stature in the Caribbean basin had never been higher.

He walked the streets each morning in Managua. "We found the people as we had been in Puerto Rico thirty years ago," Vera Clemente remembered. "Roberto saw himself in the boys in the streets—without shoes, living in a one-room house with ten people—much like it had been when his father worked for the sugar mill in Carolina."[5] When word of his quiet philanthropy leaked, the press dubbed him "El Angel Moreno." A few weeks later an earthquake rocked Nicaragua. The Clementes, from their home in Puerto Rico, worked sixteen-hour days gathering aid shipments, only to find that dictator Anastasio Somoza's military was pilfering the supplies upon arrival. With people in Nicaragua clamoring for his intervention, Clemente boarded an overloaded DC-7 on New Year's Eve: the airplane vanished into the sea soon after takeoff. Manny Sanguillen, his Panamanian teammate, joined divers trying to recover his body. It was never found. "He was everything to Latin ballplayers," Sanguillen said.[6] Indeed, he was everything to many people, whatever their nationality or race.

When Pittsburghers awakened on New Year's Day 1973 to news of Clemente's disappearance into the sea, few held back their tears. By then, Roberto Clemente had transcended confining definitions based on race or culture—and not just in Pittsburgh, but throughout America and across the Caribbean. Forty years later, that love affair with a man whose off-the-field presence eclipsed his Hall of Fame career endures.

Notes

1   Myron Cope, *Sports Illustrated,* 7 Mar. 1966.
2   Howard Kohn, *Sport,* quoted in Kal Wagenheim, *Clemente!: The Enduring Legacy* (Chicago: Olmstead, 2001), 82–83.
3   Quoted in "Roberto Clemente," dir. Bernardo Ruiz, Juan Gonzalez interview, *American Experience*, PBS: 2007.
4   Quoted in ibid.
5   Vera Clemente, interview, Managua, 10 Apr. 1989.
6   Rob Ruck, "Remembering Roberto," *Pittsburgh,* Dec. 1972.

ICHIRO SUZUKI

—

BORN A SAMURAI

"You were born into a royal Samurai family…but we will see in the coming years how weak or strong our families genes have gotten through you."

—Samurai Bushido proverb

KERRY
YO
NAKAGAWA

Magoichi Suzuki, a legendary Japanese samurai, would be filled with "spiritual" pride knowing that his great-great-grandson would be a Hall of Fame-worthy baseball player in two countries. Like his royal ancestors, who faced their destinies through war, each baseball game Ichiro Suzuki plays is filled with calculations and preparations in varying environmental conditions. He must account for all situations and the vast number of possible scenarios that might take place moment to moment. Taking the field could be your last day as a player or as a warrior. Your duty is to be fierce, competitive, and accomplished; but the team is paramount over individual achievement.

Ichiro's reverence for the game, his mitt, and his bats, coupled with his passion and heart, keep him on course to enter Cooperstown's "Shrine of the Eternals" and Japan's Baseball Hall of Fame. His warrior spirit on the green battlefields of any stadium is legendary.

After leaving a nine-year Hall of Fame career with the Orix Blue Wave team in Japan's Nippon Professional Baseball, Ichiro joined Major League Baseball's Seattle Mariners. The first Japanese-born position player in the American League, Ichiro led the American League in batting average and stolen bases, in addition to being named the league's Rookie of the Year and Most Valuable Player. He has the Major League Baseball record for hits in a single season, with 262; won the Gold Glove Award in each of his first ten years in the major leagues; was named an All-Star ten times; and won the 2007 All-Star Game Most Valuable Player Award after a three-hit performance that included the game's first, and only, inside-the-park home run. Ichiro had ten consecutive two-hundred-hit seasons, the longest streak by any player, surpassing the Negro League All-Star Wee Willie Keeler's streak of eight. In his rookie season he won the James "Cool Papa" Bell Legacy Award from the Negro League Baseball Museum for leading the American League in stolen bases. John "Buck" O'Neil, founder of the museum and Negro League ambassador, beamed when he said in 2001 that "Ichiro won the award and is coming to our museum."[1]

"With Buck, I felt something big," Ichiro said. "The way he carried himself, you can see and tell and feel he loved this game. And when you see that presence, it makes you want to know more about him. That's what I looked to. We're all trying to play better baseball. Make it a better sport. That's what I see, and that's what I look forward to doing."[2]

In 2009, Don Wakamatsu became the first Japanese American manager in the major leagues, for the Seattle Mariners. As Ichiro's new manager, Wakamatsu said about him: "After helping Japan win the World Baseball Classic twice in a row, he came to spring training ten pounds lighter. I wanted to rest him up and keep him out of the lineup, but he refused. We found out he had a bleeding ulcer, and Ichi continued to play through the terrible pain. That tells you how dedicated he is to his teammates and to the organization. It was also very moving to find out he went to visit George Sisler's grave site to pay respects to the man that had the total hits record for over eighty-four years till Ichi broke it."[3] About this visit, Ichiro told MLB.com, "I wanted to do that for a grand upperclassman of the baseball world; I think it's only natural for someone to want to do that, to express my feelings in that way."[4]

As early as 1914, a steady flow of Japanese American teams traveled as American ambassadors to play Japan's universities, as well as company/

Seattle Mariner Ichiro Suzuki prepares to bat during the first inning against the Detroit Tigers, September 4, 2006

merchant teams throughout Asia, Korea, China, and Russia. The first Nisei (American-born Japanese) team to go to Japan was Frank Fukuda's Seattle Asahi (Rising Sun). Fukuda was considered the father of Japanese American baseball in the Northwest, and he described the tour's two major purposes: "to make our young players understand their mother country more deeply and to also study the current situation of Japanese commerce." One Asahi player, a Mr. Nakamura, said, "The most important objective is to learn 'Yamato Damashi' (way of the Samurai) in order to become a Japanese American-born Japanese, rather than to become an 'Americanized' Japanese. And if we do something in American style with the Japanese way of thinking, we believe we can produce a superior combination of those two cultures." Efforts to bridge American culture and Japanese heritage, to blend the two cultures without losing the Japanese identity, were important to many semipro, prewar Nisei teams that traveled to Japan.[5]

Many Nisei in the 1940s hoped to make the leap to Major League Baseball; the talent was surely there, but the war dashed all such hopes. Japanese Americans were rounded up and placed in concentration camps throughout the desert wastelands of the American West. Interned because of their race, they nevertheless kept the American pastime alive in the barbed-wire cities. George Omachi, a Nisei scout for the Milwaukee Brewers, San Francisco Giants, and Houston Astros, believed that "if it weren't for...World War II, we would have had a Nisei ballplayer in the major leagues before Jackie Robinson."[6]

Guadalupe YMBA (Young Men's Buddhist Association) team, ca. 1944. During World War II, this semipro Nisei team was interned at Gila River, AZ in what is now referred to as a concentration camp, where it won the camp championship. Masao Iriyama is in the bottom row, fourth from the right

"Perhaps the most impressive thing I've seen is his eternal quest for perfection and performance with a dignity and grace seldom seen in professional sports."

Masao Iriyama was an All-Star shortstop for a semi-pro Nisei team before World War II, then played in the concentration camps, and, after the war, was again a Nisei All-Star. During the war years, he helped his Young Men's Buddhist Association (YMBA) team, Guadalupe, to win the camp championship and received a handmade wooden batting trophy. He was also given a telegram to deliver to his parents at their barrack, where the family was devastated to learn that his oldest brother, Minoru, had been shot down and killed over Tokyo during the Doolittle raid. "Minoru was with the Army Air Academy, and I was playing ball inside the barbed-wire fence...very sad day for us." Masao felt that a few of the Nisei ballplayers he competed with could have been good major leaguers, but prejudices prevented them from playing professionally. "Ichiro is my favorite player because he can do it all," he stated with pride. "[He can] run, hit, throw, bunt, golden glove, and his size gives us all hope, no matter how small you may be physically. It gives me great pride knowing he is Japanese and is one of the best in the Major Leagues."[7]

Tony Attanasio, who has been Ichiro's agent for fifteen years, said, "Perhaps the most impressive thing I've seen is his eternal quest for perfection and performance, with a dignity and grace seldom seen in professional sports. I was with him in an interview by Bob Costas in which Bob asked him why he never threw his bat after striking out, and his response was as disciplined and unique as he himself is. Ichiro looked Bob right in the eyes and said: 'My bats are made by professionals who care about their performance in making the bat, and they provide for me the best possible tools to perform at the level to which I strive. The bat did not make a mistake; I did. Why should I put marks on the bat or toss it away as if it intentionally did not perform; it was me that failed at that moment, not the bat, and it would be an insult to the bat maker if I were to toss his honest labor away and place blame on it when it had nothing to do with that moment in time.' Bob was (as was I) so impressed with his explanation; it quite frankly put just about everything into perspective."[8]

Ichiro Suzuki has had a unique alacrity and maturity at every level of his professional life. Inside and outside the lines, in Japan and challenging the cultural barriers in the United States, he is an exceptional person. In every arena of human endeavor, there are icons of skill and artistry: Rudolf Nureyev in dance, Bruce Lee in martial arts, and Ichiro Suzuki in baseball. He is a Blue Wave, Mariner, WBC Champion, Yankee, Hall of Famer...but always a "Samurai."

Notes

1   Buck O'Neil, personal interview, Feb. 2002.
2   Jeff Passan, "Ichiro Draws Lessons Learned from Friend Buck O'Neil as He Ponders Future with Mariners," Yahoo Sports, Web, 12 July 2012. http://sports.yahoo.com/news/ichiro-draws-from-lessons-learned-from-friend-buck-o-neil-as-he-ponders-future-with-mariners.html.
3   Don Wakamatsu, personal interview, 17 Nov. 2013.
4   "Ichiro Breaks George Sisler's Record," MLB.com, 2004.
5   Kerry Yo Nakagawa, *Through a Diamond: 100 Years of Japanese American Baseball* (San Francisco: Rudi, 2001).
6   George Omachi, interview, June 1994.
7   Masao Iriyama, personal interview, 1 Dec. 2013.
8   Tony Attanasio, personal interview, 19 Nov. 2013.

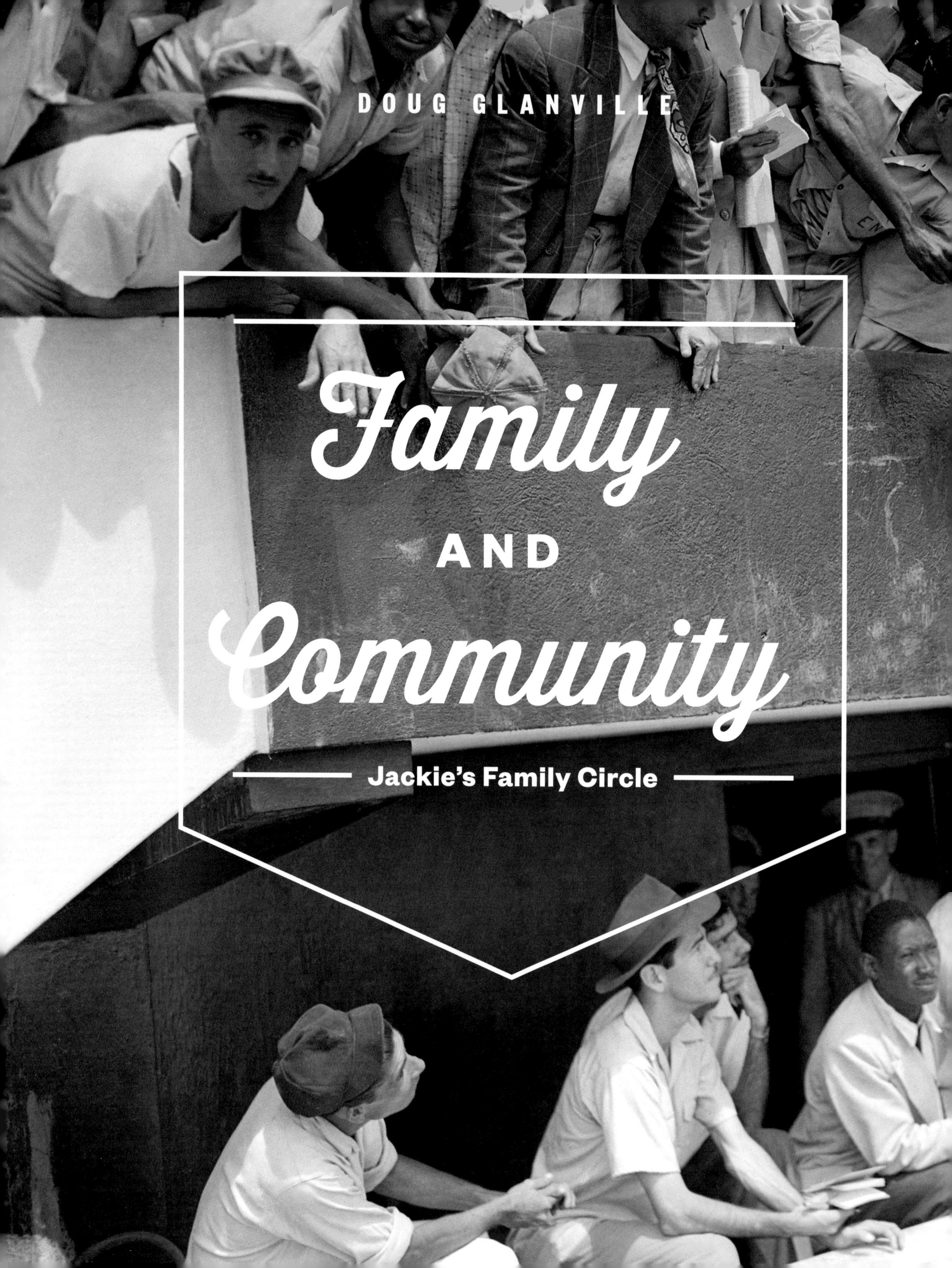

DOUG GLANVILLE

Family
AND
Community

— Jackie's Family Circle —

Jackie Robinson signing autographs on the first day of spring training in Santo Domingo, Dominican Republic, March 6, 1948

I WAS NOT BORN when Jackie

Robinson made his major league debut in 1947, but baseball offers a unique gift that allows me to be Jackie's brother, part of the lineage of baseball history, flowing through the hereditary pipeline that makes baseball a family game.

My brother, Ken, was not born either, but long before I made it to the major leagues, baseball defined our relationship. He taught me the game through board games and rain-soaked sessions of Wiffle ball on the driveway as soon as I could walk. Before I put on my first uniform, we communicated

Doug Glanville and his brother Ken, 1971

through our own scorecard, encrypted by a Morse code of dots of statistics and dashes of our favorite team's postseason possibilities. By the time any given game day had ended, we would have already spent hours walking through play-by-play accounts of what had happened, from the first pitch to the last.

Our seven-year age difference never mattered much. Baseball was a language of equality, spoken in a poetic harmony that often tempered seniority, bridged maturity levels, blurred the lines of age, and brought everyone into the same living room. We could talk on par, the only difference being the number of stories we had in our archives. Once a story was told, it became common property, available to be retold by anyone. We may have bickered over team loyalties, we may have disputed how to make the game greater, but we were from the same cloth and we both wanted baseball to endure.

So Jackie Robinson's story was shared with me by many people: by my parents; by Jackie's daughter, Sharon, who I later worked with on charitable causes; by history; and by his widow, Rachel, during my humble meeting with her. He and I were connected through these stories they shared, ultimately making him ever present and coursing in my life—because we were both ballplayers, both fans of the game, but also because he led and persevered through the most trying times of race relations in the United States. He made baseball speak the language of equality, which then made my career as the first African American to make it to the major leagues with an Ivy League degree possible.

Baseball tends to do that—to be at the front door of social change, to be at your dinner table. It speaks the unspoken and makes you feel like you have lived its stories your entire life even if so much of it was lived vicariously. You were there, even when you weren't, because somewhere in your own life experience there was a moment that felt the same. I was ten years old when my favorite team, the Philadelphia Phillies, won the 1980 World Series, and Tug McGraw patted his leg to victory. I was thirty-eight when the 2008 Phillies took the World Series, and Brad Lidge kneeled to glory. The feelings were eerily similar.

Robinson is the middle name of my son because, even within my own family, we knew that his legacy represented everything we loved about family. No elder was insulted when we named our son after someone we had never met or seen play in person—because it was understood that Jackie had a dignity worth modeling, and, in baseball and in life, was part of us. We shared with him the struggle for racial equality that shaped my mother, born in Oak City, North Carolina, and my father, who came from Trinidad and had to navigate a new land with glass ceilings framed by visible—and often invisible— walls to opportunity. Robinson's voice was one of inspiration, matching action to principle, and his voice stopped time in its tracks.

Robinson's presence in our lives is fitting, given that baseball has no clock. No one is late; no one is early. No one tells us "you are here," because it is everywhere at every time. Its continuity erases constructs like "before" and "after." It is one dynamic flow of events with its loyal followers able to teleport between points by a simple anecdote. Along the way we are chasing perfection, chasing equality, chasing the dream of defining the best of what baseball has to offer. We are tapping its ability to change midstream and let a man of color like Jackie Robinson walk in the whitewashed door of homogeneity, then in a blink of time make it unimaginable for the game to exist without him.

After years of falling short in the final act of many seasons, the Dodgers became World Series champions in 1955, at the tail end of Jackie's career. The Dodgers' victory was both the culmination of the team's developing a concept of family and a window into the greatness of baseball. You can bring immense change to a team and a nation divided, and within a short period of time you can overcome monumental adversity to become a perennial champion, a world champion. It was a lesson that

Jackie Robinson, 1952

subtly seeped into America's consciousness, reaching the depths of young African American baseball fans like my brother and me, and ultimately all fans generations later. Through Jackie, we were able embrace the idea that anything is possible, that character and caliber supersede race when determining who can be a champion at the highest level. Robinson's endurance granted freedom of a pervasive and persuasive kind that instantly turned the previous realm of possibility upside down.

———

Even though he had a Hall of Fame career, Pee Wee Reese was equally noted for his gesture that brought Jackie Robinson into the Dodger family circle. When he put his arm around Robinson in the face of a hostile crowd, he sent a message to the racially polarized nation that the time had come. Even a man like Reese, who hailed from an area of the country that was particularly unwelcoming to men like Jackie, recognized history in Jackie. Reese's embrace was made possible because of the respect Reese had gained from Jackie's fortitude and what Reese saw day in and day out about Robinson's character—a man who had the ironclad constitution you aspire to have on your team, regardless of color.

During my own years as a professional player, my understanding of being a good teammate, a good person, developed alongside my skills. No one benefited more from those kinds of lessons than Robinson's teammates: Koufax, Drysdale, Roseboro, Gilliam, to name a few. Some of the greatest players of that era faced their own personal demons, in the end using the trials they overcame to provide lessons for the next generation of players, on and off the field.

Sandy Koufax dealt with many of the social issues that plagued Robinson and other black players, enduring the antisemitism that flowed through baseball's ranks. He often connected with black players because they too understood what it was like to be ostracized.

Yet on the field, Koufax had a partner in Don Drysdale, the other half of the Dodger one-two punch of a starting rotation. Both began their Dodger careers in their teens. The Dodgers won the World Series in Koufax's first season, and four years later they did the same, with their aces smashing strikeout records. In Drysdale's final full season in 1968, he would notch a fifty-eight-inning scoreless streak on the back of six straight shutouts. The following year would be his last, with arm troubles wrapping up his career at the young age of thirty-two. Koufax was thirty when he retired.

When Drysdale was laboring through his final season, Dodger rookie Bill Buckner was about to make his debut. He only got one at-bat in '69, but it was the start of a long career of solid hitting that produced 2,715 hits by 1990. Buckner was known for his consistent line-drive stroke. He scrapped, he never gave up, and he always played hard in a remarkable twenty-two seasons of major league performance.

Buckner learned from the quiet toughness of managers like Walter Alston, but in a game that thrives on mentorship and passing down wisdom from generation to generation, he found lessons from all corners of the game. He gained insight from witnessing the "togetherness" in which players and staff of all levels ate together, played Ping-Pong together, celebrated fun-filled holidays together. "There wasn't this distance between management and players as it stands today," said Buckner. Players could also depend on continuity as opposed to the constant turnover that characterizes the game today.

Bill Buckner's upbringing in the game celebrated the baseball "family," and he credits Maury Wills and Robinson teammate Junior Gilliam with helping him learn how to play baseball the right way. "Gilliam spent a lot of time in the game before he got his big shot," said Buckner. With many Negro League and minor league stops along the way, Gilliam arrived to the big leagues (Rookie of the Year in 1953) polished, "understanding how to do the little things...and he was very team-oriented."

Sure, whenever he battled through a slump, at times, Buckner's frustration spilled over into a helmet thrown in disgust, that is, until the day Richie Allen approached him after such an episode and asked, "Don't you think you'll get a hit the next time?" There would be lots of next times for Bill Buckner; and his openness to learning how to be a complete professional, from all players, no matter where they were coming from, no matter what race, made him a better ballplayer. Jackie Robinson opened the door that allowed men like Gilliam, Wills, and Allen to make an impact on Bill Buckner, and Buckner paid it forward.

Even though Allen had encouraged Buckner not to blatantly display his frustrations, Ryne Sandberg, a "student" of Buckner, was actually encouraged to throw his helmet.

Sandberg, who met Buckner in his first major league season, started the year at zero for his first thirty-two at-bats. With not a hit in sight, he was demoted to hit eighth in the lineup. Then, over a two-week period, he got hot and was promoted to second in the order, hitting in the same batting-practice group as Bill Buckner.

Sandberg watched Buckner like a hawk. Buckner's approach was exact and well-planned. He took batting practice seriously, concentrating on turning every swing into a crisp line drive. From this discipline Sandberg learned that you can set the tone for a great game by how you handle the first pitch in batting practice. He saw that Buckner never gave up an at-bat, always fought until the last strike.

Sandberg described Buckner as a "walking scouting report" in an era when players kept their own reports and were not necessarily generous about sharing them. Buckner, however, talked openly about opposing pitchers to help his team and to help Sandberg learn how to best his opponent. Their time together helped shape the player Sandberg would eventually become.

By the time I met Ryne Sandberg, he had already become a legendary player, an icon in real life as well as in my Strat-O-Matic memories. I had seen him play at Shea Stadium as a kid; and during my simulated games I had cheered dice into resting on another triple to hopefully beat my brother in my last living-room at bat.

My first major league spring training was in 1994. When I walked into the locker room on day one of that year, my enthusiasm was sobered by seeing Ryne Sandberg's jersey hanging next to my locker. Number twenty-three. This dream was now for real.

The rookie silence that I was expected to keep allowed me to listen closely, to capture the off-the-field education that is the school of baseball. Between stentorian-voiced Shawon Dunston and his bickering partner, Mark Grace, my notebook filled with wisdom. But Sandberg said hardly a word. Observation was the key to understanding what he most had to offer; and given that my locker was right next to his, I had a front-row seat. He wasn't walking around with an aura of unapproachability, but instead one of almost shyness, of humility. I saw the discipline, I filed away that a great player can dominate and not break bats after a strikeout or make everyone around him feel secondary. He watched like a panther, waiting for the right time, then he would bury his opponents with quiet precision.

It was what I needed to see at that time: wisdom through action. As a young hitter, I appreciated seeing a variety of ways to handle the inherent frustrations that counterbalanced the euphoria of baseball's emotional roller coaster. When I was a player, people believed that emotion had to be shown outwardly. You had to be loud and boisterous, strut your stuff, make sure your audience of managers and coaches knew that striking out with the bases loaded bothered you. There was no backing down, no "oh well, get 'em next time."

But I, too, had a quiet nature and was at the stage in my career where labels were starting to stick, not all of them positive. I saw that maybe Ryne Sandberg

During my own years as a professional player, my understanding of being a good teammate, a good person, developed alongside my skills.

Red Sox first baseman Bill Buckner playing against the Kansas City Royals, Fenway Park, May 28, 1984

Ryne Sandberg connects during the All-Star home run contest at Chicago's Wrigley Field, July 10, 1990

was not breaking helmets. His reticence allowed him to focus his power of observation and his ability to take advice and replicate great habits. His Hall of Fame induction spoke volumes as to how well he knew himself.

By 1993, ten-plus years into his major league career, Sandberg was arguably the best all-around player in baseball. Then Sandberg's misfortune became my fortune. In spring training of that same year, a pitcher hit him with a pitch and broke his hand. This forced him to miss the beginning of the season and go on a rehabilitation assignment in the minor leagues. One of his stops was Daytona Beach, Florida.

In my second full season in the minor leagues, I reported to Jackie Robinson Stadium as a member of the Daytona Cubs. It was at the height of my negotiating "passive" labels and receiving suggestions from my manager to display more emotion; so, like Sandberg, I began to experiment with throwing helmets or making lots of noise when a runner was in scoring position and I did not get a hit. I didn't think it made me a better player, but it did let my teammates know that I "cared" when I didn't produce. At least so went the theory.

Then Ryne Sandberg became my teammate in Daytona. He quietly showed up, crept around doing drills off the tee, spoke softly if at all—all the while garnering respect and instilling fear in young opposing pitchers.

I learned from him that there was not one way to be a major league ballplayer; in fact, I saw very quickly that it took all kinds of personalities to make a team's engine run—as long as there was respect. When I would eventually get my first call to the "show" in 1996, I would unequivocally thank "Ryno" for validating that the way I engaged in the game had

had already navigated some of those labels. Too quiet means aloof, or lackadaisical. Maybe even lacking the fire of passion that makes enduring this four-season sport possible.

At one point in his minor league ascension, Sandberg came across Bill Dancy, a first-year manager in Spartanburg, South Carolina. Dancy suggested that he show more fire, using words that I would hear a decade later: "You need to break a helmet once in a while." So Sandberg thought about it, and despite feeling like it would be a better idea to take his frustrations out on the opposing pitcher and the baseball, he decided to take Dancy's advice. After grounding out to the shortstop a few games later, he came back to the dugout and smashed his helmet into bits against a nearby brick wall. Then he realized he didn't have a helmet anymore and asked himself, "What did that really prove? Well, it proved I could break a helmet."

Sandberg's silence was never a weakness, and fortunately he had advocates like his first year manager, Larry Rojas, and mentors like Bill Buckner to make it known that he had a future even when he

One joy of being a professional baseball player is the access it gives you to the players you grew up admiring, the chance to engage in and around the game of baseball with favorite players from your childhood.

strengths. From Sandberg, I learned that I too could win and be a productive major league player by killing teams softly with sportsmanship. It made me reflect back on my competition with my brother. My respect and love for him did not preclude beating him to a pulp in a game of Wiffle ball or Strat-O-Matic. Even though I was seven years his minor, he did not show me mercy out of sympathy; he gave me his best effort so that when I won, I knew I had won and it meant something.

A few seasons later I was traded to Philadelphia, where I enjoyed some of my greatest moments as a part of the baseball family. This trade also brought me closer to my parents in New Jersey, while allowing me to walk in the footsteps of my baseball idols, right in my college town, a train ride from the Wiffle ball field in front of my parents' garage door. I would be embraced as the boy next door coming home, the local son; and that sentiment gave me strength.

One joy of being a professional baseball player is the access it gives you to the players you grew up admiring, the chance to engage in and around the game of baseball with favorite players from your childhood.

Often, in the path to the big leagues, your coaches and managers were players from a generation or two before you. Jay Loviglio taught me how to steal bases; Billy Williams was my first hitting coach; Jimmy Piersall was my outfield coach; Sandy Alomar Sr. was my mental guru. They were everywhere. Players jumped off my Strat-O-Matic cards and sat right next to me in the dugout or on the team bus. I was picking the brains of legends on a daily basis.

Once I started my Phillies years, I had the chance to play center field in the steps of Garry Maddox, to hear Mike Schmidt tell stories of facing Fernando Valenzuela, and to catch the ceremonial first pitch from Steve Carlton. It did not take me long to realize that these players were not just figureheads; they knew the game, they loved the game, and they all sensed the critical importance of passing it on.

No one did more for me in Philadelphia than Garry Maddox. He took the time to sit with me just to talk, to help me see my experiences in baseball as connected to my past and my future. It could be about baseball, but mostly it was about life, about setting yourself up for the inevitability of the game

Philadelphia Phillie Garry Maddox arrives safe at third base on a throwing error, May 22, 1985

ending and tapping into those relationships that want to see you transition in a healthy way. I got relationship advice, and I also got business advice that he had gleaned from Joe Morgan.

Keep in mind that Maddox was one of my favorite players growing up. Here he was taking the time to help me learn the game and then set myself up for a better life after it was over.

In 2003, I became a free agent for the first time in my career. I had the rare chance to pick my employer while keeping the uniform on. I had been disenchanted with my 2002 season for a whole host of reasons. Besides the trauma of losing my father during the season's last game, I did not play well that year until the very end of the season. Larry Bowa was my manager, another legend from my fandom past, but he was not penciling me into the lineup as often as I had hoped.

When the season ended and I had the chance to go where I could play again consistently, I took that opportunity.

But shortly after the Texas Rangers made me an offer that I liked, I met with Garry Maddox in downtown Philadelphia. He took me to a dinner party to feel the love, to see how much my work as a Philadelphia Phillie had meant to my community, my city. I spoke to a mix of people in all fields, from all walks of life, and was reminded of the great Jackie Robinson adage: "A life is only important in

Doug Glanville celebrates with his teammates after his winning walk-off home run against the Montreal Expos, April 18, 2004

the impact it has on others." Maddox pointed out that I could go to Texas and maybe make more money, maybe be told (not guaranteed, keep in mind) that I would play, but Philadelphia was home. Home literally, home figuratively, my alma mater; and my now-widowed mother was less than two hours away. Texas was an entire country away, comparatively. I could have the greatest impact "right here" in my own backyard.

Knowing that I was leaning toward going to Texas, Maddox eventually cornered me with an editor from *Philadelphia* magazine to take her pulse on my situation. He put her in my shoes, and she glowingly responded to the question "Would you stay if you were him?" with a resounding "Yes!" But Maddox had left something out. I would start in Texas, but in Philly I probably would not. Learning this, the editor revised her answer, and I thanked her.

Garry Maddox may have wanted me to stay. He was certainly sure that the best career move was to stay in the known environment that had been critical to ten years of my life. He did exactly what a mentor

in the family of baseball does all the time—put a mirror up in your face and make you state your case, make you take a stance, but with access to veteran wisdom to chew on. He helped me solidify my position, as hard as it was for me to leave the comfort of Philadelphia.

But there was something else I needed to do.

Jimmy Rollins was called up to the major leagues in 2001, my fourth season in Philadelphia. He was brash, even brazen at times, and absolutely infectious. He loved the game, he loved to compete, and he loved the idea of being a star. I knew the moment he walked in that he would pit old school against new school. He was here to push the envelope, to challenge the idea of being seen but not heard.

In his first days, I feared for him. The veterans were watching and wanting to take him down a few pegs. Out of excitement and even a twist of nervousness, he talked incessantly. It was as if he were doing a documentary on his career from the moment he got that first call.

One day our All-Star third baseman Scott Rolen, Rollins, Bobby Abreu, and I were in a hitting group together. Rollins was describing in great detail every ball he hit during batting practice. He talked to the baseball in flight, egged it on, called an imaginary game full of colorful commentary. But Rolen had reached his rookie talking-limit.

He called a meeting to take a vote to set up the coup d'état. "We need to kick him out of our group," said Rolen. Abreu seemed indifferent, but would support Rolen; and I understood the old-school sentiment, even though I wanted to keep Rollins close so I could help him adjust. Eventually Abreu's and my neutrality led Rolen to take the lead, so Rollins was out.

For the next few days, Rollins looked like a kicked puppy. He was quiet for days, which was not really his personality. But eventually, with his success on the field, he could not contain his enthusiasm for what was about to be a long and successful career. Even then, he never stopped talking. It would appear that as much as Sandberg and Glanville needed to be quiet observers, Rollins needed to be a vocal pot-stirrer; and if that is his game, that is his game.

And Rollins backed it up with solid achievement. An MVP trophy and World Championship ring showed that he had found his rhythm and a safe path for him to do his job in his style. He was able to do so while maintaining his voice, which he employed to forge great personal and team success. He was able to be himself; and more importantly, he was comfortable with himself.

Baseball is a continuum. The relationships one forges in the game are eternal, even those unplanned and by happenstance.

In the middle of the 2013 season, Charlie Manuel, the manager responsible for the Phillies' 2008 World Championship, was let go and in walked my former teammate Ryne Sandberg to manage the 2013 Phillies. He would now be managing a mix of players that included Jimmy Rollins—longtime shortstop, a position Sandberg had once played as a young player in the Phillies' minor league system.

No matter which two players you choose, and from whatever era, you can bridge them, you can connect their stories, even when the details may make them seem diametrically opposed. In those stories are the fiber of the game's innate ability to mentor, to pass down its lore from generation to generation.

When Jackie Robinson broke in with the Dodgers, no one could say for sure where it would take our country, our game. But the magnetic core of baseball is greater than any moment, even one as great as Jackie Robinson's turned out to be. This dynamic allowed the first black baseball player to impact a future Hall of Famer, Ryne Sandberg,

Philadelphia Phillies player Doug Glanville congratulates his teammate Placido Polanco during a game against the San Diego Padres, August 5, 2004

who debuted nearly forty years later. It can be done without direct conversation, through generations of players, through Junior Gilliam, Sandy Koufax, Maury Wills, Richie Allen, Bill Buckner, and a whole host of others.

It is the baseball family that sustains the game, that keeps tradition alive, that keeps players connected to every era.

This game can take the story of a man unfairly pinned for the fate of the 1986 Red Sox and realize that as a Los Angeles Dodger he was one degree from Jackie Robinson and was able to gain from Jackie's teammates a lesson that helped him communicate to Ryne Sandberg the keys to professional success in the game. It shows that Bill Buckner's legacy was written in much bigger letters than those that stenciled his fielding error in the 1986 World Series. Long before his ignominious moment, he had helped Hall of Famers, won a batting title, was a humble rookie, made an All-Star team; and in time what he showed Sandberg, Sandberg showed me, which I showed Jimmy Rollins, who in turn showed Domonic Brown....

It does not stop. It loops around to perpetuity, willful and accidental, loving and sometimes even under the guise of a saboteur. It works with perspective and even with immediacy.

It is the baseball family that sustains the game, that keeps tradition alive, that keeps players connected to every era; and I imagine that when Rollins walks away from this game, his impact will have only just begun and will one day boomerang around and hit him right in the heart and soul.

And when it does, consciously or not, he will recognize the great debt he owes to all those who came before him. From Jackie Robinson to the family of teammates, coaches, managers, and opponents who he touched. Even to two brothers who battled it out in Wiffle ball in their front yard while dreaming that one day they could be part of the family that began with a seemingly impossible hope for integration in America.

PLAYING CATCH WITH MY DAD

ONE SHABBAT MORNING AT DAWN

JOSHUA PRAGER

I am typing in Jerusalem when I see that my father is online six thousand miles away. I have the thought that I would like to talk to him. And then I remember what he said to me twenty-three years ago when I was off to Israel after high school and we parted at the airport: "Don't call home more than once a month." International calls had a high cost back then. But so did his words.

When I then returned for Passover seven phone calls later, he and my mother overslept and were hours late picking me up.

But our month together was restorative. So far away, I had begun to feel closer to my father, to admire his thoughtful practice of religion and medicine. And one afternoon, we walked into the backyard with our mitts, six thousand miles reduced to sixty feet. I threw a baseball and he threw it back.

My control was good. That was why on a Friday afternoon two years before, my coach had pleaded with my mother to let me finish what I had started. She was hesitant, but acquiesced and drove home and the sun set and I continued pitching and we won and I was the hero. Then I walked the few miles home in my cleats and opened the door and interrupted Kiddush and my father wouldn't talk to me.

Our baseball catch continued. I began to throw hard. I asked my father to make me dive, to throw balls to my right and my left. I gloved nearly every hard grounder he threw—my body parallel to the ground, my mitt outstretched—and whipped them back so fast that his mitt popped and his palm hurt and he laughed and called me Jake, as he did when he was happy. I saw that my father was appreciating me, marveling at me.

Then I hugged my father and the rest of my family, and my cat, Peach, and returned to Israel. I was nineteen years old.

Two weeks later, after a night of basketball and a morning of study at my yeshiva, I boarded a minibus. We were a thousand feet shy of Jerusalem when a runaway truck bore down on the rear of the bus where I sat.

Bang! The nape of my neck snapped back over my seat. My body jerked like a wound towel. I landed two seats to my right. I was numb. And I could not move.

A teenage Joshua Prager playing catch outside New York's Ramaz School

In time, my right side returned to life. And after months in hospitals and years in wheelchairs, I rose to my feet for good, walking with a cane and ankle brace. But time passed felt like time wasted; every anniversary of the crash recalled to me only what had been. And I mourned my lost body, mourned that it was slowly disintegrating within me like some radioactive atom.

But then more years passed. And I saw that I was happy. And I remembered that the decay of radioactive atoms is asymptotic; what forever divides by half will never disappear. There would always remain in me a piece of the past.

I took comfort in that thought and in the thought that my body had spent fewer days disabled than not. And it was then I began to wonder of the moment when I would have lived exactly as long after my neck broke as before. I called that moment my half-life.

I was born at 2:00 a.m. Mountain Standard Time on April 11, 1971. My neck broke at noon Israel Standard Time on May 16, 1990. I had thus lived, pre-crash, one Metonic cycle—the 235-month sequence of the Hebrew calendar—plus thirty-five days and zero minutes.

I asked a friend to pinpoint my half-life. He told me that I would tip at 5:00 a.m. on June 20, 2009. And so a morning years away supplanted my annual May tolling of the crash. It loomed as a sort of über-anniversary, a hinge in my life.

An engineer named Robert Lemlich studied what he called subjective time.[1] He noted that the perceived duration of time decreases as we age. And so, the point that people feel to be the halfway mark of their lives arrives much earlier than the actual midpoint.

There was meaning for me in this. And when an equation Lemlich created to measure subjective time put the midpoint of the life of an American man at precisely nineteen, I nodded.[2] And when author Lorrie Moore said that it was at precisely this midpoint, this hinge, that a person attained the full depth of his being, I nodded again. "It's the age at which nature and form come together," she said, "and your individual passion achieves its final shape and expression."

And so an engineer and an author testified that I had already been the me I was to continue to become when my neck broke.

I was in my mid-thirties when I began to mull how to spend my half-life. It ought to be lived pertinently, I thought. Should I be riding in the back of a bus? Jumping from a plane? Writing? Having sex? I didn't know. And then I did, the thought born as I contemplated, one month shy of thirty-eight, who I had been at age nineteen.

Minutes before dawn, on a Saturday in June 2009, my father and I stepped outside. The Sabbath sky was turning pink, and we walked where we had walked and stood where we had stood. Then I put a glove on the hand I had not then gloved and threw my father a baseball.

We were quiet as we threw. We were quiet just as my father had been quiet when he got yelled at by an embarrassed doctor after turning my oxygen up and saving me when I was blue in the face in the ICU, just as he had been quiet when two large Caribbean women showered me in a net of metal and mesh and he stood nearby as I had asked him to and his slacks and shirt got wet from the spray, just as he had been quiet when he wheeled me nineteen blocks from the hospital to a synagogue and I barked with every jerk in the sidewalk. Nineteen years after a first catch, it was now the son appreciating the father.

The sky lightened. We threw harder, and I asked my father to throw the ball a body length to my right. He did, and I dove. I missed the ball, got up, got it from the ivy, threw it back, and asked for another. He obliged and I lunged seven or eight times toward a clump of larches whose golden needles had long ago blanketed Peach. One ball I gloved neatly and threw back from my knees.

> ## The sky lightened. We threw harder, and I asked my father to throw the ball a body length to my right. He did, and I dove.

There was another ball my father threw faster and farther from me than the others. I took a big quick step to my right, thrust myself headlong, and fell with outstretched arm and glove, my jaw, shoulder, and head hitting the ground hard. I deflected the ball. I prevented a double, my dad said. I had. My best play in nineteen years.

I got up slowly. We continued our catch.

Then I knew that we were done; my half-life had passed. I caught the next throw, took off my glove, and picked up my cane.

Wrote Colson Whitehead:

> *There are unheralded tipping points, a certain number of times that we will unlock the front door of an apartment. At some point you were closer to the last time than you were to the first time, and you didn't even know it. You didn't know that each time you passed the threshold you were saying goodbye.*

I dial my dad to say hello and wonder to what I am nearer than farther.

Notes

1   Robert Lemlich, "Subjective Acceleration of Time with Aging," *Perceptual and Motor Skills 41*, August 1975: 235–38.

2   Based on average life expectancy of seventy-six years.

"SHOULD CHILDREN PLAY BASEBALL?"

THE BINTEL BRIEF, *JEWISH DAILY FORWARD*, AUGUST 6, 1903

ABRAHAM CAHAN

A father writes to ask advice about baseball. He thinks that baseball is a foolish and wild game. But his boy, who is already in the upper grades, is very eager to play. He's not the only one. The majority of our immigrants have the same idea about it. They express it in an interesting fashion, in such a way that it's possible to see in him clearly how the parents in the Yiddish neighborhood feel about baseball.

"It is said the one should teach their child how to play chess or checkers or goat & wolf [*tsig un volf*] or at least a game that sharpens the mind. That would be appreciated," writes the father in his letter. "But what value does a game like baseball have? Nothing more than becoming crippled comes out of it. When I was a young boy we used to play 'rabbits' chasing and catching one another. But when we got older we stopped playing. Imagine a big boy in Russia playing tag, we would have treated him like he was crazy. And here in this highly educated America adults play baseball! They run after the stupid ball made of hide and are as excited about it as little boys. I want my boy to grow up to be a *mentsh* not a wild American runner. He's making me miserable, I can't take it anymore."

This part of the letter captures the point of the question posed by the boy's father. And the writer of this article has but one answer:

Let your boys play baseball and even become outstanding players as long as it doesn't interfere with their studies and doesn't make them keep in the company of bad influences.

This issue arises for nearly half the families of the Jewish quarter. And this is the writer's advice to all of them. Think this issue over carefully.

The father who wrote this aforementioned letter spoke about educational games like chess. But to only be occupied with academic work is also not good! One also needs to develop one's physique. Jews are the most intellectual people in the world. There's no doubt about that. When child development is discussed, especially in the big cities of New York or Chicago, Mr. Reynolds, Mayor Lowe's current secretary, (while he was head of the University Settlement on Delancey Street and then on Eldridge Street) in a published article of his said the following as paraphrased:

Lewis Hine, *Playground in
Tenement Alley*, Boston, 1909

Let's not raise our children to be foreigners in their own country. An American who isn't agile and strong in hands, feet, and his entire body is not an American.

It is remarkable to compare the Jewish boys to the Irish boys. The Irish boys are attracted to boxing gloves (gloves used to fight). And the Jewish boys are drawn to debating.

Much has been written in the American newspapers and journals about the debating clubs and all manner of literary societies of the Jewish quarter. You can find this enthusiasm in these things all over America. And naturally this is very good. But just developing the mind is not enough. Baseball is a good way to develop the body. It's better than gymnastics. First of all it's out in the fresh air. Secondly it develops the hands and feet and the reflex responses of the limbs and eyes. Why shouldn't the children play this these days? Football, the "aristocratic" sport of the colleges, now there is a wild game. You fight with each other like Indians, and often one is left with a broken foot or hand or gets wounded. But there is no danger in baseball.

Most importantly it's a mistake to keep the children confined at home. Therein lies the difference between a Jewish and a Christian boy in Russia or Poland. The Christian goes out looking for birds, climbs trees, and other such activities whereas the Jewish boy is cloistered. The only critical issue here is to make sure the Jewish boy doesn't get in with bad influences such as thieves or similar street gangs. Here in New York such gangs are just as horrible as everywhere else. If you know that your boy is going to play baseball with other upstanding youths, why wouldn't you let him? Let him in a genteel way go and have this "sport." As long as he doesn't become an athlete as a result. A young man who was the best student in college but who spent his entire life squeezing a bench at home, isn't so well prepared for life as he could be if he had also been strong and agile. The Jewish young man who recently was awarded the Cecil Rhodes prize was the best student not only in all intellectual endeavors, but also in such things as baseball and crew. "A healthy mind lives in a healthy body" In an agile body—an agile mind.

Let's not raise our children to be foreigners in their own country. An American who isn't agile and strong in hands, feet, and his entire body is not an American. Unfortunately these qualities have more value than the true assets of a citizen. Raise your children as educated and thoughtful; as people filled with the true heritage of humanity and fellowship for which they are ready to fight. They should also be healthy and agile youth who shouldn't feel inferior to others.

Reprinted translation with permission courtesy of the Forward Association.

DORIS KEARNS GOODWIN

Wait Till Next Year

WHEN I was six, my father gave me a bright-red scorebook that opened my heart to the game of baseball. After dinner on long summer nights, he would sit beside me in our small enclosed porch to hear my account of that day's Brooklyn Dodger game. Night after night he taught me the odd collection of symbols, numbers, and letters that enable a baseball lover to record every action of the game. Our score sheets had blank boxes in which we could draw our own slanted lines in the form of a diamond as we followed players around the bases. Wherever the baserunner's progress stopped, the line stopped. He instructed me to fill in the unused boxes at the end of each inning with an elaborate checkerboard design which made it absolutely clear who had been the last to bat and who would lead off the next inning. By the time I had mastered the art of score-keeping, a lasting bond had been forged among my father, baseball, and me.

All through the summer of 1949, my first summer as a fan, I spent my afternoons sitting cross-legged before the squat Philco radio which stood as a permanent fixture on our porch in Rockville Centre, on the South Shore of Long Island, New York. With my scorebook spread before me, I attended Dodger games through the courtly voice of Dodger announcer Red Barber. As he announced the lineup, I carefully printed each player's name in a column on the left side of my sheet. Then, using the standard system my father had taught me, which assigned a number to each position in the field, starting with a "1" for the pitcher and ending with a "9" for the right fielder, I recorded every play. I found it difficult at times to sit still. As the Dodgers came to bat, I would walk around the room, talking to the players as if they were standing in front of me. At critical junctures, I tried to make a bargain, whispering and cajoling while Pee Wee Reese or Duke Snider stepped into the batter's box: "Please, please, get a hit. If you get a hit now, I'll make my bed every day for a week." Sometimes, when the score was close and the opposing team at bat with men on base, I was too agitated to listen. Asking

197

my mother to keep notes, I left the house for a walk around the block, hoping that when I returned the enemy threat would be over, and once again we'd be up at bat. Mostly, however, I stayed at my post, diligently recording each inning so that, when my father returned from his job as bank examiner for the State of New York, I could re-create for him the game he had missed.

When my father came home from the city, he would change from his three-piece suit into long pants and a short-sleeved sport shirt, and come downstairs for the ritual Manhattan cocktail with my mother. Then my parents would summon me for dinner from my play on the street outside our house. All through dinner I had to restrain myself from telling him about the day's game, waiting for the special time to come when we would sit together on the couch, my scorebook on my lap.

"Well, did anything interesting happen today?" he would begin. And even before the daily question was completed I had eagerly launched into my narrative of every play, and almost every pitch, of that afternoon's contest. It never crossed my mind to wonder if, at the close of a day's work, he might find my lengthy account the least bit tedious. For there was mastery as well as pleasure in our nightly ritual. Through my knowledge, I commanded my father's undivided attention, the sign of his love. It would instill in me an early awareness of the power of narrative, which would introduce a lifetime of storytelling, fueled by the naive confidence that others would find me as entertaining as my father did.

Michael Francis Aloysius Kearns, my father, was a short man who appeared much larger on account of his erect bearing, broad chest, and thick neck. He had a ruddy Irish complexion, and his green eyes flashed with humor and vitality. When he smiled his entire face was transformed, radiating enthusiasm and friendliness. He called me "Bubbles," a pet name he had chosen, he told me, because I seemed to enjoy so many things. Anxious to confirm his description, I refused to let my enthusiasm wane, even when I grew tired or grumpy. Thus excitement about things became a habit, a part of

Ebbets Field in Brooklyn, New York, October 7, 1952

Game 3 of the World Series between the Brooklyn Dodgers and the New York Yankees, Ebbets Field, October 7, 1949

Red Barber, 1945

my personality, and the expectation that I should enjoy new experiences often engendered the enjoyment itself.

These nightly recountings of the Dodgers' progress provided my first lessons in the narrative art. From the scorebook, with its tight squares of neatly arranged symbols, I could unfold the tale of an entire game and tell a story that seemed to last almost as long as the game itself. At first, I was unable to resist the temptation to skip ahead to an important play in later innings. At times, I grew so excited about a Dodger victory that I blurted out the final score before I had hardly begun. But as I became more experienced in my storytelling, I learned to build a dramatic story with a beginning, middle, and end. Slowly, I learned that if I could recount the game, one batter at a time, inning by inning, without divulging the outcome, I could keep the suspense and my father's interest alive until the very last pitch. Sometimes I pretended that I was the great Red Barber himself, allowing my voice to swell when reporting a home run, quieting to a whisper when the action grew tense, injecting tidbits about the players into my reports. At critical moments, I would jump from the couch to illustrate a ball that turned foul at the last moment or a dropped fly that was scored as an error.

"How many hits did Roy Campanella get?" my dad would ask. Tracing my finger across the horizontal line that represented Campanella's at bats that day, I would count. "One, two, three. Three hits, a single, a double, and another single." "How many strikeouts for Don Newcombe?" It was easy. I would count the Ks. "One, two...eight. He had eight strikeouts." Then he'd ask me more subtle questions about different plays—whether a strikeout was called or swinging, whether the double play was around the horn, whether the single that won the game was hit to left or right. If I had scored carefully, using the elaborate system he had taught me, I would know the answers. My father pointed to the second inning, where Jackie Robinson had hit a single and then stolen second. There was excitement in his voice. "See, it's all here. While Robinson was dancing off second, he rattled the pitcher so badly that the next two guys walked to load the bases. That's the impact Robinson makes, game after game. Isn't he something?" His smile at such moments inspired me to take my responsibility seriously.

Sometimes, a particular play would trigger in my father a memory of a similar situation in a game when he was young, and he would tell me stories about the Dodgers when he was a boy growing up in Brooklyn. His vivid tales featured strange heroes such as Casey Stengel, Zack Wheat, and Jimmy Johnston. Though it was hard at first to imagine that the Casey Stengel I knew, the manager of the Yankees, with his colorful language and hilarious antics, was the same man as the Dodger outfielder who hit an inside-the-park home run at the first game ever played at Ebbets Field, my father so skillfully stitched together the past and the present that I felt as if I were living in different time zones. If I closed my eyes, I imagined I was at Ebbets Field in the 1920s for that celebrated game when Dodger right fielder Babe Herman hit a double with the bases loaded, and through a series of mishaps on the base paths, three Dodgers ended up at third base at the same time. And I was sitting by my father's side, five years before I was born, when the lights were turned on for the first time at Ebbets Field, the crowd gasping and then cheering as the summer night was transformed into startling day.

When I had finished describing the game, it was time to go to bed, unless I could convince my father to tally each player's batting average, reconfiguring his statistics to reflect the developments of that day's game. If Reese went 3 for 5 and had started the day at .303, my father showed me, by adding and multiplying all the numbers in his head, that his average would rise to .305. If Snider went 0 for 4 and started the day at .301, then his average would dip four points below the .300 mark. If Carl Erskine had let in three runs in seven innings, then my father would multiply three times nine, divide that by the number of innings pitched, and magically tell me whether Erskine's earned-run average had improved or worsened. It was this facility with numbers that had made it possible for my father to pass the civil-service test and become a bank examiner despite leaving school after the eighth grade. And this job had carried him from a Brooklyn tenement to a house with a lawn on Southard Avenue in Rockville Centre.

> **I believed that, if I did not recount the games he had missed, my father would never have been able to follow our Dodgers the proper way, day by day, play by play, inning by inning. In other words, without me, his love of baseball would be forever unfulfilled.**

All through that summer, my father kept from me the knowledge that running box scores appeared in the daily newspapers. He never mentioned that these abbreviated histories had been a staple feature of the sports pages since the nineteenth century and were generally the first thing he and his fellow commuters turned to when they opened the *Daily News* and the *Herald Tribune* in the morning. I believed that, if I did not recount the games he had missed, my father would never have been able to follow our Dodgers the proper way, day by day, play by play, inning by inning. In other words, without me, his love of baseball would be forever unfulfilled.

I had the luck to fall in love with baseball at the start of an era of pure delight for New York fans. In each of the nine seasons from 1949 to 1957—spanning much of my childhood—we would watch one of the three New York teams—the Dodgers, the Giants, or the Yankees—compete in the World Series. In this golden era, the Yankees won five consecutive World Series, the Giants won two pennants and one championship, and my beloved Dodgers won one championship and five pennants, while losing two additional pennants in the last inning of the last game of the season.

HANK AND ME

Arn Tellem with his aunt Natalie, his mother, Gerrie Stern, seated with his sister, Roni, and grandparents, Fanny and Ellis Seltzer, on a trip to the Baseball Hall of Fame, August, 1965

I grew up in a Russian Jewish enclave of southwest Philadelphia, smack in the middle of one of the largest Catholic parishes in the United States. The only sport in which my family excelled was chess.

Sundays were spent indoors *patzering* with my uncle, my father, and my father's father. Max Tellem and his brother fled the poverty and pogroms of Lithuania for refuge in faraway lands. Max decamped for Philly, where he worked as a tailor; his brother went to Palestine and became a rabbi. A Talmudic scholar, Max helped start the first yeshiva in the City of Brotherly Love.

My other grandpop, Ellis, was an Eastern European immigrant. Whenever I think of him, I'm reminded of the virtues by which he lived: caring and perseverance, fairness and integrity — virtues that defined his everyday life. Honesty was more important to him than how much you made, where you lived, or what school you went to. Titles, degrees meant *bupkes* — you were measured by your impact on others.

Though the lives of both sets of grandparents revolved around the synagogue, they were proud to be American citizens. They loved sports, especially baseball, and they encouraged me to share that love. My grandparents empathized with the struggles of the Phils, for whom disappointments always lurked around the corner. During the '50s and early '60s, the team set a record for most consecutive last-place seasons. One second baseman, Danny Murtaugh, said: "If Philadelphia even won two games in a row, it would be grounds for a congressional investigation." After a 9–4 drubbing on opening day in 1960, our manager, Eddie Sawyer, retired, saying he was forty-nine years old, and wanted to live to be fifty.

Having made something of their lives in the United States, after arriving with next to nothing, my grandparents admired Franklin Roosevelt as a leader who cared about the dispossessed. They adored Jackie Robinson, too. Both exemplified qualities that they valued, qualities of tolerance, equality, and inclusiveness. My grandparents always encouraged me to speak out for the less fortunate.

They were equally moved by Hank Greenberg and Sandy Koufax, mythical Jewish ballplayers whose achievements went far beyond any of our expectations. Greenberg — the Hebrew Hammer — embodied my grandparents' hopes of assimilation: this talented, handsome, smart gentleman who had even married well. Koufax — the Left Arm of God — won their eternal respect in part by declining to pitch the opening game of the 1965 World Series because it fell on Yom Kippur.

In Philly, our local Jewish sports heroes were Eddie Gottlieb, the owner of the Warriors in the NBA; and Harry Litwack, the Temple University coach. Neither of them looked like Greenberg or Koufax. They looked like they belonged behind a deli counter slicing smoked whitefish. So it should come as no surprise that in our neighborhood any Jew who was successful, athletic, or good-looking was treated with both admiration and fascination.

My father died during Hanukkah in 1966, two months before my bar mitzvah. On the final day of that mournful holiday, my grandfather Ellis and grandmother Fanny gave me the book *The Jew in American Sports*. I read it over and over — no doubt the stories led to my own career in sports. I treasured the chapters on boxers Benny Leonard and Barney Ross, quarterback Sid Luckman, basketball greats Dolph Schayes and Red Auerbach, and, of course, Sidney Franklin, the greatest matador ever to come out of Flatbush. In the section on chess I learned about the prodigies Sammy Reshevsky, Emanuel Lasker, and Bobby Fischer. Notwithstanding Fischer's slow descent into reclusion and madness, his rise to the highest summits of the game remains one of the touchstones of my youth.

I practically memorized the chapters on Koufax and Greenberg. I was already intimately acquainted with Koufax, having written letters asking him to date my mother's unattached sister, Natalie. He didn't take the bait. In reading and rereading about Greenberg, I learned that he had three children: Glenn, Steve, and Alva. They weren't much older than me. Maybe I'd marry Alva? Maybe Glenn and Steve and I would meet someday over a bowl of matzah ball soup. I actually fantasized about such things.

But I never dreamed that twelve years after my dad's death I would be offered a job at a Los Angeles law firm in which Steve Greenberg was an associate. I jumped

BELOW

Arn Tellem with his mentor and colleague, Steve Greenberg, 1981

OPPOSITE

Hank Greenberg card, APBA board game, 1938

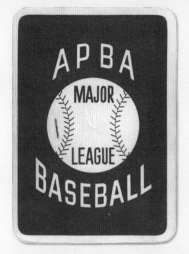

Bats: Right   Throws: Right
Height: 6-3½   Weight: 215
Born:1-11-11 New York City, N.Y.
Henry
"Hank"

GREENBERG

Firstbaseman (4) (OF-1)

11 - 1	31 - 9	51 - 8
12 - 25	32 - 26	52 - 27
13 - 14	33 - 1	53 - 14
14 - 30	34 - 31	54 - 32
15 - 10	35 - 9	55 - 8
16 - 28	36 - 14	56 - 34
21 - 41	41 - 24	61 - 24
22 - 4	42 - 14	62 - 13
23 - 37	43 - 12	63 - 20
24 - 13	44 - 6	64 - 14
25 - 8	45 - 14	65 - 35
26 - 13	46 - 13	66 - 1

My bride, Nancy, asked what I was up to. "I always sleep with Hank next to my bed at night," I said. "Not anymore," she said.

at the opportunity. As well as becoming a close friend and mentor, Steve was my boss in my first baseball practice. I owe him my career.

Through Steve, I befriended Hank, who was larger than life—and at 6 feet 4 inches and 250 pounds, a great deal larger than me. He had a sharp mind and an even sharper sense of humor. I loved to hear Hank reminisce about Lou Gehrig, Babe Ruth, Ted Williams, Joe DiMaggio, and the gefilte fish his mother made him for every home run he hit in 1938. "That was fifty-eight dingers," he told me, "and fifty-eight gefilte fish."

When I got married in 1979, I carried in the breast pocket of my wedding suit a Hank Greenberg card from APBA Major League Baseball, the tabletop game to which I lashed my adolescence. The card lists his statistics during the 1938 season, in which he smacked fifty-eight home runs. I'd wanted Hank to share the most important day of my life.

That night I propped the cherished card on the nightstand next to the conjugal bed. My bride, Nancy, asked what I was up to. "I always sleep with Hank next to my bed at night," I said.

"Not anymore," she said.

A compromise was reached—sort of. I moved Hank to a drawer where Nancy couldn't see him.

In 2006, I became vice chairman of the Wasserman Media Group, a global sports and entertainment marketing agency headed by Casey Wasserman. My focus has been expanding our representation of athletes around the world. Recently, I joined a group that purchased the Hapoel Jerusalem basketball team. This pivot to the front office combines my love of sports with my ties to Israel and my Jewish heritage. I hope to help foster the growth of basketball in Israel, and to bring together people from diverse backgrounds and divided communities.

Hapoel Jerusalem plays in an arena not far from the cemetery in which two of my grandparents are buried. Their plots overlook the Old City and are close by Hadassah Hospital, the most cherished charity of my grandparents Fanny and Ellis. Not long ago, during a visit to Israel, I remembered an encounter with Hank Greenberg. We were having lunch when a woman, a Holocaust survivor, approached our table and told Hank that he was her hero. Deeply touched, Hank thanked her and later told me, "*She* is the true hero." When I think of Hank, my grandparents, their generation, and the adversity they confronted, I'm stirred by their indomitable spirit. Their lives and their actions inspire me to dream more, do more and become more.

SANDY KOUFAX

———

BEST BAT MITZVAH
GUEST EVER

JANE
LEAVY

Sandy Koufax ruined me for other men.

At the beginning of our relationship, I wouldn't have predicted that.
I wouldn't have predicted any relationship at all. At the beginning, before I
was sure I could or would or should write his biography, I told him I hated
his guts because of what he did to Mickey Mantle in the 1963 World Series.

Mickey was my guy. Or: I was a Mickey guy. Either way, I was pretty
sure I was the only Jewish kid on Long Island not rooting for Koufax when
he turned the Cathedral of Baseball into his own personal congregation
during Game 1 of the 1963 World Series.

It was the Dodgers' first appearance at Yankee Stadium since the
Diaspora: NYC versus LA, East Coast establishment versus Hollywood
hip, Koufax versus Mantle. Teachers dragged black-and-white TVs into
classrooms throughout the metropolitan area. A special citywide telephone
number was set up to provide updates. The odds posted against a Dodger
sweep: 25–1.

I worshipped Mickey Mantle from my grandmother's parlor in the
Yankee Arms, an apartment building one very long, very loud foul ball
from home plate. One fine spring day, when I was five, opening day of the
baseball season, we took the CC train downtown to Saks Fifth Avenue to
buy a baseball glove. My grandmother didn't know from sporting goods
or sports—she never crossed the threshold of the the House that Ruth
Built—but she wanted the best for me.

The subway cars still had those old straw seats with bristles that caught
in my tights. We almost missed the stop while trying to untangle me. I
often got tangled up when I tried to be a proper girl. We bought a mitt, the
only one they had, a Sam Esposito model, which was firmly attached to
the hand of a mannequin in the store window. No matter how many times
the salesman demurred—"Madam, it's not for sale"—my grandmother
would not be deterred. I took Sammy home with me and everywhere
else, including to the High Holiday services held in the ballroom of the
Concourse Plaza Hotel at the corner of 161st Street just up the street from
the Stadium. While my grandmother prayed for my future, I prayed for
the Mick.

"Pitching for the Health Department," Sandy Koufax with Jose Henandez, Daniel Bicciche, and Don Lyle Jr. publicizing Dodger immunization clinics, June 5, 1966

Prayer was not enough on October 2, 1963. On that balmy Bronx Wednesday afternoon, in front of sixty-nine thousand new true believers, Koufax declared his preeminence by striking out the first three Yankees he faced on twelve pitches. By the time Mantle led off in the bottom of the second, the Dodgers were leading 4–0. It was one thing for Koufax to have his way with Tony Kubek, Bobby Richardson, and Tom Tresh, but this was the Mick.

This at bat would set the tone for all the innings to come.
Swing and a miss. Strike one.
High with a fastball. Ball one.
Foul back on the screen. Strike two.

"Then he struck him out with a fastball around the letters," the late Dodger catcher John Roseboro told me. "Mantle looked back at me and said, 'How in the fuck are you supposed to hit that shit?'"

He couldn't. They couldn't. The afternoon waned. Shadows cut the diamond in half, engulfing the plate in an early gloaming. With the ball emerging out of the sun and the white shirts in the center-field bleachers and each pitch coming over the top with a perfect and repetitive motion, Koufax lulled and dulled Yankee reflexes. His fifteenth strikeout, with two outs in the bottom of the ninth, broke Carl Erskine's record, set in the 1953 World Series between the Yankees and the Brooklyn Dodgers. In the locker room, Koufax told Erskine, "You know, Carl, in the eighth inning I just thought to myself how great it would be just to share that record with you."

After the Yankees lost the next game to Johnny Podres, there was little to do but pray. "Aren't there any more Jewish holidays?" Yankee third baseman Clete Boyer asked aboard the team bus. "You mean like Yom *Koufax*?" Mantle replied.

Don Drysdale shut out the Yankees in Game 3 in Los Angeles. Koufax punctuated Mantle's futility in Game 4 with a ninth inning curve that broke like a comma over home plate, and sentenced my Yankees to a winter of wishful thinking. Mickey would never be the same again.

The next year, Koufax pitched the third no-hitter of his career, struck out more than two hundred batters for the fourth consecutive season, and was diagnosed with traumatic arthritis in his left elbow: a diagnosis then without a cure. Koufax and the Dodgers would have to wait until next year—to see how much more he had left in his left arm.

The National League pennant had yet to be decided when Major League Baseball announced on September 9, 1965, that the first game of the World Series would be played on Yom Kippur. That evening Koufax pitched a perfect game against the Chicago Cubs and told reporters, "I'm praying for rain."

Three weeks later, he achieved another kind of perfection. When he refused to pitch Game 1 of the Series against the Minnesota Twins, he was inscribed forever in the Book of Life and in popular culture. John Goodman's character distilled his importance in *The Big Lebowski:* "Three thousand years of beautiful tradition: from Moses to Sandy Koufax." He became a New American Patriarch: Abraham, Isaac, Jacob, and *Sandee,* a pitcher defined as much by what he refused to do as by what he could do with a baseball in his left hand.

The Jewish community laid claim to him, including several rabbis who swore, erroneously, that he was in their synagogues that afternoon. But he was more dutiful than devout, respectful of his parents and his community. He had never pitched on the High Holidays and saw no reason to change just because of the World Series. *What's the big schmeer? So Drysdale will start Game 1 instead.*

Drysdale got hammered. The score was 7–1 when Alston came to the mound to relieve him. "Hey, Skip, bet you wish I was Jewish today, too," Drysdale said. For Jews, the loss was a win. If Big D, the big goy, could joke about being one of the Chosen People, that was already something, a tacit acknowledgement of their acceptance into the mainstream. *Shtetl, farewell.*

It would take years for Koufax to assimilate the meaning his gesture had for others, in part because it was so reflexive for him. His long-held silence was far more eloquent, in my view, than the comments he made for the 2010 documentary *Jews and Baseball: An American Love Story.* Typical Koufax: he didn't like the first take and offered to come back and redo the segment. "I had taken Yom Kippur off for ten years," he told producer Peter Miller, the second time around. "It's just something I'd always done as respect. But I could always do something about it. There was always a game the day before. So I'd move up and pitch on two days rest so I wouldn't miss a start at the end of the season. But this day there was no game the day before."

He pitched Game 7 of the 1965 World Series on two days' rest, and he was pitching on fumes—as well as Codeine and Butazolidin, an anti-inflammatory drug so toxic it has since been taken off the market. When he walked two batters in the first inning, Drysdale got up in the bullpen. He was a two-pitch pitcher without a second pitch. Roseboro went to the mound for a conversation. For the first time, Koufax acknowledged how bad his elbow was—in fact, he had already decided that the 1966 season would be his last. "He said, 'Rosie, my arm's not right. My arm's sore,'" Roseboro told me. "I said, 'What'll we do, kid?' He said, 'Fuck it, we'll blow 'em away.'"

He did. It was his second shutout in four days and twenty-ninth complete game of the year. At the end, he was too tired to celebrate.

Koufax didn't just challenge batters; he challenged stereotypes of Jewish beauty and toughness and athleticism. "Think of the stereotype of the Jew in literature, the ugly avariciousness of Shylock," said my rabbi, M. Bruce Lustig. "Here was a good-looking Jew, a lefty, very powerful on

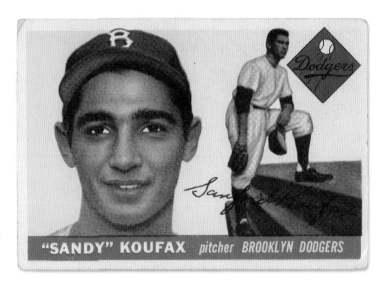

"SANDY" KOUFAX *pitcher* BROOKLYN DODGERS

Koufax didn't just challenge batters; he challenged stereotypes of Jewish beauty and toughness and athleticism.

ABOVE

Sandy Koufax rookie card, Brooklyn Dodgers, 1955

OPPOSITE

"It's a Perfect Night at Dodger Stadium: Koufax Becomes the First Player to Pitch Four No-Hitters," *Los Angeles Times,* September 10, 1965

IT'S A PERFECT NIGHT AT DODGER STADIUM

Koufax Becomes First Player to Pitch Four No-Hitters

JIM MURRAY

The Law Breaker

If the Pittsburgh Pirates win the 1965 National League pennant—and shop for a price if you think—don't bother to send champagne for the victory party. There won't be any.

And, if the Pittsburgh Pirates don't win the 1965 National League pennant, it will be because they won the 1960 N.L. pennant—and had a victory party.

It was on the bus back from the pennant-clinching win in Milwaukee. A few of the boys were whooping it up; the champagne was flowing, laced with beer. Elroy Face took his teeth out and put his hat on sideways, a quartet got going, off-key, in the back of the bus and everybody was happy.

Or, almost everybody. In a front seat, the team's most valuable member, the pitcher who was to win the Cy Young Award and beat the Yankees twice in the upcoming World Series, looked more like a guy who had just heard Paris fell.

When anyone sits this sombre in the midst of a gay party, you all know what the next scene is: some guy with a lampshade on his head and wearing a grass skirt, with his glasses fogged up, comes along and shouts, "Shay! You don't look like you're havin' fun!" And he empties a bottle of champagne over your new suit, or pushes you in the pool or dumps a giggling girl in your lap just as your wife enters the room.

A Playful Yank Proved Expensive

They didn't exactly do this to Vernon Sanders Law that September afternoon in 1960. But a utility player whose contribution to the victory that season could not be found without a microscope, came playfully up to Law and grabbed him by the foot. He gave it a yank—the most expensive leg pull in history. He not only sprained Law's ankle, he fractured Pittsburgh's pennant chances for four years.

Vernon Law pitched in the World Series, favoring an ankle that made him wince on every follow-through. What happened next is what always happens next when a pitcher favors an injured leg—the unnatural motion tore a rotator muscle in his shoulder. He beat the Yanks twice, but each pitch shortened his career. The next spring he showed up in camp with an arm so stiff and sore, it looked as if it were tacked on his side. The 20-game winner in 1960 became a 3-game winner in 1961. He pitched only 59 innings, but he had to clench his teeth to keep from screaming during most of them.

Vern Law occupies the same unique position on the Pittsburgh Pirates that Albie Pearson does on the Angels, Don Demeter on the Tigers, Bobby Richardson on the Yankees and a handful of other players around the leagues. He is a tither, a teetotaler. The Pirates call him "Deacon," because ballplayers call anybody "Deacon" who goes to church on Sundays and to bed before midnight.

Profanity Cut to a Minimum

Actually, Vern Law is an ordained Elder in the Mormon Church. The Pirates respect him for his beliefs even though they know if he wandered into Frankie's Band-Box saloon in Pittsburgh, it would be to use the phone or to get out of an earthquake. The profanity is cut to a minimum in his corner of the locker room where the scholarly Bob Veale and the abstemious Del Crandall also suit up. It is a section of the dressing room one of the players refers to affectionately as "The Monastery" and where he has recommended stained-glass windows for their shower.

Although Vern Law is the most expensive casualty of the post-pennant victory party, he is not the only one. In 1941, Leo Durocher's Brooklyn Dodgers were rolling south from Boston on the New York-New Haven-and-Hartford Railroad and the grape was flowing and the hats were on sideways. When the victory train rolled into 125th St. owner Larry MacPhail, never a man to pass up a drink, wanted to get aboard. "Drive on!" Leo instructed the trainmen. And they did—leaving MacPhail sputtering on the platform. Leo Durocher was the first manager ever to get fired while he was being carried off on the shoulders of his countrymen.

In 1960, when the Yankees celebrated winning their pennant, the pitcher, Ryne Duren, elected to push a lighted cigar into the mouth of a bullpen coach. The bullpen coach turned out to be Ralph Houk, and, the next season, Ralph Houk turned out to be the Yankee manager, and it turned out if he wanted to chew tobacco he didn't want it to be lighted, and Ryne Duren turned out to be on the Los Angeles roster by late spring.

Houk didn't get much for him, but rumor had it, he didn't want much for him—just a lot of geography. The feeling was Houk just traded him as far away as he could without a passport.

If the Pirates win this year, (and if they do, the biggest part of the reason will be the 16 games Law won this year between arm twinges) the victory party won't be bobbing for apples at the YMCA, or fruit punch and sarsparilla, but you can bet me that the Pirates' general manager, Joe Brown, will make sure anything his athletes do is not against the Law.

Ralston Suffers Upset

STORY ON PAGE 5

HAPPY SANDY — Dodgers' Sandy Koufax is congratulated by teammates Willie Davis and Ron Fairly moments after Sandy had completed hurling a perfect game agains the Chicago Cubs. It was Sandy's fourth major league no-hitter, an all-time baseball record.

UPI photo

Los Angeles Times

Sports

PART III BUSINESS & FINANCE

CC FRIDAY MORNING, SEPTEMBER 10, 1965 2†

Hendley Loses, 1-0, on 1-Hitter

BY FRANK FINCH
Times Staff Writer

A Michelangelo among pitchers, Sandy Koufax produced his masterpiece Thursday night when he pitched a perfect no-hit, no-run game against the Chicago Cubs.

The score was a nervous 1-0, as Koufax's opponent, Bob Hendley, allowed Los Angeles only one hit in eight innings.

The game's sole tally was unearned.

Lou Johnson drew Hendley's only walk to begin the fifth inning. Sacrificed to second by Ron Fairly, the speedy outfielder then stole third base and kept on coming when catcher Chris Krug's hurried throw sailed into left field.

Johnson also blooped a double in the seventh for the thriller's only hit.

Huge Roar

A crowd of 29.139 fans rocked Dodger Stadium with their roaring as Koufax struck out the last six batters for a total of 14—the 79th time in his career and the 18th time this season Sandy has fanned 10 or more batters in a game.

Koufax finally attained his 22nd victory after failing in five previous attempts and now leads both majors in wins and strikeouts. Juan Marichal of the Giants notched his 21st victory Thursday afternoon as the Giants remained a half-game ahead of Los Angeles and Cincinnati.

Tension in the last two innings was almost unbearable as the Cubs attacked Koufax in a vain effort to break his magic spell.

Banks Fans

In the eighth inning, he threw a called third strike past Ron Santo and sent Ernie Banks and rookie Byron Browne down swinging.

Now he needed just three more outs to become the first pitcher in history to record four no-hit games.

The first batter in the ninth was Krug, and he struck out swinging.

A tough pinch hitter, Joe Amalfitano, fanned on three serves.

..... And It's Over

Another crafty batsman, Harvey Kuenn, batted for Hendley. With a count of two balls and two strikes Kuenn swung viciously at a fast ball—and missed it by a mile.

Sandy danced off the

Please Turn to Pg. 2, Col. 4

Counting the House

Thursday's attendance	29,139
1965 attendance, 65 dates	2,077,238
1964 attendance, 65 dates	2,021,112

WOW!

CHICAGO	ab	r	h	bi	LOS ANGELES	ab	r	h	bi
Young cf	3	0	0	0	Wills ss	3	0	0	0
Beckert 2b	3	0	0	0	Gilliam 3b	3	0	0	0
Williams rf	3	0	0	0	Kennedy 3b	0	0	0	0
Santo 3b	3	0	0	0	Davis cf	3	0	0	0
Banks 1b	3	0	0	0	Johnson lf	2	1	1	0
Browne lf	3	0	0	0	Fairly rf	2	0	0	0
Krug c	3	0	0	0	Lefebvre 2b	3	0	0	0
Kess'ger ss	2	0	0	0	T'cewski 2b	0	0	0	0
Am'f'ano ph	1	0	0	0	Parker 1b	3	0	0	0
Hendley p	2	0	0	0	Torborg c	3	0	0	0
Kuenn ph	1	0	0	0	Koufax p	2	0	0	0
Totals	27	0	0	0	Totals	24	1	1	0

Chicago .... 000 000 000—0
Los Angeles .... 000 010 00x—1

E—Krug. LOB—Chicago 0, Los Angeles 1.
2B—Johnson. SB—Johnson. S—Fairly.

	IP	H	R	ER	BB	SO
Hendley L, 2-3	8	1	1	0	1	3
Koufax W, 22-7	9	0	0	0	0	14

T—1:43. A—29,139.

Alston Would Prefer Twins to White Sox

BY CHARLES MAHER
Times Staff Writer

Walter Alston inspected the remaining National League schedule and conceded at once that Pittsburgh, among the five contenders, has the best of it on paper.

But Wlter Alston dosen't believe everything he reads on paper.

The Pirates have 19 games left. Except for three with Cincinnati this week, they're all against second-division teams.

"I don't think that means a helluva lot," the Dodger manager said. "For one thing, there's not that much difference between the top clubs and the rest of them, with maybe one or two exceptions.

"Like I've said before, I'd rather have my own club going good and playing the best of them than have it going not so good and playing the weaker ones. If you're not going good, about any of them can beat you."

Alston was asked which of the other four contenders concerns him most.

"Milwaukee has been the toughest for us to beat," he said. "But I think I'd agree with what Tom Haller (the San Francisco catcher) said the other day—that Cincinnati has the best balance."

The Dodgers, of course, are not without arresting attributes themselves. They have pitching and speed. Moreover, they have successfully inverted the formula of their gasoline sponsors and are eminently entitled to acclaim as the team that took the Pow! out of Power.

If their attack should develop enough thrust to put them in the World Series, Aston would rather have them play the Minnesota Twins than the Chicago White Sox. Minnesota's power worries him less than Chicago's lack of it.

"With our pitching," he said, "I'd just as soon play the hard-hitting club. Turning it around the oth-

Please Turn to Pg. 3, Col. 3

Juan Cheered, Whips Astros for No. 21, 4-0

SAN FRANCISCO (AP) — Right-hander Juan Marichal made his first start in San Francisco's Candlestick Park since his Aug. 22 battle with John Roseboro and hurled the National League-leading Giants to a 4-0 triumph over Houston.

The crowd of 20,076 cheered Marichal when he went out for his pre-game warm-up and when he faced the first Houston batter.

Marichal notched his 21st victory of the campaign and his 10th shutout, limiting the Astros to four hits.

The Giants won their sixth straight, jumping into a two-run lead in the second inning on a walk to Willie McCovey, a triple by Len Gabrielson and Tom Haller's sacrifice fly.

HOUSTON	ab	r	h	bi	SAN FRANCISCO	ab	r	h	bi
Maye lf	4	0	0	0	Schofield ss	4	1	1	0
Morgan 2b	4	0	0	0	J.Alou rf	4	0	1	1
Wynn cf	3	0	1	0	Mays cf	3	0	0	0
Bond 1b	4	0	1	0	Hend'son cf	1	0	0	0
Aspro'te 3b	3	0	0	0	McCovey 1b	2	1	1	0
Staub rf	3	0	1	0	Hart 3b	3	0	0	0
Brand c	1	0	0	0	G'br'ls'n lf	3	1	1	1
Adiesh c	2	0	1	0	Haller c	2	1	1	2
Kasko ss	3	0	0	0	Lanier 2b	3	0	0	0
Bruce p	2	0	0	0	Marichal p	3	0	0	0
Gentile ph	1	0	0	0					
Totals	30	0	4	0	Totals	28	4	5	4

Houston .... 000 000 000—0
San Francisco .... 020 020 00x—4

Errors—None. DP—San Francisco 1. LOB—Houston 4, San Francisco 2.
2B—Schofield, Wynn. 3B—Gabrielson. HR—Haller (12). SB—Wynn. SF—Haller.

	IP	H	R	ER	BB	SO
Bruce L, 9-18	7	5	4	4	1	4
Raymond	1	0	0	0	0	2
Marichal W, 21-10	9	4	0	0	1	5

WP—Bruce 2. T—1:55. A—20,076.

TODAY IN SPORTS

HORSE RACING—Del Mar, first post 2 p.m.

BASEBALL—Houston vs. Dodgers, Dodger Stadium, 8 p.m.

MOTORCYCLE RACING—Ascot Park, National AMA 8-mile qualifying, novice program, 7 p.m.

AUTO RACING — Southgate Raceway, NMRA midgets, 8 p.m.

RADIO-TELEVISION

BASEBALL — Angels at Washington, KMPC, 5 p.m.; Houston vs. Dodgers, KFI, KWKW, 8 p.m.

ALL AGREED

Even Koufax Admits Game 'Nearly Perfect'

BY CHARLES MAHER
Times Staff Writer

Sandy Koufax is normally as modest and unassuming as Clark Kent, but even he had to agree with the scorebook, which said the game he pitched against the Chicago Cubs Thursday night was nearly perfect.

"You mean," someone asked, "that there wasn't a pitch you didn't want back right after you threw it?"

"No," Koufax said, "I don't think so. Well, there was one I threw to Byron Browne in the second inning that I didn't want back as soon as I let it go. But I wanted it back after he hit it."

Four No-Hitters

Browne hit it on a line to center fielder Willie Davis, coming as close as the Cubs got to a hit all night.

Koufax has pitched a no-hitter a year for four seasons and he said this gave him more satisfaction than the first two (against the Mets and the Giants) and as much as the third (against Philadelphia).

He conceded the fourth one should be most gratifying because no one else has ever pitched more than three. "But the third," he said, "was equally thrilling."

Good Fastball

"I think the stuff I had tonight was the best I've had all season," he said. "I had a real good fastball, and that sort of helps your curve. I thought the fastball was really working best the last three innings.

"You always know when you've got a no-hitter going, but you don't particularly pay attention to it early in the game. In the seventh, I really started to feel as though I had a shot at it.

"But I still had only one run to work on. I still had to win the game."

Koufax offered his sympathy to Bob Hendley, who followed the Dodgers only one hit, the bloop double in the seventh by Lou Johnson.

Unearned Run

The hit would have been meaningless if it hadn't broken up Hendley's no-hitter because the Dodgers scored their only run two innings before on a walk, a sacrifice, a stolen base by Johnson and a throwing error by catcher Chris Krug on Johnson's steal.

"It's a shame Hendley had to get beaten that way," Koufax said. "But I'm glad we got the run or we might have been here all night."

Wanted Hit

Koufax came closest to losing his perfect game in the seventh, when he went three balls and no strikes to Billy williams.

"I threw him two curves low," Sandy said, "and then I was high with a fastball."

Williams was asked if he was looking for a walk at this point.

"I was looking for a base

Please Turn to Pg. 4, Col. 1

BASEBALL STANDINGS

NATIONAL LEAGUE

	W	L	Pct.	GBL
San Francisco	79	59	.572	
DODGERS	80	61	.567	½
Cincinnati	80	61	.567	½
Milwaukee	77	62	.554	2½
Pittsburgh	77	66	.538	4½
Philadelphia	71	68	.511	8½
St. Louis	70	71	.496	10½
Chicago	65	77	.458	16
Houston	60	81	.426	20½
New York	45	98	.315	36½

Thursday's Results

DODGERS 1, Chicago 0
Cincinnati 3, New York 2
Philadelphia at Milwaukee, postponed, rain
San Francisco 4, Houston 0
Only games scheduled

Today's Schedule

Houston (Roberts, 9-8) vs. DODGERS (Drysdale, 18-12), Dodger Stadium, KFI, KWKW, 8 p.m.

Milwaukee (Blasingame, 16-9) at New York (Fisher, 8-19), night.

St. Louis (Gibson, 17-10) at Philadelphia (Short, 16-9), night.

Cincinnati (Jay, 9-8) at Pittsburgh (Veale, 15-10), night.

Chicago (Ellsworth, 13-13) at San Francisco (Herbel, 9-1), night.

AMERICAN LEAGUE

	W	L	Pct.	GBL
Minnesota	89	54	.622	
Chicago	82	61	.573	7
Baltimore	80	60	.571	7½
Cleveland	77	63	.550	10½
Detroit	78	64	.549	10½
New York	69	75	.479	21½
ANGELS	66	77	.462	23
Washington	62	80	.437	26½
Boston	56	87	.392	28
Kansas City	51	89	.364	36½

Thursday's Results

ANGELS 7, Kansas City 2
Minnesota 10, Chicago 4
Only games scheduled

Today's Schedule

ANGELS (Brunet, 8-10) at Washington (Richert, 12-10), KMPC, 5 p.m.

Kansas City (Sheldon, 7-7 and Hunter, 6-6) at Baltimore (Pappas, 12-7 and J. Miller, 6-3), twi-night doubleheader.

Minnesota (Perry, 9-6) at Boston (Lonborg, 9-15), night.

Detroit (Lolich, 11-8) at Cleveland (Siebert, 14-8), night.

New York (Stottlemyre, 18-8) at Chicago (Peters, 9-11), night.

Versalles, Desire Make Twins Tick

BY JOHN HALL
Times Staff Writer

CHICAGO — What puts the tick-tick in the American League time bomb known as the Minnesota Twins?

Al Campanis, L.A. Operator 007 whom the Dodgers dispatched here to investigate the lonely leaders in their latest moment of truth with the White Sox, opened his case full of charts and diagrams Thursday and delivered a preliminary diagnosis.

"Zoilo Versalles, underrated pitching, timely hitting and big desire," capsuled the chief of the Dodger scouts.

"But without Harmon Killebrew their power isn't overwhelming, their defense is average and they have real speed in only a couple of spots," he said.

"If the Dodgers can make it home in the National, it's going to be interesting to see what our pitching can do to their hitting. Dodger Stadium isn't going to help the Twins."

Without saying directly, Campanis gave the impression he agreed with the general suspicion that winning the World Series will be a much better bet for the Dodgers than surviving in the National League.

Nonetheless, the Twins continue to demonstrate they are tough to master.

Making it a two-in-a-row sweep over the suddenly flat and fractured Sox with a 10-4 death rattle Thursday, Minnesota moved a safe seven jumps ahead of Chicago and 7½ in front of the idle Baltimore and impressively erased all remaining doubts.

Sam Mele's lineup was the same for both battles at Comiskey Park, and it will probably be the same for the World Series opener Oct. 6 in Metropolitan Sta-

Please Turn to Pg. 4, Col. 3

Sandy Koufax pitching against the
Minnesota Twins in Game 7 of the
1965 World Series

the mound; a perfect player, a man who didn't reach for fame or money. He broadened the concept of what a Jew is."

A year after the publication of *Sandy Koufax: A Lefty's Legacy*, my daughter became a bat mitzvah. Like most overly indulgent Jewish parents, I told her she could invite anyone. In the stack of envelopes she handed me a month later, I found an invitation for Sandy Koufax.

By then I knew Koufax well enough to know that he is "a very Jewish being," as his friend New York Mets owner Fred Wilpon put it, but he is not a practicing Jew. I also knew him well enough to know that being the center of attention of two hundred fifty Jews of a certain age is not his idea of a good time.

But I had promised my daughter.

I called Sandy and told him he was going to get an invitation. I told him he didn't have to come. "You don't have to do this," I said.

I remember his reply. "I'll be there for Emma. After all, I'm the guy who's taken her mother away from her for the last two years."

Who knew I was rooting for the wrong guy?

Despite a five-hour drive from his home in Pennsylvania, he and the woman who would become his wife were the first guests to arrive. I saw him standing alone, impeccably dressed, reading the synagogue bulletin as the horde descended. I grabbed his elbow and dragged him into the rabbi's study.

Every bar or bat mitzvah in every *shul* in America would kill (commandment violation) to have Koufax in attendance, if only because every parent and every rabbi would kill to have him in the congregation. Our rabbi was no exception. As a young boy, Bruce Lustig snuck a transistor radio into the sanctuary during Game 1 of the 1965 Series, running the wire up the sleeve of his white dress shirt. When the congregants were called to stand and pray, the earpiece came loose and Vin Scully's voice crackled through the congregation. His mother banished him to the library, where the TV was tuned to NBC's coverage of The Game Koufax Refused to Pitch.

In Lustig's study at Washington Hebrew Congregation, Koufax signed baseballs for the rabbi and the cantor, for Emma's four grandparents, and for the family of the young man who shared the bimah with her that day. He also offered an impromptu tutorial on the mechanics of throwing a curveball and potential injury to young soft tissue, thereby providing the rabbi with new material for future sermons on the godliness of Sandy Koufax.

When the service ended, Sandy got in his car and drove home. The party went on without him, on a paddleboat that set sail an hour late on the Potomac River. This was two weeks after 9/11, and I'm thinking, "Oh my God, we're sitting ducks." On board, I was greeted by well-wishers with other concerns. "Too good for us, huh?" they said, as if offering condolences.

Their knowing cynicism was as unseemly as it was unwarranted. I knew Sandy's decision had nothing to do with the guest list or the decidedly unkosher menu of barbecued chicken and ribs. (The rabbi promised to look the other way if I did when he helped himself.)

He chose not to attend Emma's party because, having lived in the hot center of unwelcome attention for so long, he knew that his presence would have deprived my daughter of her star turn.

Sandy Koufax holds up twenty baseballs in the dressing room after becoming the first major league pitcher to achieve that many wins in the 1965 season, August 11, 1965

Koufax is the rare public figure who eschews public life as it is led on Page Six (now appearing on page thirteen) of the *New York Post* or on the proliferating websites devoted to consuming what little is left of American privacy. This is not because he is a recluse or a misanthrope or a snob, but because, in defiance of modern convention, he refuses to trade parts of his soul for "mentions" and "items" and "sound bites." His ego does not require those ministrations.

Nor did he need baseball to know who he was, making him one of the true athletic elite: those who absent themselves when the consequences of playing on outweigh the psychic or monetary benefits of doing so. He quit at the height of his popularity and success after winning twenty-seven (complete) games in 1966. He could still pitch but he could no longer straighten his left arm. He could not envision a whole life of not being whole. Quitting was an act of imagination and emancipation. It required the ability to conceive of an existence as full and as important as the one he had so publicly led.

The day after my daughter's bat mitzvah, I returned to my desk to finish writing the biography he didn't want written. I didn't tell this story in the book, in deference to his privacy as well as Emma's, and I hope they will forgive me for telling it now. But his absence aboard the *Cherry Blossom* made his presence felt in what I wrote: "To the extent that he removed himself from public view, it was not so much because he believed there are no second acts in American life as because he was determined to have one."

More than a decade has passed since my daughter was called to the Torah. We survived the cruise. Sandy survived the publication of what he sometimes calls "an unauthorized biography by a very nice lady." I wanted to call it *Sandy Koufax: Past Perfect*. The publisher objected—"sounds like a French novel." Koufax would have objected on other grounds.

People ask me all the time what he thought of the book. I always reply that as far as I know, he hasn't read it. If he were the kind of guy who wanted to read 266 pages about himself, he wouldn't be the guy I described in the book: a guy who called attention to himself at a charity golf tournament only after Bob Costas neglected to introduce him in alphabetical order along with the other celebs. Costas got all the way to the R's before he realized his mistake.

"And, of course, who could forget the great Sandy Koufax?" the mortified emcee said, having done just that.

Koufax was delighted. For once, he was an afterthought. "Bob! Bob!" he said, rising from his seat. "K comes after R in the Jewish alphabet!"

I often think about the prescient words offered by a friend while I was wrangling the final Koufax manuscript to the ground: "You have no idea how lucky you are to be writing about someone you like."

Now I know.

The only thing wrong with Sandy Koufax is that he isn't single.

MINOR LEAGUERS

CHASING THE DREAM AND TOUCHING HOME

WILLIAM RESSLER

The traditional story arc is well known: Jews come to America, Jews play baseball, Jews feel more American. In the late nineteenth and early twentieth centuries, that narrative made sense. Today? Not so much. Lengthy interviews with fifty-four Jewish minor leaguers, conducted between June 2011 and October 2013, reveal a different story line. They came to baseball already feeling American but—given the demands of baseball—with less time for Jewish involvement. Then they reach the minor leagues, and—not all, but more than one might expect—they look for ways to reconnect with the Jewishness of their youth. At some point, the narrative flipped, and baseball went from a way for American Jews to feel more American to a way for Jewish Americans to feel more Jewish.

RECAPTURING JEWISH IDENTITY

On the surface, it makes little sense. Life in the minor leagues should make Jewish identification less likely. Players endure long bus rides, cramped and often squalid living conditions, and bad food, while playing "in different geographic locations [where] it's almost frowned upon to be Jewish."[1] In short, "it's really not an ideal way to live." It's certainly not an ideal way to live Jewishly. With their Jewish expression tied to home and family, living far from both adds to the challenge. "We try to celebrate anything we can as much as we can. It's always tough, 'cause I'm always on the road, I'm always gone."

Despite these obstacles, many Jews in the minors express a renewed Jewish identification. "Since I got in pro ball, I've gotten back into helping the Jewish community." They reclaim Jewish identity. "Once I started playing pro baseball, it kind of came back." Why? Explanations come from Jewish minor leaguers themselves and can be grouped into five categories.

THE DYNAMIC NATURE OF JEWISH IDENTITY

Although they come from a range of Jewish backgrounds, Jewish minor leaguers begin their baseball journeys with meaningful Jewish identities strongly tied to family celebrations and community involvement. For observant and nonobservant Jews alike, this changes at about bar mitzvah age, thirteen, when "baseball kinda takes over." Friday-night dinners, Hebrew school, and synagogue attendance give way to practices, games, and travel. That is not to say that young Jews who choose to play baseball competitively stop feeling Jewish. Many continue to look for ways to express their Jewish identities, but for those who aspire to the highest levels of the game, baseball takes precedence. "I didn't lose [my identification with being Jewish], but I didn't practice it as much after my bar mitzvah, and I started making decisions about what I wanted to do, and eventually it just turned into such a time-consuming thing, playing baseball, that I wasn't around on Saturdays to go to temple, [and] I wasn't around on Friday nights as much."

Because Jewish identification is "not a time line, [but] a big circle, it's never too far away." Jewish ballplayers are ready, then, for changes that occur as they reach the minor leagues, changes that cause them to look inward and to reconnect with dormant Jewish identities.

Some suggest that being in the minors coincides with a time in their lives when they begin to contemplate starting a family. That leads them to reexamine a part of themselves that they strongly associate with family—Jewish identity.

Others believe that professional baseball encourages exploring identity. "That's when you find out more about yourself, because a lot of professional baseball is soul searching, [and] if you don't find out who you are—minor league baseball's a tough road.... You want to find out more about yourself; you want to find out more about where you come from."

Many feel that fan reactions prime this exploration. "Until I started playing professional baseball, I didn't realize how important [I would be] to the Jewish community." That, they say, feels good. Community interactions rekindle childhood memories that connect baseball, family, and heritage, leading minor leaguers to recall the "generational love for baseball in the American Jewish community" that "makes me want to have a stronger connection to my heritage."

THE UNFORGIVING NATURE OF PLAYER EVALUATION

The intense competition and high probability of failing—day to day and year to year—create tremendous pressure. Baseball's obsession with reducing a person to a complex set of formulas is especially frustrating. "We're identified for one thing and one thing only—how we're performing—and that's one of the things about the game that I dislike: it's just about statistics." Jewish identification can help minor leaguers cope when those numbers go down as well as when the numbers come back up.

Slumps, of course, are inevitable. "It's a cruel game. It's a game of failure." Mired in a slump, statistics can become stifling. Jewish minor

PREVIOUS

Harbor Yard ballpark with the Bridgeport power station in the background during a game between the Bridgeport Bluefish and York Revolution, Bridgeport, Connecticut, April 28, 2013

RIGHT

Minor league player Jake Lemmerman praying at the Western Wall while on a Taglit-Birthright Israel trip, Jerusalem, Israel, ca. 2012

"A lot of heritage and religion comes into the mental game.... It's just more peace of mind." That peace of mind is part of the emotional and mental strength necessary to reach the major leagues.

leaguers say they "need a balance," and Jewish identity provides it. "A lot of heritage and religion comes into the mental game.... It's just more peace of mind." That peace of mind is part of the emotional and mental strength necessary to reach the major leagues. "[Minor league baseball] is for strong people, and if you're not strong, it's gonna be tough." Standing out as a *Jewish* ballplayer directs attention to minor leaguers' personal selves, allowing them to see themselves and to be seen by others as more than just athletes, more than just a set of numbers. That helps give them the inner strength necessary to advance. "I think that's what makes people reconnect and feel more Jewish."

At the other extreme, during times of success, minor leaguers fear that their accomplishments will get lost within the indistinguishable mass of players and numbers. Being openly Jewish can draw attention to on-field successes. "They always say in the minor leagues, 'What way can you distinguish yourself from other players?' because that's what will get you to the big leagues. So [being a Jewish baseball player] on top of the skill set that you have, you put yourself in a pretty good position.... They'll notice you more."

THE CHANGING NATURE OF BASEBALL

Baseball's status as national pastime may be in flux. Its appeal seems less and less national and increasingly local, and the minor leagues embody and embrace this trend. Indeed, minor league teams are referred to as the community's front porch because they thrive on and strengthen feelings of community. Jewish minor leaguers acknowledge that they play within and for an additional community, the Jewish community, which feels local yet cuts across location.

The 2012 Qualifiers of the World Baseball Classic (WBC) underscored this. American Jewish minor leaguers who participated felt that even while wearing "Israel" on their chests they were "Team Jew" too. "I think people from all over the country will feel like they're rooting for their hometown team when they see us playing." Beyond the WBC, some ballplayers feel their Jewish identity more strongly because they feel part of the Jewish community's "hometown team," wherever they are in the minor leagues. Playing professionally places them on the American Jewish community's front porch.

THE SUPPORTIVE NATURE OF JEWISH COMMUNITY

Jews in the minor leagues express their appreciation for the "special bond [Jews] share"; the ability to "immediately identify"; the sense that "you've always got someone in your corner"; and the feeling that "we're all one and we're all part of the same thing, same family." Many Jews in the minors, especially in the low minors, benefit from support that they see as unconditional. For example, although major leaguers certainly receive attention from fans, only certain minor leaguers do. "Top prospects get [mail from fans] every day, but I never get that, but [a fan wrote me and] said he was Jewish and he followed me because I was a Jewish baseball player and wanted my autograph, so that was like the coolest thing that's ever happened by far." Fan support contributes to the inner personal-professional balance that minor leaguers seek: Jewish players are reminded that Jewish fans look up to them as Jews, not just as ballplayers. One player, who sees himself as a role model for Jewish identity, declared he is "making it cool to be Jewish."

Relationships with other Jews in the minor leagues are especially beneficial in the "selfish, cutthroat" world of minor league baseball. "We're all watching out for each other a little bit." Jewish minor leaguers describe themselves as "a fraternity," as "brothers" or "cousins"—"you feel like family, right off the bat." When Hebrew-speaking members of Israel's World Baseball Classic team wanted to introduce their American Jewish counterparts to Hebrew, one expression that the Americans seemed to remember most was *ach sheli*. "I love that one—'my brother.'"

THE FAMILIAL NATURE OF JEWISH – AND BASEBALL – BEGINNINGS

Jews in the minor leagues say that both their Jewish identification and their baseball careers are rooted in family. One player feels that his Jewish upbringing, guided by his father's love, made him a better ballplayer. Another identifies baseball with "hearing my dad always talk about Sandy Koufax," adding, "I guess that would be who I would recognize the most [as my hero]." When asked which one he meant, his dad or Koufax, he smiled: "My dad. Definitely my dad."

Reconnecting to Jewish identity, through interactions with fans and with other Jews in the minor leagues, allows Jewish minor leaguers to recapture the personal and interpersonal joys that, together with their families, they originally found in baseball. It is why, far from home, Jewish minor leaguers welcome connections that feel like family, that offer reassuring continuity. "It's a very family-oriented religion, and it's always great to see family come in, come watch me play, and get to be together…. Getting to be a role model for [them]—it's a blessing."

LOOKING BACK IN ORDER TO MOVE FORWARD

Dreaming of the future brings many Jewish minor leaguers back to Jewish identity, which, in turn, points them toward the future. Renewed identity spurs interest in Israel and raises hopes of traveling there (again, for some) with family or other Jewish minor leaguers. It fosters their

Team Israel with Jeremy Gould, number 26, celebrating their win against South Africa during a qualifying game in the World Baseball Classic, September 19, 2012

desire to resume learning about their heritage. At the same time, it helps them to become better ballplayers: psychologically stronger, more balanced.

A former minor leaguer wrote, "When you lose yourself in the game, as you must, it's all too easy to lose your sense of home."[2] Perhaps that fear is ultimately what drives Jewish minor leaguers to reconnect with their Jewish backgrounds, for in the end, playing minor league baseball is a process of returning to the place where Jewish identification and baseball careers always begin: chasing their dreams brings Jewish minor leaguers "a little bit closer to home."

Notes

1   All quotes are from Jewish minor league players and staff, interviewed by the author; names are omitted to safeguard their privacy.

2   Adrian Cardenas, "Why I Quit Major League Baseball," Web, 30 Oct. 2013, www.newyorker.com/online/blogs/sportingscene/2013/10/why-i-quit-major-league-baseball.html.

BRAD AUSMUS

A BASEBALL JOURNEY

I was not raised in a Jewish household. My mother is Jewish, and her parents raised her Jewishly. However, my father is Protestant, and other than lighting the menorah and visiting maternal relatives on the High Holidays, we didn't practice much of the Jewish faith. When asked about religion, I described myself as half-Jewish and half-Protestant, which meant I received presents for both Hanukkah and Christmas, a bonanza for a child. It wasn't until my second or third year in the major leagues that an outside media publication discovered my Jewish heritage, and from that story on, Jewish baseball fans recognized me as one of their own. I had never realized the amount of pride Jews felt toward the few Jewish major leaguers, regardless of the team for which they played. Over the remainder of my career, I often had Jewish fans approach me and wish me well, occasionally speaking in Hebrew, which I don't understand. Many young, Jewish baseball players would tell me I was their favorite player because of my heritage. I am often asked if I ever encountered antisemitism while playing in major league baseball, and the truth is that, outside of one incident that was not directed at me, the answer is no. This one incident involved an ignorant fan, not a player.

Baseball has been a part of my life for as long as I can remember. I loved the Boston Red Sox growing up. I was a rabid fan, checking the box scores every morning, and falling asleep to the radio play-by-play at night. I grew up in Connecticut, which is sort of a no-man's-land between Boston and New York. You were either a Red Sox fan or a Yankees fan, no offense to the smattering of Mets fans who were mixed in. Most of my friends chose for themselves which of the two teams to root for, but when your mother is from Brookline, just outside of Boston, there is only one option. I remember vividly the first time I walked into Fenway Park. I could not believe how green the grass was in the middle of a concrete jungle.

I can't solely point to my mother for my obsession with the Red Sox. My maternal grandfather was also a big Red Sox fan, and I assume my mother as well wasn't given much leeway in selecting her favorite team. I suppose this is some sort of forced generational love of the Boston Red Sox. Long before cable TV or the Internet, the only time I could watch the Red Sox games was with my grandfather when I was visiting him in Brookline. Channel 38 in Boston was the next best thing to being at Fenway Park.

I get the sense, after years of playing baseball, that my experience was very common in Jewish homes across America, especially in some of the larger cities.

Grandparents handed their love of the game or a team to their children, who passed the same passion on to the grandchildren. It provided a common bond across the generations, and probably occupied more dinner table discussions than other non-baseball-fan members of the family cared to listen to. Regardless, these were the seeds that grew into my baseball career.

In 2011, I received an e-mail, out of the blue, from the president of the Israeli Association of Baseball (IAB), Haim Katz. He wondered if I would be interested in being part of the 2012 Israeli team that would play in the World Baseball Classic (WBC). Truthfully, I was very reluctant to become involved, at first. I had just recently retired and wasn't sure that I wanted any overwhelming time commitments. I was really enjoying my downtime. Nonetheless, I met with Haim, and later with Shawn Green, Gabe Kapler, and Peter Kurz, the secretary general of the IAB, to discuss possibilities and ideas regarding the Israeli WBC team. Shawn, Gabe, and I walked away from the meeting having committed to help the IAB, but unsure what our specific roles were to be. The only thing I knew for sure was that I did not want to play. I felt my playing days were behind me, and had no interest in donning the tools of ignorance again. I will say that Shawn and Gabe both had an infectious excitement about working and playing with Team Israel, and it made me much more enthusiastic about my own involvement. Without their enthusiasm, I'm not sure I'd be writing this essay.

Over the next few months, Shawn, Gabe, and I e-mailed, texted, and spoke on the phone. By the beginning of 2012, we had decided on our roles. Shawn very much wanted to play (for a nearly forty-year-old guy who hadn't touched a baseball bat in years, he did some great hitting) and be the hitting coach; Gabe would play and be the bench coach; and I would be the manager. (In the end, Gabe had an injury and was unable to play.) One major perk of being Team Israel's manager was an all-expenses-paid trip to the country you're representing. Peter Kurz and Haim Katz gave my wife and me the royal treatment. We visited ancient Jerusalem, Yad Vashem, the Dead Sea, the beaches of Tel Aviv, and even met President Shimon Peres. I had the opportunity to see the country's baseball facilities and to meet the small groups of kids who play baseball in Israel. It was an unforgettable trip.

Then the hard work started. Peter Kurz and I began amassing a list of all the potential Team Israel players. We corresponded more over the next eight months than I have corresponded with anybody in my entire life. I would discover that this list was never etched in stone; it was in a constant state of flux. Names would be removed, and new names added. Putting a team together from scratch is fun, but difficult, work. Once we had the names, I began putting together scouting reports on each player, prioritizing which players we would want on the team. But because I would not be able to watch each player perform, I essentially had to make decisions based on statistics, word of mouth, and the scouting reports that I was able to access thanks to the San Diego Padres' scouting database.

Getting in touch with the players was an adventure in itself. It was not easy to get e-mails or phone numbers for every player we had listed. But, amazingly, a number of people in the baseball community — especially agents, many of them Jewish — wanted nothing more than to help. And so the recruiting began. I e-mailed the players. I called the players. I texted the players. I spoke to agents. I spoke to parents. I even spoke to an uncle.

PREVIOUS

Brad Ausmus, manager of Team Israel with catcher Charlie Cutler during the World Baseball Classic Qualifier, Jupiter, Florida, September 21, 2012

BELOW

Brad Ausmus being introduced as the new manager of the Detroit Tigers, November 3, 2013

Red Sox left fielder Gabe Kapler makes a running catch at Fenway Park, Boston, June 29, 2006

The response from the vast majority of players I contacted was positive. They were, as a group, very excited about the possibility of playing for Team Israel. As the date grew nearer, we whittled down the list, and finally we put together the roster that would represent Israel at the 2012 WBC Qualifier in Jupiter, Florida.

To play for any country in the WBC, a player must be eligible for citizenship in that country. Normally, that simply means the player, one of his parents, or one of his grandparents would need a birth certificate from that country. To be eligible for citizenship in Israel, a person only needs to have a parent or grandparent who is Jewish. But proving one's religion is where things get much more difficult, and interesting. We saw everything from Israeli passports to bar mitzvah certificates to circumcision affidavits in Hebrew.

I know this for sure: the players, whether American or Israeli, practiced, played, joked, laughed, hung out, and ate meals together like they had known each other for years.

When the team arrived in Florida to begin workouts, I wasn't sure what to expect. We had put together twenty-five or so Jewish American minor league ballplayers, with a few Israeli players, and asked all these strangers to become a team. In addition, the Israeli national team would also be sharing facilities and working out with all the WBC players. I was concerned that the team would have no chemistry, and with only ten days together, no bonds would form. I was wrong. I cannot say with any certainty why this group of strangers immediately hit it off so well. It may have been their common heritage, the game they all love to play, or some combination of both. I know this for sure: the players, whether American or Israeli, practiced, played, joked, laughed, hung out, and ate meals together like they had known each other for years. Team Israel may have lost in the championship of that qualifying tournament, but I'm willing to bet the memories and sense of pride that each of those players and the staff felt will stay with them for a lifetime. It was probably the greatest Jewish baseball team ever assembled.

HOW A JEWISH KID FROM CONNECTICUT MADE IT TO THE MAJOR LEAGUES

ADAM
CHANDLER

Josh Zeid plays for one of the worst teams in baseball but still says he's living the dream.

Your parents may have already told you this, but the odds of becoming a professional baseball player are infinitesimal. Historically, if you're Jewish, that number gets even smaller. A hundred times smaller. The 2010 documentary *Jews and Baseball: An American Love Story* estimated that Jews account for only about one hundred sixty of the nearly seventeen thousand current and former players of Major League Baseball.

The ones who make it achieve legend status almost instantly. Ask a Jewish sports fan about America's pastime and you will be regaled with the heroic feats of players like Hank Greenberg, Al Rosen, and Shawn Green. The most famous of them all is Sandy Koufax, who refused to pitch Game 1 of the 1965 World Series because it fell on Yom Kippur, making him a hero to generations of Jewish kids. One of them is Josh Zeid, who considers Koufax to be the greatest ballplayer of all time.

If you haven't heard of Josh Zeid yet, it's probably for two reasons. Zeid only made his major league debut in late July, and Zeid pitches for the Houston Astros, one of just a sad handful of teams in baseball history to lose more than a hundred games in a season three seasons in a row. But Zeid throws a wicked slider and a four-seam fastball that averages close to ninety-five miles per hour, putting him among the top fifteen percent of major league pitchers.

Late last month, Zeid and I met in the dugout at Minute Maid Park, in downtown Houston. The team was prepping for its final series of the season, against the New York Yankees. The Disastros had lost twelve straight games, including five games by just one run along with two shutouts, a 12–0 drubbing by the Cincinnati Reds and a 10–0 beat down by their rivals the Texas Rangers. One loss in that dirty dozen has already become something of legend, after it yielded a 0.0 Nielsen rating in the local market, meaning maybe a thousand people in the country's fourth-largest city had tuned in to watch.

It's tempting to think that Zeid's story is tragic: He joined the league's worst team with the league's lowest payroll and spent his inaugural months in the majors pitching in the league's worst-performing bullpen. But Zeid is all smiles. "I'm living the dream," he told me. "You play high-school baseball, you play college baseball, you play minor league baseball, and your goal, your dream, is to play in the major leagues."

———

Zeid grew up in New Haven, Connecticut, where his father, Ira, is a dentist; his mother, Karen, works at a senior center. In high school, Zeid set a record with four hundred strikeouts, winning two New England championships along the way. *Baseball America* ranked him No. 27 on its list of top national prospects.

Zeid also made the Maccabiah baseball team, but the outbreak of the Second Intifada kept him and his peers from competing in Israel. After graduating high school, in 2005, Zeid resisted recruitment efforts by big state schools and chose Vanderbilt, where he met his wife, Stephanie, a neuropsychologist. ("She's very, very smart," Zeid told me.) But he couldn't find consistency in his game. After struggling through his sophomore year, he transferred to Tulane. "My parents didn't mind if I spent equal time with school and sports, but it couldn't be any less school and more sports," Zeid told me. "It had to be a fair and equal balance."

Things got better in New Orleans. In 2009, his senior year, the Phillies selected him in the tenth round of the draft, launching him on a circuitous route through the minor leagues with stints on teams that had unfathomable names: the Lakewood Blueclaws, the Williamsport Crosscutters, and the Mesa Solar Sox.

Farm league baseball is a timeless and inimitable American enterprise, something both native and specific to the world of baseball, a confederacy apart of miniature stadiums with aluminum bleachers and cheap admission in small cities and rural towns across the country: Altoona, Midland, Lynchburg, Stockton. For a player, the work is hard, the pay is lousy, and the path is uncertain. None of that was a problem for Zeid. "You get to travel across the country, you get to see the biggest cities, you get to see the smallest cities, you get to meet some amazing people, you get to meet some people who might not be as privileged as others," Zeid explained. "You can be president, you can be a rabbi, you can be someone who actually has a platform, but to so many kids out here, we may be someone they look up to."

Zeid used the experiences as fodder for a blog he started publishing on the MLB Network in 2010. In his inaugural entry, Zeid wrote about his Jewish heroes and reminisced about his childhood pitching days:

> Like I was back in New Haven, CT, playing for the Andy Papero Little League on a Tuesday night. Where the only bit of constructive criticism during my coach's mound visit was: "Hurry up now, my macaroni's getting cold!" He would then smile, and jog off the field.

Zeid also detailed how his path had diverged from those of the kids he grew up with in New Haven:

> **"You can be president, you can be a rabbi, you can be someone who actually has a platform, but to so many kids out here, we may be someone they look up to."**

Josh Zeid at his bar mitzvah, *kippot* painted by Karen Zeid

Growing up in a Jewish household, we focused on having a sound foundation based on private schools and living very close to my extended family. I only had Sandy Koufax and Hank Greenberg to look up to as legitimate Jewish heroes, so in the back of my family's mind was a hesitation and a desire for me to focus on getting a good education. Where I grew up Jewish kids dreamt of playing pro sports, but in reality, becoming doctors, lawyers, accountants, or real-estate entrepreneurs was more realistic. I felt I had a platform to be different, and I had the support from my parents and sister to do that.

After reading the blog, I thought about Philip Roth's book *American Pastoral*, the plot of which centers around a character called the Swede. Like Zeid, the Swede is Jewish, a star high-school baseball player, and a Mets fan who comes of age just outside of New York. The similarities end there—the Swede played first base and eventually has his life trampled by the mayhem of the 1960s. But in an early scene, Roth's narrator, Nathan Zuckerman, describes a book in the Swede's adolescent library wedged between two bookends in the shape of Rodin's *The Thinker*.

The book, *The Kid from Tomkinsville*, is about a young pitcher from Connecticut whose journey to the big leagues is laden with its share of challenge and heartbreak. Calling it "the boys' Book of Job," Zuckerman notes that what the book's primitive illustrations make "graphically clear is that playing up in the majors, heroic though it may seem, is yet another form of backbreaking, unremunerative labor."

In 2011, Zeid and three other players were traded to Houston in a deal that sent the Astros' last marquee player—Hunter Pence—to the Phillies. Zeid pitched for four more teams: the Salt River Rafters, the Corpus Christi Hooks, the Oklahoma City RedHawks, and the Israeli national team.

The last Jewish player to grace the roster of the Houston Astros was the catcher Brad Ausmus, who caught games from the likes of Roger Clemens, Andy Pettitte, and Roy Oswalt on the Astros' march to their sole World Series appearance, in 2005. Last year, Ausmus managed the Israeli national team on its fruitless inaugural quest to qualify for the World Baseball Classic. Only three players on the twenty-eight-man roster were Israeli. The rest were Americans, who like Zeid, had at least one Jewish grandparent.

In the team's first ever game—played in Jupiter, Florida—Israel was clinging to a 1–0 lead over South Africa when Zeid was called in to pitch in the bottom of the sixth inning. South Africa had runners on second and third and only one out. Zeid, facing the heart of the South African lineup, struck the first batter out and intentionally walked the next batter. With the bases loaded, Zeid ended the inning by forcing a pop-out. Israel held the lead and went on to win the game. "Zeid's inning-plus there was probably the turning point of the game for us," Ausmus said after the game.

"One thing you notice right away is his ability," Ausmus told me last week. "He's got a strong right arm that touches the upper-90s, and he gets strikeouts with his slider. We immediately slotted him in the back of our bullpen."

In the second game, Israel defeated Spain, with Zeid pitching again and earning a save. Having beaten both teams in its pool, Israel seemed poised to advance. But tournament rules stipulated that even though Israel was

undefeated, Spain and South Africa would play each other for the right to face
Israel in a winner-take-all game. Spain beat South Africa and then bested
Israel, 9–7, in an epic five-hour, ten-inning battle. Zeid pitched the Israeli team
through the ninth inning, getting three straight batters out. In the top of the
tenth, Zeid gave up a walk to the first batter, much to the chagrin of Israeli
catcher Charles Cutler, who was ejected for arguing calls with the umpire.
Zeid hit the next batter and then got the next two out before Spain scored the
decisive two runs on a single off of Zeid.

Almost a year later, he finally got his call from the Astros. At twenty-six,
Zeid is still a young player, but old for a rookie. This year, on an Astros roster
with an unprecedented twenty rookies, Zeid's experience lent him some
perspective on the struggles of the young players. "Instead of having three good
outs, they'll have two good outs, and then there will be that mental lapse," Zeid
said. Then, with his characteristic optimism, he added, "This year is going to
make everyone good for next year."

Zeid wears two items around his neck when he pitches: his wedding ring
and a Star of David. "People say, 'You should be careful, a lot of people don't
know Jewish people or they don't understand Judaism, they associate you with
the Middle East,'" Zeid said. "You know, everyone wears a cross, but you don't
ever see anyone wearing a Star of David or anything for any other religion."

Baseball has a Jesus-heavy essence. After Zeid left to go warm up, Astros
skipper Bo Porter, the steward of Houston's slow rebuilding process, joined
reporters in the dugout to talk about the season's endless disappointments,
including the twelve-game losing streak. Porter, at forty-one, still looks like a
ballplayer. While the team had just come back from a losing road trip, bringing
home a palpable sense of weariness, Porter seemed excited. Accordingly, the
coterie of sportswriters around him had long stopped asking questions about
strategy and moved on to pop psychology. "When you go through what it is
we've been through this year," Porter said, "it really made me take a step back
and realize how God prepared me for this
position because without the preparation,
there's no way we would have made it
through all the ups and downs this year."

Despite the historic futility, the Astros
are considered a team whose farm system
will produce some winning seasons with
enough time. After the press conference,
I asked Porter for his thoughts on Zeid.
"He's done a tremendous job," Porter said.
"He's been a great addition to our bullpen,
he's a workaholic. What I love about him is that he's durable. He's a bullpen guy
who can go two innings, come back to the next day, throw an inning, you give
him a day off, he's available the next day. He has that closer's mentality. He gets
after it, he's not afraid. I think he has the chance to be a pretty special pitcher
for a long time in the major leagues."

Earlier that day, Zeid had spoken with excitement about the prospect of
playing the Yankees for the first time as a major leaguer. The Yankees had just
been unceremoniously eliminated from playoff contention after an injury-
plagued season. The night before in the Bronx, the team had bid farewell to
its legendary reliever Mariano Rivera. Yankees star pitcher Andy Pettitte,

> "It really made me take a step back and realize how God prepared me for this position because without the preparation, there's no way we would have made it through all the ups and downs this year."

Josh Zeid playing for the Astros against the Washington Nationals, Osceola County Stadium, Kissimmee, Florida, February, 2011

a Houston native, would be pitching the last game of his career in his hometown. "As much as you want to idolize them, think that they're really good, you have to believe that you're just as good or better, and get them out," Zeid told me. "You have to convince yourself to get them out from the get-go."

That night, with the Astros already down in a 3–0 hole, Yankees star Alfonso Soriano hit a long double in the top of the sixth inning with one out. Porter called Zeid in from the bullpen to replace the starter, Brett Oberholtzer. Zeid induced a pop-out and then, with his slider, struck out the next player swinging to strand Soriano on base and end the inning. Zeid came back for the seventh inning where he ran the Yankees out in no time, striking out two Yankees and causing another to ground up weakly. With that, Zeid's night was done. The Astros scratched out two runs in the eighth inning and lost 3–2.

This is reprinted from *Tablet Magazine*, at tabletmag.com, the online magazine of Jewish news, ideas, and culture.

THE GIFT OF GUMP

HOW JUDAISM MADE ME A BETTER BASEBALL PLAYER, AND BASEBALL MADE ME A BETTER JEW

COLIN FRIEDMAN

I can still remember myself as a young child, playing baseball in the backyard. My dad graciously spent hours throwing heated batting practice and catching ferocious pitches. To any onlooker, it was probably just another father and son playing catch, but those moments were so much more. When I stepped up to bat, habitually tapping the outside corner of the plate, I turned into Derek Jeter of the Yankees. Forget that I was two thousand miles away from New York, those face-offs were always taking place in front of fifty thousand roaring fans inside Yankee Stadium. And when I tired of hitting, I hopped right onto the pitcher's mound as Mariano Rivera, ready to close out Game 7 of the World Series.

Baseball became a part of me at an early age. My mom was never much of a sports enthusiast, and my dad played only football and basketball competitively through high school. But dribbling was never my forte, and my mom refused to let her son play football. With a clear passion and propensity for the sport, it became clear early on just how much I loved baseball. At age seven, my dad started coaching me, and nothing ever compared to those baseball-filled summers. Everything about it sucked me in, from the aroma of freshly cut grass to the crack of the ball off the bat. I simply could not get enough of all the game had to offer.

Most of all, I loved stepping onto the pitcher's mound. The world seemed to slow down, and all my troubles were cast away. To this day, nothing compares to zipping a fastball past the batter for a swing and miss on strike three. That feeling of accomplishment never fails to send a rush of euphoria. For a brief moment I am invincible, truly standing atop the world. Even the darkest of thoughts cannot penetrate me, and I feel truly unstoppable.

While I've almost always been certain of my place atop the pitcher's mound, an equally significant part of my life has not always felt so strong. Growing up in Santa Fe, New Mexico, often made it difficult to appreciate my Judaism. Through my early years in elementary schools, and then later on as I attended a Catholic middle school and high school, I did not always feel proud to recognize my faith.

My grandfather Norbert Friedman, or "Gump" as I call him, had spent a lot of time speaking about his experiences during the Holocaust. I understood the severity of the circumstances my family and millions of

Colin Friedman

others had endured, but I did not truly begin to grasp the significance of the events until reading his autobiography at age ten. Some of the stories were familiar while others were not, but through several hundred pages I gained an insight into his life story. I continually went back to that book over the next six years, often feeling ashamed about the times I was afraid to recognize my own heritage. Sharing my Judaism with others in a Catholic school did not always bring with it a sense of ease. Yet, over time, I realized this unique part of me was something to be proud of. So at age sixteen, I saw that despite having to answer uncomfortable questions, or occasionally deal with acts of antisemitism, my Judaism needed to be cherished.

Even with this realization, the social stigma regarding Jews and their limited athletic abilities still lived inside my head. I was often convinced that my religious beliefs hindered me on the playing field. However, at this time I also began lifting weights. As an athlete with dreams of playing collegiate baseball, it was time to start getting stronger in the weight room and within a year I had gained significant strength through Olympic weight lifting. Earning several state records and a top fifteen national ranking in lifting competitions not only contributed to my performance on the field, but boosted a newfound confidence that beat out my sense of inferiority.

Colin Friedman with his grandfather Norbert "Gump" Friedman

My newfound confidence as a person echoed throughout all aspects of my life, with friends, family, school, and even on the baseball field. An offer to play baseball for Johns Hopkins University arrived, along with multiple New Mexico state pitching records and even an appearance in *Sports Illustrated*'s "Faces in the Crowd." Rather than acting as a hindrance, my faith had served as a motivator, pushing me to achieve the unthinkable.

Looking back now, I realize I was motivated by a man who knew little of baseball before the war. But this same grandfather has pushed me to make the most of life, both on and off the field.

He sacrificed so much to continue living, to give future generations a life; and his strength and endurance have helped me to find my own. His wisdom will always help to guide me. Baseball and Judaism are both part of my identity, two joys that I will surely carry throughout my lifetime. I will forever be grateful as their lessons continually push me to be the best person possible, each and every day.

BAR MITZVAH TRIP
OF A LIFETIME

**MARC
APPLEMAN**

I've often told my sons, Michael and Drew, about the weekend trip I took with my dad when I was about to turn thirteen. I'd grown up in New York City and was a diehard Yankees fan. So, as a special bar mitzvah present, my dad took me to the Yankees' spring training camp in Ft. Lauderdale, Florida. Michael and Drew have heard my spring training stories many times. It's family legend.

They know that as soon as I got up in the morning, I put on my Yankees pinstripes and wore them all day. That my dad and I sat in box seats and I talked to the players while they were warming up. I got autographs of my favorite players, including Mel Stottlemyre (whom Michael and Drew knew as the Yankee pitching coach). After the games, my dad and I retrieved our gloves and a ball from the trunk of our car and played catch in the stadium parking lot.

That, in addition to watching and talking baseball, baseball, and more baseball, we went swimming in the ocean; ate roast beef sandwiches at Lum's; stayed in a hotel; and late at night, before going to sleep, talked about life in general—everything from growing up to what it means to be Jewish. I loved that weekend and never forgot a single thing about it. Once I became a father, I often thought, that's what I'd like to do with my sons someday.

That day came so quickly. It was as if, during a seventh-inning stretch, I'd gone to high school and college, begun my career (as a sportswriter), gotten married, and had two sons. In the spring of 2002, my oldest son, Michael, was twelve years old and began preparing for his bar mitzvah. He also hinted—very strongly—that it was time for us to take our father-son baseball trip. However, his idea of a trip was far grander and far more expensive than a weekend in Florida.

Instead, we hit the highway for an international baseball road trip! Over two weeks, two countries, eight states, and three thousand miles, we went to eight games in six stadiums (Doubleday Field, Parc Olympique, the Skydome, Wrigley Field, Comerica Park, Jacobs Field) and visited the Baseball, Hockey, and Pro Football Halls of Fame.

On a trip filled with adventures, Michael caught balls in Montreal, Detroit, and Cleveland. We had a blast sitting with the Bleacher Bums at Wrigley and making friends with passionate Indians fans at Jacobs Field.

A highlight of the trip was the first stop—the induction ceremony
of my mentor and good friend, the late sportswriter Joe Falls, at the
National Baseball Hall of Fame in Cooperstown, New York. My dad and
my younger son, Drew, joined us in Cooperstown. In addition to spending
one-on-one time with Joe, we were given passes that allowed us access to
the hotel lobby at the Otesaga Hotel. The Otesaga is a turn-of-the-century
landmark, and the lobby is a majestic place. And it is the place to be
during induction weekend.

The Otesaga lobby is where the Hall of Famers gather to share stories.
It was also the place where Michael and Drew met Hank Aaron, Bob Feller,
Sandy Koufax, Whitey Ford, Harmon Killebrew, Yogi Berra, and Stan
Musial. The boys said hello and shook hands politely, but Musial had a little
fun with them. His handshake was a bone crusher. Several hours after
meeting Musial, their "Musial hands" still ached.

Another Hall of Famer who had fun with Michael was the late Warren
Spahn, who was eighty-two at the time. The winningest left-hander in
baseball history was sitting on the porch at the Otesaga when Michael
approached him. As Michael tells the tale:

> I saw Warren sitting by himself and held out a ball and pen and
> asked him for his autograph.

Marc Appleman on his bar
mitzvah trip to Yankees spring
training with his father, Herb
Appleman, Ft. Lauderdale,
Florida, 1970

He said, "Why didn't you come into town and buy it?"

I said, "I was at the Hall of Fame."

He said, "Then you missed your chance."

So I said, "Maybe you can give me a chance now."

He said, "Why should I do that?" Then, he started asking me a lot of questions. "What's your name? Where do you live? What do you want to be when you grow up?"

I answered him, finishing up with "I want to be a Major Leaguer one day."

He said, "What makes you think you're good enough? The odds are probably a thousand to one against you. You know that?"

I said, "I'm pretty good for my age."

So he said, "That doesn't mean anything. Lots of kids are good for their age. If I were you, I'd think of doing something else."

I said, "I'm getting tired, Mr. Spahn. Do you think I can have your autograph?" Then he laughed and said, "I gave you a hard time, didn't I?"

I said, "Yes!" Then he took my ball and pen and signed his name. And he said, "Was it worth it?"

And I said, "Sure. You're one of the all-time great pitchers."

Then my dad and Drew came along and Spahn said to Drew, "Are you his brother?" Drew nodded. Then Spahn said, "I suppose you want an autograph too?" And Drew nodded again and held out a ball and pen, and Spahn took it and signed his name for Drew. And I got mad because Drew didn't have to do anything for the autograph, and I had to answer a hundred questions.

The time in Cooperstown was particularly special because it was shared by three generations of Applemans connected by baseball—my dad, my two sons, and me.

After the induction ceremonies in Cooperstown, Michael and I headed out on our special adventure. However, just like my trip to Florida with my dad, the trip with Michael was about a lot more than baseball. It was about hot dogs, pizzas, laughs, talks, adventures, and misadventures—the stuff that memories are made of.

Memories such as when Michael called Mrs. Braunstein, his bar mitzvah teacher, on his cell phone. "Mrs. Braunstein? We're on our way to Toronto. I've been practicing my *haftarah*. Here goes...." And Michael began chanting. Mrs. Braunstein would make some comments, and he'd repeat his chanting. "Thanks, Mrs. Braunstein. I think it's OK, don't you? I'll call again soon."

The boys said hello and shook hands politely, but Musial had a little fun with them. His handshake was a bone crusher. Several hours after meeting Musial, their "Musial hands" still ached.

During batting practice at Wrigley Field, our friends in the bleachers took off their shirts, started drinking beer and prepared for the opening pitch with one-liners that were as funny as they were uncensored. It was a perfect father-son baseball moment.

During our trip, we saw Mark Prior pitch a thirteen-strikeout game, a complete game; Vladdy Guerrero hit a walk-off homer; Randy Johnson strike out fifteen; the Angels beat the Tigers behind rookie pitcher John Lackey; and C. C. Sabathia pitch seven strong innings in Cleveland.

Stories of our special father-son trip passed down to Michael's younger brother, Drew. Three years after Michael and I hit the road, Drew and I were on a flight from New York to California. We drove down the California coast—laughing, eating a lot of crab, and going to major league games in Oakland, San Francisco, Los Angeles, and San Diego. It was the first time that Drew had been to any of these stadiums.

My trip with Drew was special and unique, just like the trips with my dad and Michael. Before a game between the Royals and A's in Oakland, Drew caught a ball during batting practice (both boys learned the key to positioning and boxing out when it came to catching balls) and also got autographs. We saw the Royals snap their nineteen-game losing streak with a 2–1 win. In San Francisco, we saw the Giants beat the Phillies 5–0 on an eerie, but fun, foggy night at AT&T Park. Once we got to Southern California, we followed the Rockies—we saw them beat the Dodgers, at Dodger Stadium, and then the Padres, at Petco Park.

Marc Appleman with his father, Herb, and sons Michael and Drew at Game 3 of the World Series between the New York Yankees and Atlanta Braves, October 26, 1999

Along the way, we also went swimming in a river in Coloma, explored the Bay Area, went hiking at Muir Woods, drove down the scenic Pacific Coast Highway, stayed in the memorable Jungle Room at the wild Madonna Hotel, ate at a Mexican restaurant on Olivera Street in Los Angeles, went bodysurfing, and even won $130 on the seventh race at Del Mar Racetrack.

Throughout my trips with Michael and Drew, we often talked about my days as a sportswriter. On our trips, we were basically on the same type of schedule that players and sportswriters are on during road trips, the difference being that we woke up early each day.

We also spent a lot of time talking about the special times we shared on the fields at Westport—with dad as coach and Michael and Drew as very good players. We also discussed the times we all shared at Yankee Stadium—Michael and Drew were spoiled by a dominant team that enabled them to go to playoff and World Series games almost every year. Baseball was a big part of the Appleman family.

From the Yankees spring training camp to Wrigley Field to Dodger Stadium, three great baseball trips showed how a special game can become intertwined with family, friendships, and a career.

Material for this essay includes excerpts drawn from *Dad, Are You Pumped? A Father-Son Baseball Odyssey*, written by Marc Appleman and published by iUniverse in 2005.

WHY I HATE
SANDY KOUFAX

WILLIAM CHOSLOVSKY

As a kid, I was consumed with baseball, but I peaked athletically around the age of eleven.

If I ever got down about sitting on the bench, my father would say: "Be ready. Just as it takes ten men to make a minyan, it may take ten players to win a baseball game if someone gets hurt."

Did my father's statement ease the pain of not playing? Not really, but I am sure hidden in there was some obscure message about Jewish resilience.

THE OLD COUNTRY

My father, Sydney Choslovsky, the oldest of four children, was born in Winnipeg, Canada, in 1930 to Bella and Maurice Choslovsky, his immigrant parents from Belarus—what some call White Russia. Maurice was a junk dealer with his brothers, starting with a pushcart.

A Depression-era baby, my father had a modest childhood with little fanfare. He went to medical school for the most noble of reasons: because his mother told him to. And as a sign of the changing times, his class was one of the first without restrictive, unofficial quotas against Jews.

After a stint as a country doctor in North Dakota, my father moved to Chicago for his radiology training, becoming a US citizen in 1962, his American Dream in full swing.

And what could be more American than baseball?

SUNDAY, SEPTEMBER 25, 1966, WRIGLEY FIELD, CHICAGO

In 1966, Yom Kippur, the holiest day of the Jewish year, ended at sundown on Saturday, September 24. The next day my dad, a big baseball fan, decided to take his father, who was in town for a holiday visit, to Wrigley Field.

While the Cubs were in last place riding out another miserable season, the Dodgers were chasing a pennant. And there sat my dad, a day shy of his thirty-sixth birthday (double chai), with his father on one side and young son on the other, both attending their first Cubs game.

Most amazing that day were the starting pitchers: Ken Holtzman for the Cubs and Sandy Koufax for the Dodgers. "Yes," that Sandy Koufax. The

Ken Holtzman pitches for the Oakland A's in the fifth inning of Game 1 of the 1973 World Series, October 13, 1973.

contrast could not be bigger. Holtzman was a rookie, while Koufax was already a legend, having compiled a list of statistics that would soon make him the youngest player ever voted into the Hall of Fame.

Besides being lefties, the two pitchers shared something else in common: they were both Jews! Jews who a day earlier might have been sitting in temple praying, no different than the Choslovsky men.[1]

Just one year prior, Koufax had made history by sitting out Game 1 of the 1965 World Series to observe Yom Kippur.[2]

And now—just one year later—sat three generations of Choslovsky men getting ready to watch Koufax face Holtzman. Suffice to say, life was good.

Though the game was meaningless to the Cubs, Holtzman did not pitch like it. He carried a no-hitter into the ninth inning and actually outdueled Koufax, winning 2-1.

One week later Koufax pitched the last game of the regular season on just two days rest to clinch the pennant for the Dodgers. Though he was again brilliant, his arm almost literally fell off. Published reports say his shoulder "popped" in the fifth inning, but he still pitched the entire game, sending the Dodgers to the World Series for the third time in four years.

On October 6—exactly one year after he sat out Game 1 of the 1965 World Series—Koufax pitched Game 2 of the 1966 World Series against

Baltimore. Though he gave up just one run in six innings, the Dodgers lost, and went on to be swept by the Orioles.

And then Koufax abruptly retired. Done at thirty. His wicked curveball that made him, ultimately ended him.

He has been a living legend ever since, with his quiet humility and disdain for the public spotlight only enhancing his mystique and iconic status.

It is interesting to now think that just two weeks before Koufax retired, Jews everywhere were in temple on Yom Kippur reciting the *Unetaneh Tokef* prayer. The prayer acknowledges G-d's power to determine our destiny for the coming year, including "who shall live and who shall die." Though G-d presumably had better things to do that Yom Kippur than debate whether Koufax's career was ending, you never know.

As for Holtzman, he went on to enjoy a fifteen-year career, and like Koufax, won four World Series rings. In the 1973 World Series, he accomplished the rare feat of starting three games, winning the decisive Game 7.

In the end, Holtzman actually won more games than Koufax—174 to 165—making him the winningest Jewish pitcher of all time.

But who could know back on that fall day in 1966, when Koufax was winding up his career and Holtzman beginning his, that the torch was being passed from one Jewish star to another. *L'dor v'dor*: from generation to generation.

SPRING 1978, TUESDAY AND THURSDAY AFTERNOONS AT AM ECHAD SYNAGOGUE, PARK FOREST, ILLINOIS

As a kid, I heard a lot about Sandy Koufax. More than I wanted to.

I was actually a pretty good Little League baseball player, and nothing was more important than baseball back then. I remember riding my bike everywhere with my glove weaved around the handlebars and a baseball tucked in the spokes of the front wheel.

Besides playing baseball whenever we could, we breathed it too, listening on the radio and collecting baseball cards. I must have swallowed hundreds of pieces of the thin, pink, concrete hard, rectangular chewing gum that came in each pack of Topps baseball cards.

I actually learned math-percentages by following the standings in the sports page each day. And growing up in Chicago, we'd hustle home after school to catch the end of the Cubs game, and then watch the White Sox at night.

It was against this backdrop that my Hebrew school education collided.

Back then, we carpooled to Hebrew school on Tuesday and Thursday afternoons. It was pretty miserable, but it was simply what you did.

Though I could bear Hebrew school in the fall, come spring, when I got my Little League schedule, there was trouble. With Hebrew school running until 6:00 p.m., and my weekday games starting at 5:30, something had to give.

And unfortunately for me, it was my baseball games.

I protested, and even lied at times, telling my parents Hebrew school was cancelled for some obscure reason. But my parents had none of it.

My father was a tough love kind of guy. When I really pushed the issue, I remember him saying: "If Sandy Koufax could miss pitching Game 1 of the World Series, you can miss your Little League game."

No matter that Koufax missed his game for Yom Kippur while mine was just another boring Thursday afternoon Hebrew school class. The point was made, and how could you argue with Sandy Koufax?

Looking back, I am sure my father made the statement not only to end the "discussion," but to instill some sort of Jewish pride in me.

But all I remember from those days was sitting in Hebrew school thinking, "I hate Sandy Koufax. But for Sandy Koufax, I'd be playing baseball now!"

Though humorous now, it was anything but funny to me back then.

FRIDAY, JUNE 24, 2005, 7:35 AM, NORTHWESTERN HOSPITAL MATERNITY WARD, CHICAGO

What a day—the birth of my son—Aiden Phillip. Aiden is named after my wife's grandfather, Phillip Weinstein, who was an observant Jew with many abilities, baseball not being one of them.

I grew up in Chicago's south suburbs, and was raised, and remain, a White Sox fan. Though Jewish values teach that one should not get pleasure from another's misfortunes, I must confess that a Cubs loss gives me almost as much pleasure as a White Sox win.

My wife, on other hand, is from Chicago's northern suburbs, so she was raised a Cubs fan. We entered our marriage hoping this would be the largest divide we ever faced.

Our son was born at 7:35 a.m., and I actually had tickets to watch the Cubs play the Sox at Comiskey Park that afternoon. With interleague play still a novelty and the Sox sporting the major league's best record, little could be better than this crosstown rivalry.

Then again, it was (literally) my firstborn son, so I passed on the game.

At the hospital it hit me: what could be fairer than Aiden becoming a fan of whichever team won that day, the day of his birth? Destiny calling! Plus, when it comes to something as sacred as choosing a baseball team, no child should have free will.

Normally my wife would never agree to such a plan, but having just given birth, she was vulnerable, so she agreed. The covenant—OK, not that Covenant—was made.

And the result?

The Sox spanked the Cubs, winning 12-2.

Though my wife tried to retrade the deal afterward, I had none of it. As I condescendingly explained to her, whether it is accepting G-d's tablets on Mount Sinai or choosing a baseball team, you don't mess with destiny.

With Aiden now a White Sox fan, the team won the World Series four months later, sweeping the Houston Astros and ending an eighty-eight year old drought. Coincidence? I think not.[3]

> No matter that Koufax missed his game for Yom Kippur while mine was just another boring Thursday afternoon Hebrew School class. The point was made, and how could you argue with Sandy Koufax?

William, Carli, Aiden, Wendy, and Ellie Choslovsky (left to right) at Denver's Coors Field to see the Colorado Rockies face the Philadelphia Phillies, June 14, 2013

SUNDAY, MAY 5, 2013, OZ PARK LITTLE LEAGUE, CHICAGO

Just like me, my son Aiden loves baseball. And so far he is good at it, even making the Little League All-Star team.

Like Koufax, Aiden is a lefty and pitches.

But one game proved problematic. On Sunday, May 5, 2013, his undefeated team was set to play at 10:00 a.m. But Sunday mornings also meant…Sunday school.

And like my father before me, the decision was easy: Sunday school trumps baseball.

Needless to say, Aiden was disappointed. Trying to make it a "teachable moment," I said to him, "I know you are disappointed, but you will play many more baseball games, hopefully even in the major leagues one day. But one thing I do know is that you will be Jewish your entire life."

He took the news pretty well, better than I did thirty-five years prior.

And so it goes—*l'dor v'dor*—from generation to generation.

Notes
1   Koufax was actually scheduled to pitch on Yom Kippur, but refused, thus setting up his match-up with Holtzman.
2   Hall of Fame pitcher Don Drysdale pitched in Koufax's place that day and lost 8-2. Afterward, a reporter jokingly said to Dodger manager Walter Alston, "I bet you wish Drysdale was Jewish too."
3   My father, brother, nephew, and I—again, three generations—attended Game 1 of the World Series, which the Sox won 5-3. The Astros (Jewish) catcher was Brad Ausmus, now the manager of the Detroit Tigers.

CELEBRATE YOUR BIRTHDAYS

Honestly, my mom always made me feel special on my birthday, March 14. When I was a young boy, she used to wake me up at the exact time I was born: 7:36 A.M. As I grew older and moved out of the house, it became the phone call at 7:36 A.M. Even after I got married and had kids of my own, I always woke up looking forward to her call — it started the day off on the right foot. I put that tradition into City Slickers, with Jayne Meadows's voice playing my mom on the other end of the line. Mom's been gone since 2001, but come March 14, I still get up early and look at the alarm clock, and at 7:36, in my mind I hear the phone ring. Her call always ended with her saying, "Do something special." I didn't even mind that she called collect.

The most special thing I ever did on my birthday was when my life's dream came true: I got to play for the New York Yankees.

In 2007, I was in Costa Rica for Christmas vacation and could feel my birthday looming. I was anxious about turning sixty — it felt like a huge number. Derek Jeter happened to be at our hotel. I'd known Derek since his rookie year, and we'd become friends. I told Derek I was going to be sixty and was a little freaked out about it. Jeter asked, "If you could do one thing to make yourself happy, what would it be? You should do something special." Somewhere, my mom was smiling.

———

I knew my answer to Jeter's question right away. When Joe Torre was the Yankees' manager, he had let me work out with the team many times, even before World Series games. Joe and I were very close friends, and he not only knew I could handle myself on the field but thought my presence might even relax the guys. Infield practice was the most fun. I was still a good player, having been an outstanding (if I say so myself) high school second baseman and shortstop, and had played in leagues in New York and Los Angeles into my forties. My skills, though hardly professional, were solid. I still take batting practice regularly in a cage at home, and every morning my gym workout ends with a "catch." Turning double plays with Jeter on the historic infield of old Yankee Stadium was an enormous thrill. I wanted to do it again — this time, for real.

I came up with a plan where I would get one at bat in a spring training game. Whatever happens, happens, and I then announce my retirement and throw the team a party. Jeter loved the idea, and a few weeks before my sixtieth birthday, he and George

Billy Crystal honors his sixtieth birthday by taking one at-bat as a designated hitter for the New York Yankees during a spring training game against the Pittsburgh Pirates, March 13, 2008

Steinbrenner, Lonn Trost, Randy Levine, Brian Cashman, Bud Selig, and Major League Baseball gave me the greatest birthday gift ever: the Yankees would sign me to a one-day contract, and I would play against the Pittsburgh Pirates in a spring training game in Tampa. The game was on March 13, 2008, the day before my sixtieth birthday.

The official contract was for $4 million! But the nice part was that the Yankees gave me three days to come up with the money. We worked it out so that I would be the DH—designated Hebrew. Even though I wasn't going to be in the field, I needed to prepare. As you get older, there's a fine line between getting a walk and just wandering away from the batter's box. So I went into training.

Reggie Smith, the former great player who'd trained my "Maris and Mantle"—Barry Pepper and Thomas Jane—for *61**, has a baseball academy in Encino, California. He is a great teacher, and a better man. When I told him what was happening, he was almost as excited as I was. We didn't have a lot of time, but every day I worked on my swing with Reggie and his son (also a great teacher), against live pitching. As I left the West Coast for this great moment—accompanied by my good pal Robin Williams and some dear friends from high school—I was hitting eighty-five-mile-per-hour fastballs and felt as ready as a fifty-nine-year-old comedian can feel as he's about to play for the New York Yankees.

———

Trivia freaks will know that I was the oldest person ever to play for the Yankees, and the first player ever to test positive for Maalox. I actually did have to undergo routine testing. When they asked me for blood and urine, I gave them my underwear. The day before the game, I met with Yankee manager Joe Girardi. He wanted me to lead off and play left field. I said that was too far to run. We agreed that I would lead off and DH and have just the one at bat. Joe wanted me to score a run if I could. I wasn't sure (again, that's a long way to run), so we agreed that if I did get on base, Johnny Damon would pinch-run for me. It would be more theatrical, so to speak. I signed my contract with Lonn Trost and Jean Afterman and went and got dressed in the clubhouse. I knew most of the guys in there and had been in the clubhouse many times, but this felt unreal—I was one of them. In a strange way, I was very relaxed about it. It was so natural for me to wait until everyone had left the clubhouse so I could take off my clothes and put on my uniform. Just like high school gym class.

The team was on a road trip, and I spent that day working out with Derek and José Molina, who'd stayed back in Tampa. I took batting practice with Jeter and José while a small crowd and many camera crews looked on. I was on my game, hitting line drive after line drive. I know I shocked everyone, which was a great feeling. But I was in great shape and ready. Tino Martinez was throwing me sixty-mile-per-hour fastballs while Janice videotaped from a distance. Derek saw her and motioned for her to come over by him at the cage. She whispered to him, "How fast is Tino throwing?"

"One-oh-seven," Derek whispered back.

———

I couldn't sleep that night. It was really happening. I arrived at the park early the next morning. Girardi met me and we hung out a little, and to this day I can't thank him enough for welcoming me the way he did. This was his first year with the club, and the last thing he needed was some aging leading man as his lead-off man. Yet he treated me like a ballplayer, which is what I was that day. I did my pregame stretching and conditioning drills with the club and, of course, was then ready for a nap. Batting practice was amazing. I was in the cage with Derek and Damon and Bobby Abreu and Alex Rodriguez and Jorge Posada. When the guys nodded to one another that I was okay, I was on cloud nine. The hard part was that once batting practice was over, we had about an hour and a half till game time. I could feel my sphincter tighten, as well as my lower back and hamstrings. Now it wasn't just fun, it was really on.

I had lunch with Derek and Jorge and tried to be cool, but I was getting more and more anxious. Jorge and Derek were so easy with me. We all ate peanut butter and jelly sandwiches: the same meal I always had before games in high school and all the league games I'd played in and, actually, before hosting the Oscars. After lunch I went to put my game uniform on, and that's when the pranks started. My shoelaces were cut, so when I went to tie them, they came off in my hands. The toes on my socks were cut as well, so when I pulled them on, my foot went through. I took it all in good stride, trying to act like nothing bothered me, as I knew the guys were watching. I was careful putting on my cup, as the fear of hot sauce loomed. The pranks continued—my hat switched with one that didn't fit, my glove missing, a belt with no holes—until it was time to go to the dugout.

We worked it out so that I would be the DH—designated Hebrew. Even though I wasn't going to be in the field, I needed to prepare. As you get older, there's a fine line between getting a walk and just wandering away from the batter's box. So I went into training.

The stands were full as I bounded onto the field with the team to loosen up. A big roar from the crowd made me feel great, until I realized that A-Rod and Jeter were standing next to me. The national anthem was played, and I had a tear in my eye as I looked into the stands to see my brothers, Joel and Rip, and my daughter Jenny, and of course Janice. Mike Mussina threw a perfect first inning, and then I was up. When the announcer introduced me with "Leading off for the Yankees, the designated hitter, number 60, Billy Crystal," I just about lost it. Since I'd been a kid, playing with my dad, brothers, or friends, I'd always dreamed of this moment, and now it was real. The crowd gave me a tremendous hand as I left the on-deck circle. "Hack," (meaning swing) said Jeter, patting me on the helmet.

The Pirates' pitcher was Paul Maholm: six foot two, 220 pounds, from Mississippi. Never been to a Seder. I was nervous, but the one thing I was not nervous about was getting hit by a pitch. It never entered my mind. If Maholm hit me, I'd sue. You ever see a Jew get hit by a pitch? They get plunked in the leg and they grab their neck. Whiplash! Once I'd found out the date of the game, I'd gone to the Pirates' website to see who'd be pitching. I'd then watched Maholm strike out Barry Bonds. A real confidence builder. I studied his motion and his release point and tried to visualize what hitting off him would be like. As I approached the plate, the ump greeted me, as did the Pirates' catcher. I watched Maholm's warm-up pitches, looking for the release point I had seen on the website, and told myself, I can do this.

"Play ball!"

I stepped in. Since 1956, from the time I had seen Mickey Mantle play in the first game at the stadium I'd gone to, I had wanted to be a Yankee.

So there I am in the batter's box fifty-two years after that first game, my heart beating into the NY logo on my chest. Maholm is staring in for the sign, and I'm staring back, trying to look like I belong. Here comes the first pitch: ninety-two miles an hour. Ball one. I never see it, but it sounds outside. The ball makes a powerful thud in the catcher's glove. I want to say, "Holy s__t," but I act like I see one of those every day. In fact, I do: on TV, not in the F___ING BATTER'S BOX. The count is 1 and 0. He comes in with a fastball, a little up and away, and I hit a screaming line drive down the first base line, which means I didn't hit it that hard but I'm screaming, "I hit it! I hit it!" Someone yells, "DOUBLE!" Which would be tough because I can't run like I used to and on my way to second base I'd have to stop twice to pee. The last time a Jew my age ran that fast, the caterer was closing down the buffet.

But I'm still thinking double. The ump is thinking, Foul ball. I had made contact with a major league fastball. Okay, 1 and 1. Ball inside, 2 and 1, and another ball and it's 3 and 1. I'm this close to getting to first base, just like at my prom. I look over, and Derek Jeter is in the on-deck circle yelling, "Swing, swing!"

The windup, the pitch. It's a cutter. The nastiest cutter I've seen since my bris. But I swing and miss. The first time I've swung and missed in two days at Tampa. Now it's 3 and 2. The crowd stands up. This is my only shot, my only at bat. Ever. Maholm winds, I look to the release point, and there it is: eighty-nine miles per hour, a cut fastball, the same pitch he threw to that obstructer of justice Barry Bonds. I swing over it. Strike three. I'm out of there.

I head back to the bench, but before I do, I check with the ump: "Strike?" He shakes his head no: low and inside. I'm so mad I missed it, and also mad I didn't take the pitch, that I almost don't hear the crowd standing and cheering. The guys are giving me high fives. Girardi hugs me, then Kevin Long, the great hitting coach, and then Jorge. Then, for the first time in baseball history, they stop the game and give the batter a ball for striking out. A-Rod hands it to me, saying, "Great at bat!" My teammates greet me as if I've just hit a home run. Mariano Rivera hugs me, and others keep saying the same thing:

"Six pitches, man, you saw six pitches!"

I sit with Yogi Berra and Ron Guidry for a few innings, and if that isn't cool enough, I'm asked to come up to Mr. Steinbrenner's office. In full uniform I walk into the boss's lair. He gives me a big hug and then says with a straight face that I've been traded for Jerry Seinfeld. I thank him over and over again for a chance to be a Yankee, and he says he loved it and, most importantly, the fans loved it. That's what it's really all about.

> ## The windup, the pitch. It's a cutter. The nastiest cutter I've seen since my bris.

Billy Crystal shares a moment with Derek Jeter during the Yankees spring training game against the Pittsburgh Pirates, Legends Field, Tampa Bay, Florida, March 13, 2008

DANIEL OKRENT

Greatest JEWISH BASEBALL PLAYERS

A BRACKET

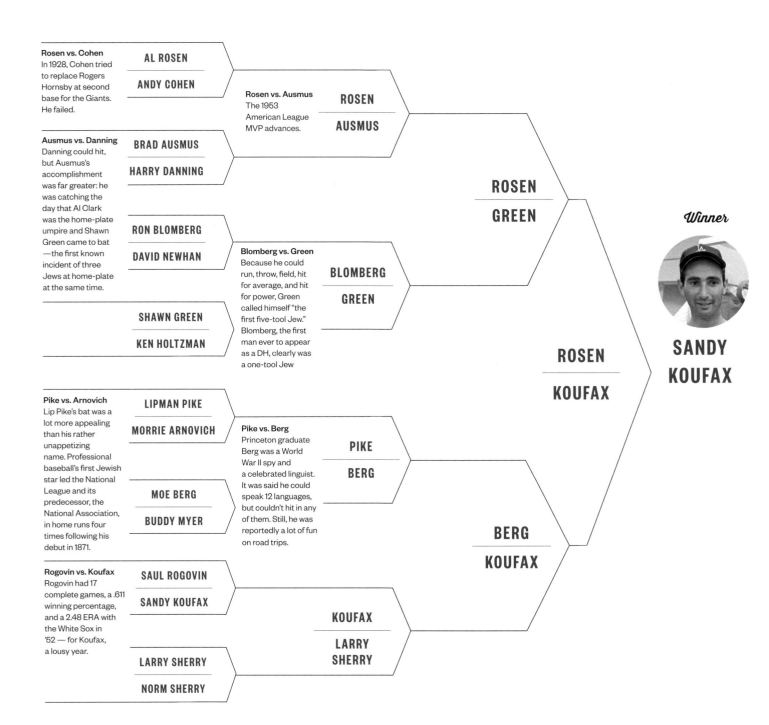

Rosen vs. Cohen
In 1928, Cohen tried to replace Rogers Hornsby at second base for the Giants. He failed.

AL ROSEN

ANDY COHEN

Rosen vs. Ausmus
The 1953 American League MVP advances.

ROSEN

AUSMUS

Ausmus vs. Danning
Danning could hit, but Ausmus's accomplishment was far greater: he was catching the day that Al Clark was the home-plate umpire and Shawn Green came to bat —the first known incident of three Jews at home-plate at the same time.

BRAD AUSMUS

HARRY DANNING

RON BLOMBERG

DAVID NEWHAN

Blomberg vs. Green
Because he could run, throw, field, hit for average, and hit for power, Green called himself "the first five-tool Jew." Blomberg, the first man ever to appear as a DH, clearly was a one-tool Jew

BLOMBERG

GREEN

SHAWN GREEN

KEN HOLTZMAN

ROSEN

GREEN

Pike vs. Arnovich
Lip Pike's bat was a lot more appealing than his rather unappetizing name. Professional baseball's first Jewish star led the National League and its predecessor, the National Association, in home runs four times following his debut in 1871.

LIPMAN PIKE

MORRIE ARNOVICH

Pike vs. Berg
Princeton graduate Berg was a World War II spy and a celebrated linguist. It was said he could speak 12 languages, but couldn't hit in any of them. Still, he was reportedly a lot of fun on road trips.

PIKE

BERG

MOE BERG

BUDDY MYER

Rogovin vs. Koufax
Rogovin had 17 complete games, a .611 winning percentage, and a 2.48 ERA with the White Sox in '52 — for Koufax, a lousy year.

SAUL ROGOVIN

SANDY KOUFAX

KOUFAX

LARRY SHERRY

LARRY SHERRY

NORM SHERRY

BERG

KOUFAX

ROSEN

KOUFAX

ROSEN

GREEN

Winner

SANDY KOUFAX

JEWISH BASEBALL PLAYERS

Once there were ballplayers with names like Harry Feldman and Moe Berg. Those days are gone, but the Jewish ballplayer remains. Only now, his name is Ryan or Ian or Scott. In this tournament of thirty-two great, good, decent, or barely adequate major league Jews (it's not as if there were thousands to choose from), face-offs are won by the better player—except when I don't like the outcome. That's when I turn to Diamond Semitology, allowing either Hebraic Pride or Yiddishe Irony to trump onfield evidence. Take your base, Mose Solomon; doff your cap, Adam Greenberg.

Adapted with the permission of Simon & Schuster Paperbacks, a Division of Simon & Schuster, Inc. from THE FINAL FOUR OF EVERYTHING edited by Mark Reiter and Richard Sandomir. Copyright © 2009 Mark Reiter and Richard Sandomir.

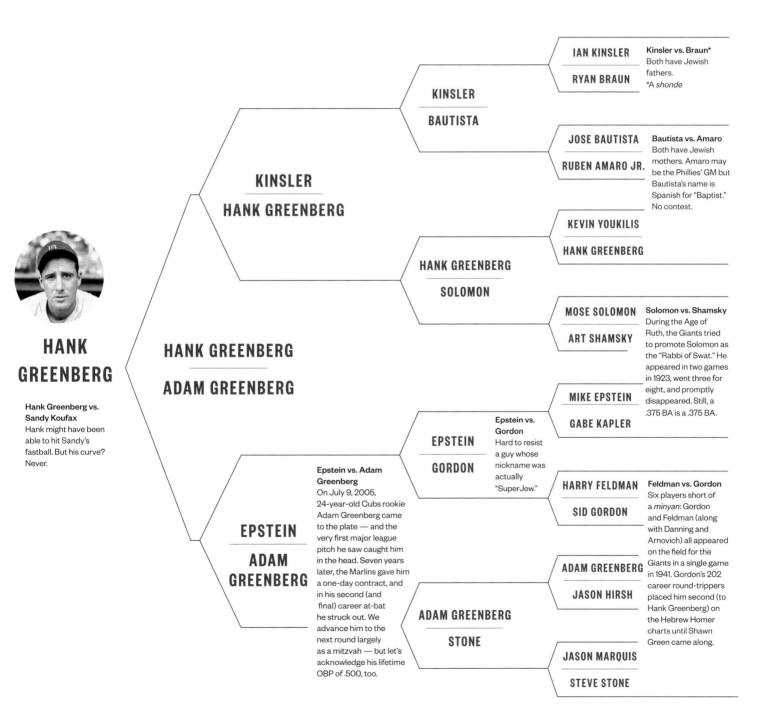

HANK GREENBERG

Hank Greenberg vs. Sandy Koufax
Hank might have been able to hit Sandy's fastball. But his curve? Never.

HANK GREENBERG
ADAM GREENBERG

KINSLER
HANK GREENBERG

EPSTEIN
ADAM GREENBERG

KINSLER
BAUTISTA

HANK GREENBERG
SOLOMON

EPSTEIN
GORDON

Epstein vs. Gordon
Hard to resist a guy whose nickname was actually "SuperJew."

Epstein vs. Adam Greenberg
On July 9, 2005, 24-year-old Cubs rookie Adam Greenberg came to the plate — and the very first major league pitch he saw caught him in the head. Seven years later, the Marlins gave him a one-day contract, and in his second (and final) career at-bat he struck out. We advance him to the next round largely as a mitzvah — but let's acknowledge his lifetime OBP of .500, too.

ADAM GREENBERG
STONE

IAN KINSLER
RYAN BRAUN

Kinsler vs. Braun*
Both have Jewish fathers.
*A *shonde*

JOSE BAUTISTA
RUBEN AMARO JR.

Bautista vs. Amaro
Both have Jewish mothers. Amaro may be the Phillies' GM but Bautista's name is Spanish for "Baptist." No contest.

KEVIN YOUKILIS
HANK GREENBERG

MOSE SOLOMON
ART SHAMSKY

Solomon vs. Shamsky
During the Age of Ruth, the Giants tried to promote Solomon as the "Rabbi of Swat." He appeared in two games in 1923, went three for eight, and promptly disappeared. Still, a .375 BA is a .375 BA.

MIKE EPSTEIN
GABE KAPLER

HARRY FELDMAN
SID GORDON

Feldman vs. Gordon
Six players short of a *minyan*: Gordon and Feldman (along with Danning and Arnovich) all appeared on the field for the Giants in a single game in 1941. Gordon's 202 career round-trippers placed him second (to Hank Greenberg) on the Hebrew Homer charts until Shawn Green came along.

ADAM GREENBERG
JASON HIRSH

JASON MARQUIS
STEVE STONE

CONTRIBUTORS

MICHAEL SCOTT ALEXANDER is associate professor of religious studies at the University of California, Riverside. He is the author of *Jazz Age Jews*, which won the National Jewish Book Award.

REBECCA T. ALPERT is professor of religion at Temple University. Alpert was one of the first women to be ordained as a rabbi in the 1970s. She is author of several books on twentieth-century American Jewish history and culture, gender and sexuality, and Jewish ethics. As an extension of these interests, she has, over the past several years, developed an expertise on Jews and sport. She is cochair of the Religion and Sport Section of the American Academy of Religion. She created and taught a course on "Jews, America, and Sport" for undergraduates at Temple University and has published several journal articles on Jews and baseball. Alpert was featured as an expert commentator in the film *Jews and Baseball: An American Love Story*. Her major work on baseball is *Out of Left Field: Jews and Black Baseball*. She is currently at work on a case-study textbook on religion and sport for Columbia University Press.

MARTY APPEL started his career with the New York Yankees responding to fan mail for Mickey Mantle, and went on to produce Yankee baseball telecasts. He helped assemble the public relations (PR) operation for the 1996 Olympic Games, directed PR for The Topps Company, and established his own firm, Marty Appel Public Relations, in 1998. Among his clients have been Team Israel in the World Baseball Classic, the Israel Baseball League, Jewish Major Leaguers Inc., the American Jewish Historical Society, and the National Museum of American Jewish History. Other clients have included Fox Sports, the Baseball Hall of Fame, the New York Yankees, the Yogi Berra Museum, *The Sporting News,* and major publishing houses. He was consulting producer to ESPN's *The Bronx is Burning,* and consultant to Billy Crystal for HBO's *61.* Appel is a regular contributor to *Yankeeographies* on YES Network and creates content for Yankees.com. He is the author of eighteen books, including a memoir, *Now Pitching for the Yankees,* and a Yankees' team history, *Pinstripe Empire.*

MARC APPLEMAN is the executive director of the Society for American Baseball Research (SABR). He has had a diverse career in sports media for more than thirty years, working for ESPN, AOL Sports, FoxSports.com, the Active Network, *Sports Illustrated For Kids,* and the *Los Angeles Times.*

BRAD AUSMUS, manager of the Detroit Tigers, has been a catcher for the San Diego Padres, Detroit Tigers, Houston Astros, and the Los Angeles Dodgers. During his career as a player, Ausmus earned three Golden Glove Awards and played on the 1999 All-Star team. After his retirement from playing, Ausmus was named special assistant of operations to the Padres front office and managed Team Israel for the 2013 World Baseball Classic. He was elected to the National Jewish Sports Hall of Fame in 2004.

MICHAEL BERENBAUM is the director of the Sigi Ziering Institute: Exploring the Ethical and Religious Implications of the Holocaust and a professor of Jewish studies at the American Jewish University in Los Angeles. The author and editor of two books, he was also the executive editor of the second edition of the *Encyclopaedia Judaica.* Berenbaum was a member of the team of historians that advised the National Museum of American Jewish History on its core exhibition. He was the project director for the creation of the United States Holocaust Memorial Museum and was president and chief executive officer of the Survivors of the Shoah Visual History Foundation. Based in Los Angeles, he still roots for the Brooklyn Dodgers.

IRA BERKOW, a former *New York Times* sports columnist, shared the Pulitzer Prize for National Reporting and was a finalist for the Pulitzer for Distinguished Commentary. He is also the author of twenty-two books, including the best sellers *Red: A Biography of Red Smith* and *Maxwell Street: Survival in a Bazaar.*

BARRY M. BLOOM is national reporter and columnist for MLB.com. Bloom has been covering baseball and other sports since 1976 and is a member of SABR and the Baseball Writers' Association of America. He holds voting rights at the Baseball Hall of Fame.

ADRIAN BURGOS JR., professor of history at the University of Illinois, specializes in US Latino history, sport history, and urban history. He has published two books: *Cuban Star: How One Negro League Owner Changed the Face of Baseball* and *Playing America's Game: Baseball, Latinos, and the Color Line,* which received the inaugural Latino/a Book Award from the Latin American Studies Association and was a Seymour Medal finalist for the best book on baseball history by the Society of American Baseball Research. His writings have appeared in the *Journal of American Ethnic History, Journal of Sport and Social Issues,* and *Journal of African American History,* as well as on MLB.com, and Progressive Media Project, among others.

ABRAHAM CAHAN (1860–1951) founded the Yiddish-language *Jewish Daily Forward* (*Forverts*). At its high point in the 1920s, the paper had a readership of more than a quarter million. Among its most beloved features was the Bintel Brief, a column that responded to readers' questions, offering them advice on dealing with the nuances of American life. Cahan was also a novelist and a contributor to various English-language newspapers. His 1917 novel, *The Rise of David Levinsky,* is considered a classic American work on the immigrant experience.

ADAM CHANDLER is a staff writer at *Tablet Magazine.* His work has appeared in the *Atlantic,* the *Wall Street Journal, New York, Haaretz,* and the *Jerusalem Post.* Chandler grew up in Houston, Texas, and currently lives in Brooklyn, New York.

WILLIAM CHOSLOVSKY is a Harvard Law School graduate who once lived in Alaska—where the Jews were called the "frozen chosen." Bill now works and lives in Chicago, and is a partner at the Chicago law firm Neal, Gerber & Eisenberg.

BILLY CRYSTAL has enjoyed a long and successful career on film, stage, and television. A former member of *Saturday Night Live,* Crystal starred in the groundbreaking sitcom *Soap* (1977) and film classics such as *The Princess Bride, When Harry Met Sally, City Slickers,* and *Analyze This.* He has hosted the Academy Awards nine times, won six Emmy Awards, received the Mark Twain Prize for American Humor in 2007, and was honored with a Tony Award in 2005 for *700 Sundays,* his one-man play about his childhood on Long Island. As a cast member of *Saturday Night Live,* he created the character Fernando, whose signature greeting, "You look mah-velous," became a part of the national lexicon.

COLIN FRIEDMAN is a college sophomore studying mechanical engineering at Johns Hopkins University. A pitcher for the Hopkins Blue Jays baseball team, Friedman hails from Santa Fe, New Mexico, where he earned All-State Honors, state records for both baseball and Olympic weight lifting, and a 2012 appearance in

Sports Illustrated's "Faces in the Crowd." Colin is a staff writer and previous sports editor for the Johns Hopkins News-Letter.

DOUG GLANVILLE played Major League Baseball for the Philadelphia Phillies, Chicago Cubs, and Texas Rangers, and is currently an ESPN baseball analyst, a regular contributor to ESPN.com and *The New York Times*, and a motivational speaker. Glanville is a featured speaker at the Tauk Baseball Event: America's Pastime, with Ken Burns, at the National Baseball Hall of Fame. Glanville is a board member of the Major League Baseball Players Association and a graduate of the University of Pennsylvania. His critically acclaimed book, *The Game from Where I Stand*, was published in 2010. Glanville authors a whimsical blog on parenting and fatherhood, *The Daddy Games*, on his website at www.DougGlanville.com/daddy-games.

DORIS KEARNS GOODWIN is a presidential scholar and the Pulitzer Prize-winning author of the bestselling *No Ordinary Time, Franklin & Eleanor Roosevelt: The Home Front in World War II*. She is also the author of the memoir *Wait Till Next Year*, as well as *The Fitzgeralds and the Kennedys: An American Saga* and the recently released book *Lyndon Johnson and the American Dream*. The 2012 Steven Spielberg film *Lincoln* was based on her book *Team of Rivals: The Political Genius of Abraham Lincoln*.

ERIC ROLFE GREENBERG was born and raised in New York, attended the University of Wisconsin and, after naval service, New York University's School of the Arts. He worked as a publicist for major film studios and as marketing director for magazine and book publishers. He joined the American Management Association's groundbreaking Institute for Management Competency in 1981 and five years later became its director of management studies, a post he left in 2001. He is the author of *The Celebrant*, still in print thirty years after its original publication and, currently available from Bison Books. *Sports Illustrated* ranked the novel among the hundred greatest sports books of the twentieth century—third among baseball fiction.

JEFFREY S. GUROCK is Libby M. Klaperman Professor of Jewish History at Yeshiva University and author of *Judaism's Encounter with American Sports*.

AVIVA KEMPNER directed and produced the Peabody Award-winning *The Life and Times of Hank Greenberg*. A new DVD of the baseball documentary containing over two hours of extras was released in 2013. Kempner produced *Partisans of Vilna* about Jewish resistance against the Nazis, produced and directed *Yoo-Hoo, Mrs. Goldberg*, and recently completed *The Rosenwald Schools* about the philanthropist Julius Rosenwald. She started the

Washington Jewish Film Festival and is a voting-rights advocate in the nation's capital.

JANE LEAVY is the author of *The New York Times* best sellers *The Last Boy: Mickey Mantle and the End of America's Childhood*, and *Sandy Koufax: A Lefty's Legacy*. Her novel, *Squeeze Play*, was called "the best novel ever written about baseball" by *Entertainment Weekly*, was inspired by her career as a staff writer for the *Washington Post*, where she covered baseball, tennis, and the Olympics.

PETER LEVINE taught American history at Michigan State University from 1969 to 2000. He is the author of numerous books, including *A. G. Spalding and the Rise of Baseball*; *Ellis Island to Ebbets Field: Sport and the American Jewish Experience*; *Idols of the Game* (with Robert Lipsyte); and a novel, *The Rabbi of Swat*. In 2000, he moved to Brooklyn in order to pursue a career as an actor. New York theatre credits include *The Madwoman of Chaillot*, *The Power of Darkness*, *The Front Page*, *Evening All Afternoon*, *Broadway Bound*, and *The Private Life of the Master Race*. Regional credits include *The Sunshine Boys*, *Cheaper By the Dozen*, *Jewtopia*, *Art*, *Angels in America*, *Indians*, and *Inherit the Wind*. He is a member of Emerging Artists Theatre, which has produced two of his plays, *The Kitchen Table* and *The Gipper*.

BERNARD MALAMUD (1914–1986) is considered one of the preeminent writers of the twentieth century. In 1967, Malamud won both a Pulitzer Prize and a National Book Award for *The Fixer*, the tale of a Jewish handyman falsely charged for the murder of a Christian boy, based on the 1913 case involving Menahem Mendel Beilis. Malamud's first novel, published in 1952, *The Natural*, was made into a hit movie in 1984, starring Robert Redford; and the film's popularity helped introduce Malamud to a new audiences.

COLUM MCCANN, originally from Dublin, Ireland, is the author of five novels and two story collections. He has won numerous international literary awards, including the National Book Award, the Pushcart Prize, the Rooney Prize, the Hennessy Award for Irish Literature, the Irish Independent Hughes, and the Hughes/Sunday Independent Novel of the Year. The short film based on his work *Everything in This Country Must* was nominated for an Oscar in 2005. His writing has been published in over thirty languages and has appeared in the *New Yorker*, *The New York Times*, the *Atlantic Monthly*, the *Irish Times*, *GQ*, the *Paris Review*, the *Guardian*, and the *Independent*, among others.

PAMELA S. NADELL holds the Patrick Clendenen Chair in Women's and Gender History at American University. A member of the team of historians that advised the National Museum of American

Jewish History on its core exhibition, she has also consulted for the Library of Congress, Beit Hatfutsot: The Museum of the Jewish People, and the Emmy Award-winning film *And the Gates Opened*. Nadell is the author of *Women Who Would Be Rabbis: A History of Women's Ordination, 1889-1985* and *Making Women's Histories: Beyond National Perspectives*.

KERRY YO NAKAGAWA is an author, filmmaker, producer, and historian. He curated *Diamonds in the Rough*, an exhibition that has been shown at the National Baseball Hall of Fame, in Tokyo, and in museums around the US. He produced and directed a companion documentary, also called *Diamonds in the Rough*, with his Godpapa Noriyuki "Pat" Morita. Nakagawa wrote the book *Through a Diamond: 100 years of Japanese American Baseball* and coproduced two curriculum guides with Stanford University's Program on International and Cross-Cultural Education. He produced the film *American Pastime*, which was an "audience favorite" at the 2007 San Francisco International Asian American Film Festival in 2007. Nakagawa founded the nonprofit Nisei Baseball Research Project.

DANIEL OKRENT's books include the baseball classic *Nine Innings*, as well as *Great Fortune: The Epic of Rockefeller Center* (a finalist for the 2004 Pulitzer Prize for history) and *Last Call: The Rise and Fall of Prohibition* (winner of the American Historical Association's Albert J. Beveridge Award for the year's best book of American history). He was also the first public editor of *The New York Times*.

JOSH PERELMAN is the chief curator and director of exhibitions and collections at the National Museum of American Jewish History in Philadelphia. He is the co-curator of the Museum's world premier exhibition, *Chasing Dreams: Baseball and Becoming American*. Under Perelman's curatorial leadership, *Chasing Dreams* was awarded a substantial grant from the National Endowment for the Humanities. He oversaw the landmark core exhibition NMAJH opened in 2010 and founded the Museum's education, public programming, and visitor services departments. Perelman has a joint PhD in Jewish Studies and American History as well as eighteen years of experience in museums and non-profit leadership. Perelman writes and lectures on topics of historical interpretation as well as the intersections of culture, politics, and art; serves on the board of directors for the Council of American Jewish Museums and Philadelphia's University City Arts League and is a member of the American Jewish Historical Society's academic council.

CHAIM POTOK's (1929–2002) first novel, *The Chosen* (1967), sold more than three million copies and stayed on *The New York Times* best seller list for thirty-nine weeks. The book explored the conflicts of observant Jews as they encountered the modern world. It was a theme Potok would tackle in later novels, including *My Name Is Asher Lev* and *In the Beginning*. From 1964 to 1975, he edited the journal *Conservative Judaism*, and he also served as editor in chief of the Jewish Publication Society (JPS) in Philadelphia.

SHIRLEY POVICH (1905–1998) was a reporter and sports journalist for seventy-five years with the *Washington Post*, forty-one of those years spent as sports editor. He was a prodigious journalist who authored over fifteen thousand columns throughout his career, the last of which he wrote on the day he died.

JOSHUA PRAGER writes for publications including *Vanity Fair*, *The New York Times*, and the *Wall Street Journal*, where he was a senior writer for eight years. His first book, *The Echoing Green*, was a *Washington Post* Best Book of the Year. His second book, *Half-Life: Reflections from Jerusalem on a Broken Neck*, was published this year. Prager has spoken at venues including TED and Google. He was a Nieman Fellow at Harvard in 2011 and a Fulbright Distinguished Chair at Hebrew University in 2012. He was born in Eagle Butte, South Dakota, grew up in New Jersey, and lives in New York.

WILLIAM RESSLER is an assistant professor in the Department of Strategic Communication at Ithaca College, focusing on sports, media, and culture. He is conducting an ongoing oral-history project with minor league players on the subject of religion, ethnicity, and identity.

STEVEN A. RIESS is Bernard Brommel Research Professor, emeritus, at Northeastern Illinois University, in Chicago, where he taught American history for thirty-five years. A former editor of the *Journal of Sport History*, his books include *Sports in Industrial America, 1850–1920*; *The Sport of Kings and the Kings of Crime: Horse Racing, Politics, and Crime in New York, 1865–1913*; *Touching Base: Professional Baseball and American Culture in the Progressive Era*, rev. ed.; *City Games: The Evolution of American Society and the Rise of Sports*; and *Sports and the American Jew*.

PHILIP ROTH first gained fame with his 1959 novella, *Goodbye, Columbus*, an irreverent depiction of Jewish life in postwar America. When he published his popular, critically acclaimed novel *Portnoy's Complaint*, in 1969 it was considered both brilliant and controversial. One of America's most decorated fiction writers, Roth has won the National Book Critics Circle Award twice and the PEN/Faulkner Award three times. In 1997, he received a Pulitzer Prize for his novel *American Pastoral*.

ROB RUCK is a professor of transnational sport history at the University of Pittsburgh. He was an advisor to the 2006 *American Experience* documentary *Roberto Clemente* and author of *Raceball: How the Major Leagues Colonized the Black and Latin Game* and *The Tropic of Baseball: Baseball in the Dominican Republic*. His documentaries include *Kings on the Hill: Baseball's Forgotten Men*, and *The Republic of Baseball: Dominican Giants of the American Game*, with Daniel Manatt.

JUSTINE SIEGAL is the first woman to pitch batting practice to a Major League team. She is the founder of Baseball for All, a nonprofit that provides meaningful opportunities and instruction in baseball, especially for girls, and is coach and technical commissioner for the International Baseball Federation. Siegal, a sought-after educator and speaker throughout the world, is the director of sport partnerships at Sport in Society, an organization working to create social change through sports.

SCOTT SIMON is well known as a journalist and host of NPR's *Weekend Edition*. He has won every broadcasting award, including the Peabody, Emmy, Columbia-DuPont Robert F. Kennedy Journalism, and Sidney Hillman Awards, among others. He is the author of the best-selling memoirs *Home and Away* and *Baby, We Were Meant for Each Other: In Praise of Adoption*, the nonfiction book *Jackie Robinson and the Integration of Baseball*, and novels *Pretty Birds* and *Windy City*.

CURT SMITH wrote more speeches than anyone for President George H. W. Bush. His sixteen books include the classic *Voices of the Game: The Acclaimed Chronicle of Baseball Radio and Television Broadcasting—from 1921 to the Present* and the upcoming *Character at the Core: George H. W. Bush's Life in Full*. Smith is an award-winning radio commentator and a senior lecturer at the University of Rochester.

ARN TELLEM is considered one of the most successful sports agents in the world. He is a vice chairman at Wasserman Media Group, overseeing the Team Sports Division. A native of Philadelphia, Tellem graduated from Haverford College and earned his law degree from the University of Michigan. He was a partner at the law firm Manatt, Phelps & Phillips, where he met his mentor and friend, Steve Greenberg. In addition to representing numerous Major League Baseball and National Basketball Association players, Tellem has written opinion pieces for the *Huffington Post* and *The New York Times*.

JOHN THORN is the official historian of Major League Baseball. Apart from his creation, with Pete Palmer, of *Total Baseball*, he is often visible on ESPN, MLB, The History Channel, and other television outlets as a sports authority and commentator. He was also a major on-screen presence in and chief consultant to

Ken Burns's eighteen-and-a-half-hour PBS series, *Baseball*. His many baseball books over the past four decades include *The Hidden Game of Baseball*, *Total Baseball*, *Treasures of the Baseball Hall of Fame*, and, most recently, *Baseball in the Garden of Eden: A Secret History of the Early Game*.

MARC TRACY is a staff writer at the *New Republic*. Previously he was a staff writer at *Tablet*, where he won the National Magazine Award for Blogging. He coedited *Jewish Jocks*, a collection of original essays about Jewish sports figures.

IVY WEINGRAM is an associate curator at NMAJH and serves as co-curator of *Chasing Dreams*. She participated in the development of the Museum's core exhibition, and plays an active role in the Museum's special exhibitions program. She has also served in the curatorial departments of The Jewish Museum, Yeshiva University Museum, and the Library of the Jewish Theological Seminary.

BETH S. WENGER is professor of history at the University of Pennsylvania, where she serves as chair of the History Department. Wenger's most recent book is *History Lessons: The Creation of American Jewish Heritage*. She also wrote *The Jewish Americans: Three Centuries of Jewish Voices in America*, companion volume to the 2008 PBS series *The Jewish Americans* and a National Jewish Book Award finalist. She also authored *New York Jews and the Great Depression: Uncertain Promise*, which was awarded the Salo Baron Prize in Jewish History from the American Academy of Jewish Research.

STEPHEN WONG is a lifelong collector of historical artifacts whose passion for baseball led him on a multiyear trek to research and write the book *Smithsonian Baseball: Inside the World's Finest Private Collections*. In addition to his work on *Chasing Dreams*, he has lent his expertise to the development of baseball exhibitions at the Chicago Historical Society, Museum of the City of New York, and the Berkshire Museum. Wong is a managing director at Goldman Sachs Asia, and lives in Hong Kong.

STEVE WULF is a senior writer for *ESPN The Magazine* and ESPN.com. Over his forty-year career he has written for various publications, including *Sports Illustrated*, *Time*, *Life*, *Entertainment Weekly*, and the *Economist*. In 1995, the Overseas Press Club of America gave him the Ed Cunningham Award for best magazine reporting from abroad for his *Time* story on the assassination of Yitzhak Rabin.

INDEX

CREDITS

COPYRIGHT

NATIONAL MUSEUM OF AMERICAN JEWISH HISTORY
101 South Independence Mall East
Philadelphia, PA 19106-2517
NMAJH.org

This book has been published in conjunction with the special exhibition *Chasing Dreams: Baseball and Becoming American* by the National Museum of American Jewish History

Book Design by Pure+Applied. The Museum acknowledges the excitement and unique creative vision Pure+Applied brought to the design of this book and of the corresponding exhibition. We are grateful for their investment in making this a truly remarkable project.

Printed in the USA by CRW Graphics.

Copyright ©2014 by the National Museum of American Jewish History

All rights reserved. No portion of this book may be used or reproduced in any manner without written permission of the publisher.

Every attempt has been made to find the copyright holders of works reproduced herein. Any omission is unintentional.

ISBN: 978-1-891507-05-2

Front Cover:
Hank Greenberg hits a third inning homer for the Pittsburgh Pirates against the Philadelphia Phillies, April 29, 1947
CB

Back Cover:
The "Miracle Mets" winning against the Baltimore Orioles at Shea Stadium during the 1969 World Series, October 16, 1969
AP

Half Title Page:
Hank Greenberg leaping for fly ball against the Philadelphia Athletics, June 20, 1946
CB

Title Page:
Shawn Green hits a single for the New York Mets against the Pittsburgh Pirates, July 24, 2007
Jim McIsaac/GT

Table of Contents:
Sandy Koufax pitches a shutout to win the 1965 World Series
CB

Endpapers:
(Front) Game 3 of the World Series between the Brooklyn Dodgers and the New York Yankees, Ebbets Field, October 7, 1949
CB

(Back) The crowd watching Game 2 of the National League Series between the Philadelphia Phillies and the Los Angeles Dodgers, Citizens Bank Park, October 10, 2008
Rob Tringali/Sportschrome/GT